Transformation of a Nerd

Aetius D. Harris

TRANSFORMATION OF A NERD

iUniverse books may be ordered through booksellers or by contacting:

iUniverse LLC
1663 Liberty Drive
Bloomington, IN 47403
www.iuniverse.com
1-800-Authors (1-800-288-4677)

Because of the dynamic nature of the Internet, any web addresses or links contained in this book may have changed since publication and may no longer be valid. The views expressed in this work are solely those of the author and do not necessarily reflect the views of the publisher, and the publisher hereby disclaims any responsibility for them.

Any people depicted in stock imagery provided by Thinkstock are models,
and such images are being used for illustrative purposes only.
Certain stock imagery © Thinkstock.

ISBN: 978-1-4917-3902-0 (sc)
ISBN: 978-1-4917-3901-3 (e)

Library of Congress Control Number: 2014912434

Printed in the United States of America.

iUniverse rev. date: 08/01/2014

Table of Contents

"Brainwashed"

This is a year-to-year memoir on being dark complexion, poor and smart in Chicago. The time period spans the mid 1970s to the mid 1980s. The main character is Columbus George aka Colo. Columbus struggles with economics, bad influences and tragedies. He has a low self-esteem because of his dark color.

There are a lot of obstacles to keep you from coming up in life. The black experience is a bitch! Three out of four blacks in the inner cities will be incarcerated, shot or killed. The other trap is to sell or use hard drugs before the age of twenty-five. Being black in color is obstacle you can't hide.

Your color was your main obstacle. Being smart was another obstacle. When you are black in America there's no roadmap left from your ancestor's history. There's nothing to aid you and your direction & development in America's Capitalistic system. Growing up on the streets of Chicago is rough. Growing up without leadership or guidance, it's virtually, futile.

There is good and there is bad coming up on any set in the city. This story is about three boys. These boys lived on 169th & Calumet St. They had no long family history, but living on that block, the people were family.

It was like they were all non-blood cousins living together in a four-block radius. The only thing they had was, love in Chicago in this time period. One place it came from was an unexpected source, through the gang organizations.

A lot of society wonders about Blacks. Why do Blacks often have such a negative outlook on life? Why do blacks rob, steal and inflict damage to their own people? Why do they tear down their own neighborhoods? Why don't they pull themselves up by their bootstraps, focus and come up?

The major factor's for the problems of today is a dysfunctional household. There aren't fathers or positive male role models in the household.

This is one of the major reasons why things have gotten out of control. Our kids growing up today don't have any strong male guidance. They are confronted with different evils of life, without a guide.

You have to learn from the guys off the corner or on the block. You learn from people who are in survival mode for your information on life.

Drugs, liquor and music videos are among the other variables. One of the main reasons is stemming from four hundred years of brainwashing. It is complicated to even think how deliberate the plans are to keep us searching.

Most of the things you've been taught in the school, some media, radio, movies, cartoons and the different TV programming. This evil programming is set up to continue programming or brainwashing our kids. There's a signal coming straight into your house. Who controls the information that gets to you? What is they're agenda?

It's a well thought out systematic plan to continue to use slave labor. Slavery has been abolished with the passing of the 13Th amendment. Due to the fact and that fact alone we came up.

There were a lot of white people who've helped black folks to freedom and equality. All people aren't the same. It's just some of the people in power wants to keep their foot on your neck.

President Lincoln a Republican president was the catalyst that helped push this amendment through. Now the Democrats are Republicans and Republicans are Democrats. Depending on the agenda those elected officials are switching sides. You don't know who's who and where's the loyalty to your people?

White folks are way ahead of the game. We have to take the blindfold off. To continue to close your eyes to the truth is our downfall. We are not questioning what's really going on!

This nation was united with the different battles of the civil war. This is a war that literally tore our country apart. This is a war that preludes the end of slavery, the year 1865.

The truth is black folks were just 3/5^{Ths} of a human being. We were close to being livestock in slave owner's eyes. You'll still hear some whites refer to us as monkeys. Still, there was mix breeding and this caused a breakdown in our color. Our skin tone was being diluted. The lighter you were the more privileges you had. This was, because you had some of Massa's blood, in you.

We were known as subhuman's or savages to some white folks in America. The descendants of those white folks are still in play, powerfully. This land was confiscated from the Indians and not founded by Christopher Columbus. It was people already here in America.

Black folks were sold or stolen from Africa. They had a slave work force that worked the land the conquerors were developing. The white folks families who orchestrated that move will never run out of plans and money. They've probably made trillions of profits off that investment and still growing. Now you have free land and you have free labor. You can't get any better than that! The seeds of slavery are still being planted; it's a diabolical plan. It is a plan to keep blacks and minorities fighting and killing each other over money.

This plan has knocked out and created self-genocide to our black leaders of the future. The descendants of those who enacted the plan still think the same way or things would be changing.

When the season changes yearly in the spring, you plant seeds. The seeds they're planting are seeds to brainwash you. When you are released out the womb your brain is wired for control.

People that are in power rarely want to relinquish it. They have the ups on the latest technology and uses it in that way.

Non-leadership is another reason why our neighborhoods have taken a turn for the worst. Lack of leadership or a concentrated effort to either lock up or kill our leaders. Who wants to be a target? Just in my time Fred Hampton, Dr. King, Malcolm X, John F. Kennedy and Robert Kennedy were all murdered.

These guys were our leaders or fought for black folk's interest. Jessie Jackson Rainbow Collation and Rev Al Sharpton are cool, but we needed more. It used to be a lot of leaders, but after those killings. Most of our leaders faded.

You have to be a strong man to put your life on the line for your cause. Barack Obama is an inspiration, he's America's first black president. Somebody got to be pulling his strings. Blacks make up about 15% of the population so black folks can't elect him alone. He had a lot of help and what's their agenda?

I was born in the year of 1968. This was a volatile year for leaders for black people. By the time I was born, our black and white leaders were slain. Fred Hampton was slain killed in his apartment by the Chicago police. He was the leader of the struggle at a young age. He was too powerful to live during those times. Mayor 'Bull' Daly was in charge of the police force that cut him down.

Dr. King and Robert Kennedy were killed right after I was born. Who was I to look up to for strength and guidance? The only person I see, who is black that lived and died naturally, was Ralph Bunche.

I didn't even know about him. I didn't learn about him until I went to college. He was our international spokesperson for the United Nations. He's the guy who helped sew up the Middle-East peace process between the Palestinians and the Israelis in the 1960s and 1970s.

After masterfully settling issue after issue in the Middle East. When he got home he couldn't drink water from the same water fountain as whites, in the American South. It didn't matter what he did globally for peace. In the South he was still just a boy!

Most black people here in the United States are descendants of slaves. Most of us have no idea of where were from, originally. We don't know who we are or our family history. Fuck shit happens to people who don't know their history. We are susceptible to what comes to us, while trying to figure life out. By then it could be too late.

We have no idea how we all got here, except for a slave ship. We have our master's who enslaved us, last name. That's all we have to go on unless you have money for a search.

During slave time most of us black Americans born here were fucked. Once the air hit our lunges. We were sold shortly afterwards from underneath our parents. Now, you don't know your mother or father anymore. Who is left to teach you your family values and history?

The long-term effect from this separation is when brainwashing takes effect. Blacks are still seeking their history. Most are wondering which way to go for success at this time? They are wondering how do you side-step some of these issues.

One of the reason white folks didn't want us to know how to read. Knowledge is power! Now our kids today don't pursue education, why? There's more than one way to skin a cat. We are left to claim street corners and blocks due to this fact.

We've been brainwashed into believing what the teachers taught us, in books as kids. We believed the media and things we saw on TV. We believed the portrayal of what white people want us to believe, we are, to be. Truth to the matter is we had to be the strongest of the strong. We had to be the pick of the litter in order to survive the ocean voyage.

Author's Comments

As a child, I felt so distant and lost. I am Columbus George. My family were scattered and my Mom settled in Chicago. Due to the darkness of my skin I felt rejection. I was a smart or above average kid. This made me kind of an outcast double-time coming up. How can I be black and smart?

I just didn't fit in with my age group as far as excelling. In school I knew the material we worked on in class already. I had to constantly go up a level to learn. Therefore, I was promoted to the upper grades. Once up there the older kids in the class rejected me immediately. It seems as, if the older kids were being attacked by the younger smarter kid's knowledge.

This rejection was not only from older kids: I experienced rejection from white people, friends, family and peers in one-way or another. I should've been proud of the darkness of my skin. That means I hadn't been diluted a great deal. I still have African features.

I was fooled into believing my darkness and my high I Q level was bad. I wished I'd known about the money and scholarships that were available to me, because I was smart. I wish I were aware about that straight out the gate. I would've taken advantage, if I'd known. Knowledge is power and knowing is half the battle.

The other part of the battle is the work. I had no problem working. All I had to do was get good grades and that was a given. I didn't know anything about a full ride in college. My grammar and high schools weren't pressing college unless you were an athlete.

Universities will pay you to go to their school, because you are smart. Had I known at the time that nerds run the world! Nerds pay the jocks. Nerds control companies and have vast amount of wealth. All this time I was trying to fit in with the people who one day will be working for nerds. I will try to answer some of these questions by the end of this book. Why!

The Setting

This is a look inside the minds of three young boy's strife and struggle in Chicago. Centering on the main character Columbus George AKA Colo. This is in an era when most of their friends had no fathers in their household.

After the Vietnam War, the structure of the household changed. You can count on one hand the kids that grew up with their father's in the house.

They are some things that are supposed to be taught to your son. Things he needs to know to build a solid base. Mom can do the best she can at rearing her son. The man is definitely needed to shape his son's foundation.

The environment is shaping the kids without fathers. TV programming plays a major part. These are the variables used in shaping our kids of the future. It was a blessing we came up in a time when people stuck halfway together. People really cared what happened to you.

There was a definite need for a father while tackling the streets of Chicago. In sort of a way the streets became their fathers. That's where they went to learn those things that their fathers didn't teach them.

Enter the term "Street Nigga". This is a guy who goes to the streets to get money and power. There is usually a criminal element to his hustle. The boys mother's prepared them as best they could for the streets. The rest they had to wing it by themselves.

They all have strong mothers and motherly figures. The mother factor was very important. They would've easily succumbed to the streets without them. The same street that did a lot of their friends in, they overcame.

The values and goals that their mothers planted in them as youngsters came through. This helped them with the life in the streets. The fathers were on the other hand, were hi and bye fathers. You can't build a foundation like that!

Now these shorties didn't grow up and accomplished any great feat. Nor have they served society to the fullest. Growing up on 169th St. confronting all those issues and making it out was miraculous. When you still have your mind together, that's a great feat in itself. These boys had a plan it wasn't drawn out, but they had a plan.

The boys knew as youngsters, they wanted to succeed in life! They didn't want to be strung out on drugs. Nor did they want to be the guy on the corner, asking for change. They didn't want to succumb to the environment that they witness day in and day out.

They had to step over dope feigns while going to hoop or playing baseball. They witness women getting the shit slapped out of them for whatever reason. They watched the pimps, the hustlers, the thieves and the bangers control the environment. They will deal with all these factors as young boys.

Throughout their young lives they'll see people rise fast. They will also, see the same people fall. They used other people experiences and learned from other's mistakes. They did this by sitting one of the main characters name John's porch watching everything go down on 169th St. or Rock Manor School. They were involved or had direct contact with the crime element and persevered. Now the boys have a chance to be part of society as positive role models.

Spiritual Battle

We are all born in a world of sin. We have to work and struggle to become righteous. We are born in a world where you have a choice to follow good or evil. I believe everyone has goodness in them.

Goodness just has to have a chance to come out. God put the tiniest fraction of himself somewhere in our body. We all can excess him, if we call upon him and believe. The devil is constantly in your ears trying to get your soul!

Parents must lay the foundation of goodness in the child from the beginning. Make sure the child understand the difference between right and wrong. We have to be taught righteousness. It seems we are all born with a selfish spirit.

We must be taught to give and to love one another. Once challenged, confronted and dabbling in evil, you must be aware. Your soul is at stake! You have to know once out in the world. The plan is to get your soul and smother your righteous spirit. Young and old prepare yourself and take Yaweh with you.

Chapter I

The Gathering of Old friends

This is a perfect example of the environment surrounding Columbus George and how it influenced him. This spurred his transformation off nerd status, to being accepted! His dreams of success were shattered by tragedies of life. He had no road map or proper guidance. He had no history to look back on for help. Gang life prepared him for the world.

He depended on his faith without knowing it, to guide him through. He constantly wanted to know why was evil, winning the battles at his core. This is the first book of a quadology of powerful and riveting 1st hand account on survival of street life. This book focuses on the early years of Columbus George.

What do you do when you're lost and stuck? What do you do when evil is permeating through your body? Let's see what Columbus aka Colo did?

Here's Colo sitting on a Southwest Airplane ready for takeoff. He just got through visiting his mother along with going through the hood. It's time for a little rest and relaxation. He's going to see his life-long friends who now live in Texas. John and Emus went to college in Austin and now have decided to stay in Austin.

These are a couple of friends who come up in the hood with him. Even though! He's known a lot of people in his short stint on earth. Those are his guys.

These two guys were with him through the bad and the good. Even though, they went their separate ways. They always had that bond and somehow always stayed tight!

Colo hears the engine revving up as the plane is taxing ready to take off leaving Chicago O'Hare. He checks his seatbelt and began to think about where he just left. Colo was wondering how his old neighborhood has deteriorated into a Cowboys and Indian type of atmosphere?

Now gun slinging and territory takeovers are prevalent in all areas. Things are popping off from one second to the next. 169th St. isn't what it used to be. He'll hate to say it, but he had his part in the destruction. People love you when you are doing evil and he did a lot of evil on 169th St.

He doesn't know too many people on the set anymore. He knows it's still evil out there prevalent though! He just don't know where it's coming from now. That is not good and he knows it.

The few people who've known him stops and gives him his respect. When he comes on the set the O.G's. has to tell the younger G's about him.

"Oh this is Colodog he helped lace this bitch up".

It's funny how your name fades and people keeps moving. Everybody's in a hurry now or can only talk for a minute. Colo asked about some of the street niggas on the block. He already knew the answer anyway. He might be dead or locked up for a long time. Maybe their on dope or something real bad has happened to a few of them. He keeps hope alive that people are on a come up.

Things are not what they use to be. He went to see his old house, only to find out it was leveled. He guessed the city came and cemented it in finally. There was empty feeling that whisked through his body not seeing his house there.

The house he grew up in was a town house. Three bedrooms upstairs and downstairs were the dining, living room and kitchen. He had a basement and a backyard. Now, it looks like he's never lived on that strip and it feels kind of funny.

Colo began to ponder heavily on what he just left and how it happened? He's gotten a chance to get away from the hood. He's been away three years at a time, six in total. Colo lived in Germany for two years as a truck driver for the army. He went to New Jersey for basic training.

After ETS out the service he came back to Chicago for four years. He attended DeVry University and graduated with a Bachelor degree in Business Operation. Now he lives in Detroit with a wife and kids.

He's gotten a chance to see some things and some other places. Now he's gotten a chance to see how other people live and their values and morals. It comes to him how people can get caught up or stuck. You know how a hamster is in a cage on the wheel.

The hamster doesn't know it's not going anywhere. No matter how fast he goes on that wheel. The hamster is still stuck in a cage on that wheel. You have to get out the cage to get away.

It's hard to get out the cage. The reason is you get smothered with day-to-day happenings. Things that seemed normal to Colo back then would have other people tripping. Shootings going on right around you, but you don't move. As long as you knew who was doing the shooting you were comfortable.

People don't go out and see anything anymore. They don't venture out anymore as an adventure of life. You rarely hear about people leaving town. Forget about leaving town. How about just going down town to hang?

Colo has been traveling the world and going to different places. When he came back home from the service, it seemed so small. It was like a jail on the outside, on the block. I'm safe, if I stay in this perimeter is what he gathered. Outside this perimeter you've got to have that missile.

When that's all you know is the hood, that's all you going to get in life, is the hood. You're trapped in the environment where its: shooting, killings, drugs, gangs, prostitution, drinking, stealing, plotting, back stabbing and just plan old game getting ran. It seemed normal to Colo though! Once you're in that atmosphere for a while things get clouded.

Being around this, everyday kills whatever good you had in you. It gets sucked slowly out of you like a mosquito, sucking your blood. I don't care how many times you keep trying to swat the mosquitoes. You kill one and another one is coming hard.

The mosquitoes keep trying to get at you to suck your blood. No matter how many you kill they keep coming to suck your blood. It's too many! You got to get out of their element or the mosquitoes are going to lump you up.

The analogy is, instead of the mosquito sucking your blood. The environment is sucking your soul out of you, turning you evil. You keep trying to swat at what's coming, but it keeps on coming. Sooner or later the environment gets you. If you stay out there the devil will get your soul. One thing about it is when you survive early life in Chicago. You can live anywhere in the world!

I think a lot of people don't venture out for fear of failure and don't try. People don't get out and see anything. If you don't see nothing you don't want nothing. You know when you were young. When you walked in the candy store with your mother? When you saw something you liked you wanted it. You didn't want it until you saw it. That's what happened to Colo. When he got a chance to see some things, he wanted it. He began reaching for those things in life.

The choices you make in life are detrimental to your well being as time goes. No matter how small, it will affect your life. There are choices that will send you on different paths. Now he knows from these few years on earth that you are in charge of your destiny.

The environment is an obstacle like any other deterrent you must overcome to succeed. There are values and the morals that your parents installed in you, since birth. This will be your foundation in helping you succeed in life. When all else fells, fall back on those righteous principles. Those principals will help steer you in the right direction. When worst come to worst, you must fall back on what you know.

This will help guide you through to be a grown man or woman. Honor, thy mother and father and your days will be lengthened. If that foundation wasn't laid properly the chances for survival diminishes.

When missing one part of the formula, it fucks you up. Just think, if you had some kool-aid and some water and mixed it together. It's still kool-aid, but it missing an important ingredient to make it good kool-aid. When it has no sugar it doesn't taste good.

Austin Texas

Screech, screech, "Damn we here already, I must have been thinking hard than a motherfucka. I hope John is waiting on me. I'm a gets off the plane and hope he is waiting around the airport".

It's a warm and sunny day people are walking with wearing skimpy summer attire. Two girls walked by with bikini tops and I almost gasped. It was a good day to fly. I'm walking through the terminal and sees John.

I shout out loud, "There's John". John is white in complexion with curly hair. He's about 5'10" tall and 185 lbs. He peeps me and we get eye contact.

I shout out, "What's up my nigga?" I noticed the people around start to look at John and then me, but keep on moving. They probably were wondering why was I calling John my nigga. John and I hug and embrace happy to see each other.

"How was the trip in?" John asked.

I reply, "Oh! It was all right, you know South West Airlines though! You have to stop in five different places before you get to your destination.

"I know what you mean", John replied.

I asked John because I was still thinking about home.

"John when the last time you been to the crib?"

He answers, "man, I went back Christmas time".

I interrupts, "John dude I just left man and each time I go back. It seems as if the hood gets worse and worse".

"The baggage claim is over here"; John says then points in that direction.

I look and spot it right away. "There's my luggage right there, right on time. I got two blue bags, grab that one John".

"Andrea is park outside waiting on us", John says, and nods his head in the direction, right outside the window.

Andrea is John live in girl friend. She's a pretty and pleasant Native American girl who works with John at Hail Corporation. She has hair that stream all the way down her back. She was a little shorter than John with a nice figure.

"You know I got a new car, a Thunder Bird" John walks and talks and points in the direction of where the car is parked.

I look at his new ride and say, "Straight up, you coming up in Texas, huh!"

"A little something, a little something," John says humbly. "Right out this door" John points and shows me the car.

I say, "Yeah, motherfuckas are coming up in Texas". I say it with a sly grin while covering my mouth, "damnnnnn nigga!"

"Hey Colo," Andrea shouts out the driver's window. You made it in all right I see. This is your first or last stop. You know how you travel".

I reply, "this is the last stop. Yeah, I stopped in Chicago to see Mom and the family, first. John I rolled through the old hood".

John opens the trunk and says, "give me the bags and go head and get in".

I reply, "Okay", after dropping the bags in the trunk. John gets in and closes the door and Andrea takes off.

I ask John, "did you go on 169th when you were there?"

"Yep," John replies, "It's gone man. The motherfucka is off the map. It doesn't feel like home anymore".

I shake my head yes in agreement.

I then say, "I know what you mean John. I remember even when I didn't live around 169th; it still was my home. Anybody who ever moved from 169th St. always came backed and kicked it. The new faces are looking at me as, if I don't belong in the hood and I know the look".

"Now you got to look for everybody and nobody got time to holler. Some of the buildings in the hood are marked up torn down or abandon". I didn't see any graffiti I had left".

"Yeah! I remember when John took me to Chicago. I wasn't impressed to see where you guys lived". Andrea comments.

I replied, "It wasn't like that a few years back before the cocaine flooded our neighborhood.

"It looks like more than cocaine hit that neighborhood," Andrea reply's.

As we pull into the complex and roll pass the basketball court. I look at the court smiles and say, "John, you know I got to hand you and Emus some court action before I go home".

Johns replies quickly, "you don't want none".

My face shows a picture of unconcern. "Back to you Andrea, it wasn't like that when we were coming up on 169th. Cocaine was the variable that broke the camel's back. Back then the families stuck together. People were much friendlier".

"We had block clubs and neighborhood watches. Now, people don't care about other people like people used to care. I'm going to tell you how it was when we were coming up Andrea".

Andrea interrupts, "I know it probably was different, but from what I've seen of your neighborhood it's hard to believe. Emus and John tells me so many stories about you. I want to hear it from you.

John pulls into his park. We jump out and get the bags out the trunk then we all go inside.

I immediately commented on the house after taking a look around. "You guys have a lovely home. You leather out with the glass and the brass. Y'all rocking the hard wood floors, floors shining like the sun".

The walls are beige with brown trimming. The house was clean and organized. John you've come a long way from 169th. What are you a big executive with the Hail Corporation or something?"

John answers, "No, but I am a supervisor moving up with Hail fast. The company is growing fast. I'm in charge of 160 people in my division".

I give John his P's. "You and Emus have come to Texas and are doing it up huh!

John cuts in, "yeah dude I've been trying to tell you to come on down. It's gravy down here. Warm all year round and Texas is a good place to raise your children down here".

Yeah, yeah! John I've still got a couple of more years in Detroit before I can make any plans like that.

"Colo I heard John's version of 169th. Tell me your view point on how it was growing up on the Southside of Chicago?" Andrea asked and continues. John told me a little something, but

he doesn't go too deep. I hear on the television news how bad it is in Chicago. Don't just tell me about the crime part. Tell me something good about Chicago.
John wants to go back and live there, but I am kind of reluctant to go".

I pause and say, "Well right now I'm living in Detroit. I'm looking from the outside in, but from what I can see. It's not too good right now living in the Chi. I don' t want to start with what's happening now. To give you a good picture I'll have to start from what I know. John you jump in whenever.

I was just on the plane and I was thinking. It wouldn't be so bad if a lot of these families had a good fatherly role model. It doesn't even have to be his father. Kids need someone to look upon positively, in the home.

A lot of our young men are handling things on their own without any guidance. It's worst now, because these are children of the cocaine era. A lot of these homes are fatherless and motherless even if they are at home.

Their parents are in jail, cracked out or dead for some of these kids. The kid's parents have given 90 percent of their life to the drugs. This leads a child into hopelessness. It's tough without a father to take you through certain things in life.

It's even tougher with a cracked out mother. Now for you to get the real picture about Chicago. You will have to go all the way back to the beginning with our child- hood. John bust open a drink I got a liter of Remy in the bag on the couch.

John looks and says, "I got you, you tell the story and I'll get the drinks together".

.

Touch Down

It was a tough road for me out the gate. The day of my birth could have been the same day I died. I was a breached baby. I was entering the world feet first. I was in there so long I was trying to walk up out the womb. This is a problem though! I could be choked to death by my mother's umbilical cord.

During this time the doctors were scrambling to turn me around. My mother prayed a prayer to God. Yaweh please! Please don't let me carry this baby for nine months and he doesn't make it. It must have been a battle between good and evil. I had a guardian angel that fought for me to be here.

The doctors flipped me around inside of her womb and I tunneled out the right way. I made it through the birth canal March 2nd 1968. This is the day I touch down in this world.

I was a born fighter, because I was fighting for my life from the gate. During the process my feet were turned backwards. The doctors turned them back the right way, but I had problems.

Once I was able to walk I had to wear special shoes. For the first few years of my life I had to work to straightened them back with my Mom's help.

I always remembered her saying, "walk straight Colo, practice walking straight".

She didn't want me to be walking slew footed or pigeon toed. After a few years you couldn't even tell I had a problem with my feet.

I had a problem pronouncing words that lasted longer. Moms worked with me on that for years! One of the words I had problem saying was fruit. She would have me pronouncing it over and over.

"Fr fru fruit is his how you pronounce it Colo".

I lived in an area called South Commons at first. I don't remember when we lived at that the address! The first house I remember living in was 314 E 170th St. We are a family of five, Arnez George, my 2 brothers, my sister and I. My sister Carmelita was the oldest.

We call her Barbara. She was like my second mother or so she thought. She's brown skinned and pretty and wore glasses. She carried a little extra weight on her when we were young. You know the first child gets over-fed.

My brother Samson was the oldest boy named after my father. Samson is the man who adopted me as his own. My bother Samson was 6'3" tall and brown skin and skinny. My younger brother was named Walley, two years my younger. He was 5'7 inches tall and has dark skin. Wally was about two shades lighter than I.

He used to say all the time. "I am black but Colo you are darkness".

Samson was the only father I knew until I was about eleven. Only to find out Columbus Cody was my father. My real father was average height dark skin and wore suits all the time. He wore suits during the week. I didn't know him as my father at first. This is a man who befriended me at church low-key.

My adopted father and mother separated. We didn't get to see him much. My adopted dad had one of those jobs where you had to stay on the premise 24 hours. What kind of job is that? Sometimes my sister would pack us up and we'd catch the bus to go see him.

He wouldn't even know we were coming. He had a nice apartment. Leather couch floor model TV. He had a Lazy Boy that sat right in front of it. What caught my attention all the time were those rifles.

He had three rifles sitting on a rack mounted to the wall. Those guns had me fascinated. When I was over there I just starred at the rack of rifles.

My adopted father didn't live with us, but he did used to come around to see us. My father was more than just a hi and bye father, at first! He called us to see how we were doing.

He would visit quite often bringing us birthday and Christmas gifts. The only thing about this is he was not in the household or in arms reach. We called him on the phone to talk to him. We couldn't knock on his bedroom door, if we wanted to talk to him.

When we were acting up or needed discipline. He had to threaten us over the phone. Instead of saying wait till I get home and I'm going to tear that ass up. You know kids will take that type of discipline, a long way.

We had a normal childhood I guess. We kept ourselves busy in the house. Our family played board games together: Battle Ship, Monopoly, Uno and Back Gammon was my favorite. We had the Atari 2600 hundred. We had the game before that which was the tennis game. We all watched TV and did everything together in the beginning. We were and still are a very close-knit family.

My mother is very religious, a god fearing woman. She doesn't smoke cigarettes. She doesn't drink nor did she curse. She didn't listen to worldly music at all. I can remember as a kid going to church constantly, almost unbearably. I liked church, but church was on Sunday.

The Chicago Bears were playing on Sunday at 12 o'clock. I think they have the football game on Sunday on purpose. It is a distraction. I'd be in church wondering about the score of the game.

We'd go to church during the week, Sunday school, morning service and afternoon service. After the long day of church she would turn around and go back to night service. She probably would have taken us to the night service too. We had to go to school in the morning, thank God. We didn't have a car at the time.

We'd prepare on Saturday everything for church on Sunday. We ironed, wash and prepare our uniforms. I remember waiting on the green limousine in the rain, sleet or snow trying to get to and from church. My mom called it our green limousine.

Moms would say, "Colo look outside on the porch and see if my green limousine is coming".

In the wintertime it was terrible. It would be cold and we'd huddle together to stay warm on the bus stop. We went through a lot just to make it to church. Mom was all we knew coming up and she guided us. When mom wasn't around the house she was working or at church.

The church is the reason why I love music so much. Our church used to be jumping. The pastor would charge everybody up by saying something powerful. You'd then here the organ start to pump along with the pastor. The congregation would be so charged up and hanging off of every word.

The instruments would start chirping. You'd hear the washboard and the fork scrapping. The drummer would begin his thing with the symbols. The guitarist would jump next. Next thing you know the church is on fire. The choir would be singing while Mr. Wooten commanded his symphony of church members with his stick. The sopranos would be chirping next the tenors. The men came in with the deep base and pastor had the spirit moving.

I'd play and watch, as the spirit was infectious to the people in the audience. I'd be playing the bongos hitting some nice sequences. Our family all came with tambourines, washboards and bongos. My brothers and I would all trade instruments just jamming in church.

I'd be like, "give me the washboard Walley". We'd switch instruments. I'd grab the washboard and start to scrub the fork on the silver metal ripples, on the beat. I had a different sweet creative sound when I was gigging with the tambourine.

My Godmother Mrs. Carmelita Frank brought me a tambourine for one of my birthdays. Mrs. Carmelita was light skin with shoulder length hair with blemish less skin. She was a very attractive lady and looked sophisticated and proud.

She didn't have any kids and that was a blessing for me. She showered me with gifts. She was one of a short list of my mother's friends. The bongos I had she bought me too. I could play those bongos pretty good not to have any lessons. I would sit up front with my bongos, along -side where the musicians setup. I would get me a short solo while everybody enjoyed me playing. I had fun while I was at church.

My sister Barbara was in charge solely, when mother was gone. My mother gave her almost the same rights she had. I would grow to hate that fact she could tell us to go to bed. Put us on punishment and chastise us if needed. She was bigger than me and could handle me quite easily when I was young. When I did go to another level with her defiantly or not listen to her.

Barbara then would threaten me with, "I'm going to tell mama on you", she'd sing it out.

Once she said that I got myself in order. Yaweh knows I didn't want her to tell momma.

My mother ruled with an iron hand. As far as discipline there was no father needed. When we got out of pocket, she would blaze us on the spot. Sometimes without her or I even knowing it sometimes.

She would say, "Boy did I just slap you?"

I'd answer, "I don't know momma". I just felt pain pulsating across my face.

I'd turn and ask her, "did you slap me? What just happen there?" I'm just joking, but my mother had a quick trigger.

While living on 170th St. was one of the best Christmas's I ever had. We got everything one year that a kid could want. The whole house got a little pool table. I got all kinds of coloring books. I always got some of those model cars you put together. I needed help so all I could do was put the stickers on them. I got a lot of things that were new.

I got my ass whipped for playing around and knocking down the Christmas tree that Christmas. My little brother got a whipped for not going to the potty. I can't forget how he looked when he felt the pain. Whack whack whack on his bottom for not going to the potty.

He had to be about one no older than two years old. Mr. Tooley the landlord stayed upstairs. Back then people didn't rent to single mothers with children. Again, this is for the fear of the kids tearing up the place.

My mother not only kept his place up; it was better when we moved. It was nothing but dirt in the backyard at one time. My Mom planted seeds for grass and watered and nurtured it. I watched the grass grow out the dirt from seeds. It was beautiful, but after she did it. Mr. Tooley didn't want us to play in it.

Our cousin Judy used to stay with us a couple of years. Judy was of light complexion and pretty.

Charles from the church would spend a night every once in a while. He was homeless. My mother used to let him sleep in the back room with us.

Charles was has light skin and where's a goatee and mustache. He was very thin and all his veins showed in his body. Charles kept his bible in his hand wherever he went.

He used to have seizures and wasn't quite right mentally. He came and spent a night one time. He had an episode while he was standing up talking to me.

All of a sudden he started to have a seizure. I'm looking at him while he was going out. His fingers were stressed like he was trying to clutch something in the air. He was trying to keep his eyes straight. He couldn't do it and they rolled to the back of his head. I guess he was trying to hold it off, but he couldn't. He falls to the floor in slow motion. I knew what it was, because he had them in church.

I called out, "momma, momma Charles is having a seizure".

That's what she told us to do, if we saw a seizure coming on! She comes in the room and just held him down. She told him to calm down. When he spent nights he never touched us. Now a day you can't do that shit.

The first time I saw Santa I was in daycare. Santa came in and gave everybody presents and I got a red plastic flute. I had some music to play. I loved that flute. I never knew how to play it. I thought this was a very special gift from Santa. When I saw him I was thrilled.

The first time I felt emptiness. My friend Star Brown left town and never came back. Star was our playmate in the hood. This girl was energetic and very opinionated. She has dark skin and long hair for a black girl. Her eyes would light up the night they were so big. All she had to do was open them wide.

The Browns stayed behind us Myra, Jake, Donna and Star. They had more brothers, but they didn't live in the house. We got so cool we used to call each other cousins from that point on!

She'd come over and play at our house and vice versa. I loved her laugh. Her laugh would just light up the world. We used to play horsey.

She used to ride me like a horse while saying, "getty up Colo", like the lone ranger.

We played all type of games together. It was Larry, John, Walley, Star and I hanging out together when we played.

Well one day I went to see her to play and her people said she'd left town. She went to California.

I asked her sister Donna, "well when is she coming back?"

Her reply, "she wasn't coming back".

I do remember just standing there trying to comprehend, not coming back.

My first day of kindergarten was horrible. My Mom dropped me off and left me at school. When my momma was leaving I tried to do the, "momma don't leave shit".

She comes back to me and said. "Do you want me to take you in that bathroom?"

I tell her, "no no mommy,"

She then says, "okay, go in the classroom, this is your teacher. She's going to teach you. I'll be back to pick you up".

I was overwhelmed at first. My teacher was white and that was fucking me up. She was the first white person I remember seeing. She was cool though! She wore rimmed glasses and spoke with a soothing voice. It was always calm I can never remember her hollering. When I enrolled in the school it was a classroom full of students just playing around.

I had on some hard bottom shoes the first day. I notice because everybody else didn't. When were playing I'd be sliding all around the floor with those slip and slides.

After a couple of days of doing this I was straight. After a few weeks of school I overheard Mrs. Young telling my mother that I picked up fast. As a matter of fact I pick up, real quick. I like to learn as a child and was a seeker of knowledge. I comprehended what she was teaching us.

Our next-door neighbors became life-long friends with us. The Harris family was a family of five. Mr. Henry, Mrs. Emma were what we called, parents. They had three kids two boys and a girl at first. The two boy names were Larry and John and the girl name was Alberta. We would hit the block as cousins. Later they had an older sister named Sabrina who came down from the South. Sabrina is short brown skin with short hair.

My mother kept us in the house, because of Mr. Tooley. She was struggling and didn't want to get kicked out. It was hard enough when her and my adopted father separated. We stayed at that address until I was about five years old. Later we moved to a bigger house a couple of blocks down and over to 356 E. 169th St.

We stayed on a side street at first and it was quiet. 169th street is a main street with a vein from the East to the West side of the area. You see a lot of live shit living on a main street. This is the street I would claim growing up 169th & Calumet.

Like I said earlier there was no need for a father, as far as discipline. I kind of wished it were somebody else to give me a whipping, instead of the G. Yeah! The G, ruled with the iron hand. When Mom came home from work and that kitchen, bedrooms and the basement wasn't clean. Whatever individually area that you were in charge of, wasn't cleaned by bedtime. Mother would come in from work and snap off immediately.

I was the kind of kid that loved to get out of doing something. Pass the work to someone else, often paying my brothers or sisters to do my work. I was the kind of kid to sweep something behind the door or under the rug. I must be a descendant of royalty or something.

My ancestors must have been kings and queens. I must be! I felt I shouldn't be doing those types of things. It was something else I was supposed to be doing, much bigger. I thought I should be practicing or playing sports. I was doing housework while people were balling at the park

Of course she would find my hiding spot sooner or later. She was the type of mother to check behind you immediately. One time when I was about eight or nine years old Mom came home singing church songs. It seemed like she would sing them to the top of her lungs. I was hoping she came right up stairs and went to bed. Nope, she started checking the areas that we were in charge of for that week.

She told us before she left. "Make sure her house was clean by the time she got home".

She walks through the dining and living room still singing. Now she's going in my area, the kitchen. She turns on the water while still singing. I can hear everything from upstairs. I'm listening to her every move. My heart is throbbing for fear that it is not up to standard. Up to standards, I knew it wasn't up to standards. I heard her open the cabinet, probably looking for a glass to get some water.

All of a sudden she stops singing and starts humming. I hear one dish hit the sink then another and another. My heart starts to race and my head get warm and wet with perspiration.

I did a rush job on the dishes, because it was almost bedtime. I wanted to watch, Starsky and Hutch so I started late and did them quickly.

I really just ran some water over them and put them in the cabinet. Mother stops humming and pauses maybe to drink the water. I hear one more dish hit the sink. Then, I hear her coming, walking heavily back through the dining room. She was almost stumping up the stairs. I knew that wasn't good. All the bedrooms were upstairs so she got to come upstairs.

I'm lying under the covers playing sleep as she walks pass my room. She stops looked in to see if everyone is asleep. I hear her walk past and she stops at my sister's room.

She's not shouting, but in a loud voice. "Who is in charge of the kitchen this week?"

I can hear the tone in her voice. She said it firmly, that's not good.

I started to shake and panic. Oh my God! I started to fear, what was coming.

My sister replied, "Colo was supposed to do the dishes momma".

She then asked my sister, "did you check behind him?"

My sister replied, "yes".

My mother then says in a heavy tone, "Well I was trying to get me a cool cup of water. I couldn't find a clean cup or a clean dish in the cabinet".

All of my dishes are dirty.

My sister reply was, "I told him to make sure they were clean". After she said that, Mom storms to her room.

My eyes are wide open under the covers hoping and praying for her to spare me. About five minutes went by and I started to feel a little easier. All of a sudden I hear her gathering or searching for whipping material.

You never knew what the whipping material was going to be. By this time you couldn't find a belt in the house. You couldn't find an extension cord or a rope nowhere in the house. We hid them all, but she would just find something else to use

I sit up on the bed damn near having an anxiety attack. I get up like I'm going to the bathroom. The bathroom was next to my room.

I look at her coming and I start saying, as if I don't know what's happening. "mama what's wrong, mama what's wrong?" My heart is thumping visibly.

She reply's as she starts swinging. "Get down stairs so I can show you".

Every time I made an attempt to go down the stairs. She would whack me one and shout, "get down stairs". She'd be holding an extension cord or a rope in her hand.

Every time she whacked me I would always repel back screaming, "please momma stop", repeatedly. "I am going to do it. I'm going to do it"

This could go on for about ten to fifth teen minutes. Until, I finally worked up enough courage to make a run for it. I got hit in the back of the head or back trying to get away. Wherever the belt, stick or extension cord would land. After I made it down stairs I would get a few more and then she would go to talking. I had to wash every dish, pot and silverware in the cabinet. I would be damn near falling asleep washing the dishes. It's something about a whipping that puts you to sleep.

My brother's were upstairs terrified. They were hoping their areas were straight. Mom would just go on to the next one. She had incredible energy.

She used to say, "I am on a warpath".

When she was on a warpath everybody is getting a whipping. I believe the only reason she stopped was when she got tired. Sometimes she would rest and come back and finish. It was a first and second half to my whippings. Just like a football or basketball fifteen-minute halftime.

When I used do something devilish she often used to say. "I'm whipping you because I love you".

You couldn't get me to believe that in a thousand years. You are inflicting damage on my ass, because you love me. I often wished she didn't love me so much.

After the whipping and tongue-lashing was over! The tongue-lashing was just as excruciating as the whipping. The lecture could go on for thirty to forty-five minutes, if she's in a hurry. I sometimes would wish her and my sister would die at that moment. God I thank you, for not answering that wish.

I later found out it was, because she really did love me. I was a scandalous little nigga, now that I think about it. She was at her wits end with me. This shit she was doing to me, was passed down from generation to generation.

It was only 100 years of us being a free people. We still were and are till this day, brainwashed on what Massa taught us. Our parents were using the techniques that Massa used to control the slave.

Later I had to realize she had to be the mother and daddy in the household. Now, don't get me wrong she banged us, but gave us much love. My mother: cut our hair, cut our finger and toenails, taught us how to cook, sew and garden. She taught us etiquette and installed morals in our psyche.

I belched at the table without covering my mouth one time. After I got off the floor from the smack across the mouth, I learned. I was supposed to turn my mouth away from the table and belch or cough into my hand. I'm a grown man and when I belch I think about getting up off the floor. Belching at the table never happened again. We knew how to set a table. When something big was going on she'd have family meetings.

My mother always gave me motivation tips. "Be better than me, because I only have a eighth grade education. I had to quit school and help out around the house. I need you all to do the best you can so you don't be in the position I am. Make me proud so I can stick my chest out. You have to be two times better than white people just to be on their level!"

"Always, remember if you are good, it's always somebody out there better than you! Never stop practicing never stop learning, because somebody will be there to take your spot. Be the best you can be in life, whatever it is. If you clean floors; be the best floor sweeper in the land".

I did not know about her leaving school in the eighth grade until later. My mother used a lot of common sense. Now that I think about it. I always stayed into reading and would read some words I didn't know. I'd ask her the meaning and she wouldn't know either. She would tell me to get the dictionary and look it up.

13

I'd say, "Mom I don't know how to spell the word how am I going to look it up?" She told me to sound it out and that's what I did. I didn't find all of them, but some of the words I did by using this method. Once I found the word I would have to go and tell her so she'd know what it meant. "Mom it's spelled like this and this is what it means".

She'd say, "good one, now we are more, smarter today than we were yesterday".

It seemed to me, my mother could do anything. She moved big furniture around and taught us how.

She always would say, "bend your knees when picking something up heavy. You don't want to mess your back up, bend your knees".

She showed us angles on how to maneuver big furniture through door openings. She painted, she worked and she did construction. She was always working around the house. When she needed to hammer and nail something. She would do it. She was left-handed so it looked funny when she did things. She would work that left hand till it worked.

Every two weeks we got our hair cut. We never saw the barber for my first ten years of life. My Mom cut my hair. This used to be almost as terrifying as getting a whipping. First of all, I didn't want my haircut. I wanted to where a natural. My mother wanted my hair low like a white boy so we met in the middle.

While she had the clippers she always told me keep still. Sometimes when I moved she'd cut a gap in my head with the scissors.

She'd tell me after she gapped me. "Boy you better stop moving you see, I already cut a gap".

That means she has to go lower or she has to leave the gap. I would feel the gap and the tears would stream down my face. I was scared to look in the mirror. I went to school many of days with a gap in my head.

My classmates would say, "your momma must of cut your hair," and it was the truth.

Most of the time, if I didn't move, she did a good job on my hair.

I used to think the things she did was wack. My Mom made her own clothes, fur hats and coats. Everybody else went to the store and got their clothes. My Mom would be sewing some mink pieces together instead of buying mink.

Now they are buying my mother's fur accessories she makes. She's got some outfits she made that are sweet. I know she could have been a clothing designer with guidance.

My momma amazed me. I knew other women of her caliber wouldn't be doing these things. She used to pride herself on not having to call men to help her. A man wants something in return and she could do it herself. We called the plumber when needed and my Mom didn't know about cars. That's it she did everything else herself.

She had Elroy change her tire when we had gotten a car. Wait a minute, about the plumber. He was only called after we couldn't snake it ourselves. The basement flooded she'd have us down their filling buckets up and dumping the water outside.

She'd say, "come on boys let's get to moving. You got to be strong, can't let your momma beat you".

She knew how to motivate me I can't let my momma beat me. I got to be stronger than my momma.

Mom only called for help with the car and sometimes the plumber. Anything else in the middle she was going to find out how to do it. My mother could do all of that and she was beautiful. My mother had a Coca Cola bottle shape, but you couldn't tell. Reason being she never wore pants. She had four kids and her stomach was still flat. She worked out to keep in shape.

My Mom never wore pants. Instead of pants, she used to where those leggings in the winter under her dress. She was brown to dark skin with a unique color. She has a lot of Indian in her. She puts me in the mind frame of Jackie Brown the black exploitation film star.

My mother could dress her butt off. She loved to look beautiful when she wanted too.

Anytime she walked out the door she'd ask. "Does your momma look good? Is everything's in place?"

We boys would look her over to make sure her slip or no strings were hanging.

My mother was definitely a jack-of-all-trades. Mom showed me how to hustle, a legal hustle. The Bud Biliken parade came before every school year. My mother would be out there, getting money.

She would bake her goodies the day before. She had these homemade apple pies she used to make. They were good as hell. She would go out to the farm and get a few barrels of apples. Bring them back home peel, cut and bake the pies in individual crusted shells.

She'd prepare everything the night before. We would line up everything in the hallway. We loaded up early and rode out to park before sunlight. Once out there we'd pick a spot and hustle those pies and snow cones all day. Next, thing you know, we picked it up. We started hustling icy cups out the house as kids. My Mom did anything you could do, to make a legal buck.

It was plenty much love there, but if we've gotten out of pocket. We would be discipline severely. If I would be a smart ass in school or caught doing something bad. If I stole, cursed or anything of the sort. Mom would take care of her business when she or I got home". Sometimes she couldn't get to us then she'd add them up for when she had energy.

Sometimes she would be tired and say, "I'll get you later".

When she had time to or when my next fuck up happened. She'd call them off during the chastising. "Remember this, remember that, you thought I forgot? I told you I would get to you".

I often hated those, because she would call you at any time. It could be weeks later. That was a mental hell. You never knew when the hammer was going to fall. It was going to fall, you just didn't know when. All it takes is something to tick her off. It could be the smallest of things and next thing you know. She's sending me off for whipping material.

That is very challenging for a kid. She's sending me off to go get my own whipping material for a whipping. I never could find any whipping material. I always came back saying, "I can't find anything momma".

Now, I'm realizing my mother was born just two generations out of slavery. During slavery time, if some of the men were rebellious or wasn't going with Massa's flow. To keep the rest of the slaves in line the slave would be whipped publicly.

After the public whipping the rest of the slaves would do just about anything not to get whipped. I believe the women and men were ingrained with this method of discipline in the genes. They were brainwashed into believing that this is how you keep young men in check.

This was laid into our genetic makeup. After slavery was abolished the mind frame on disciplining your children or property was the same. After all, we had to learn everything from the whites once they stripped us of all knowledge, family and history. Therefore, I don't blame my mother for the abuse. I made it out and I know she loved me. If this is all you know, this is all you know!

I got a whipping for what the neighbors told her. I was throwing rocks or something at the neighbor's dog. She came home, the usual time and just started taking care of business. Bang@#* booM**!!

She 'd asked us, "why were you throwing rocks at the dog?"

When we tried to lie and say we didn't do it, it was more to come. Bang @#*#BOOM@* Boom. We'd tear the house up, with me trying to escape my mother's wrath. After that we had to clean up the collateral damage.

I often wondered how she knew we were throwing rocks? I didn't know while she was at work, we were on the scope. Whenever she was gone, she had someone watching us from afar. She gave them the number to wherever she working. They would call her right away, if we were really, mischievous. Yeah the neighbors called, if we got out of pocket. I didn't know she had that ace for years.

She often said though, "I don't even have to be around and know your every move".

I still don't know which neighbor it was telling on us. Yeah, my mama was strict then a motherfucka. The things I wanted as a kid. Mom wouldn't let me have them.

I wanted the water guns. Oh! I wanted that cowboy outfit, with the plastic gun, belt and gun holster. I couldn't have the outfit, because of the guns. You had the cap guns nope I couldn't have it. I wanted a slingshots and nope I couldn't have that either.

Anything that a little boy could want that was violent or of a violent nature I could not have it. She did not want me playing with guns or weapons of any kind. I just couldn't understand it. Everybody gets the cowboy outfit, with the gun and holster. This just would intensify my desire to have them later.

I used to come up low-key and buy me a water pistol. I would trade something for one or buy it when I had a chance. When mom caught me with these items it would get taken, crushed and thrown away. I had to watch it happen was the bad part.

That's not only it; it was going to be a punishment for disobeying. I had to have those things, if I had to buy them myself. Mom was a private investigator. She would find my play heaters I'd have duffed somewhere. I stayed on punishment once they were found. I couldn't leave my room for years.

This was torture for my mind. It was solitary confinement. It was nobody to talk to and nothing to play with, to pass time. All you could do was lie in the bed and think. I had these glow in the dark stars, moons and planets on the ceiling.

I used the ceiling to travel somewhere else. This was jail I couldn't take it. It was worst, when I couldn't read my comic books either. She would take them and lock them up in her closet.

I was a highflying eagle, but I'm in a cage all the time! I couldn't watch TV. I couldn't go outside. I just couldn't do anything. I was in solitary confinement for real. Up till about eleven I didn't know what, you can, meant. I stayed on punishment.

Now knowing that I'm a get my ass kicked, on the other side of the moon. I'd still do whatever I could to get out my room. My room was on the second floor. I would slip out the window onto the back porch grab onto the banister. Jump on our porch, then jump on the neighbor's porch and scale down to the ground. Go out their gate, hit the gangway and I'd be on the Met chilling. I had to time it right if found outside I was through.

I had balls, I guess I figured, I can't do shit anyway. It's worth the whooping just to be outside. When I had money I would run to the store real quick and come back. Most of the time I didn't have money and I still ran to the store anyway. Ooh wee! I used to tear the store up on King Drive. They had the ice cream freezer as soon as you come in the store and off to the right. The register is off to the left on a 45-degree angle from the ice cream freezer.

I had a compartment I had made in my pants. My thing was to lean over in the freezer once Jessie wasn't looking. Slip the ice cream in my pants low-key. I kept a big shirt on when I did it. I would duff four ice cream sandwiches, the push up and those strawberry short cakes.

The underlay would be, to take two other ice creams up to the counter. Take one back and then buy the one. Get a snicker and a Twix, which then cost 15 cents apiece. You know kids can't make up their mind. I would play it full hilt. I had to buy something couldn't just come in and leave out without buying nothing out the store.

This went on a while until Jessie caught me. Jessie was Black tall and thin. He had the store before the Arabs came in the hood. He damn near couldn't believe it. He caught me trying to get extras. I already had enough I went for too many, being greedy.

Jessie yelled, "give me that stuff you put in your pants".

I pulled it out and gave it to him and then kept coming out with shit. Jessie was disappointed at me. I saw it in his face. I was taking him to the bank. He borrowed me from the store and told me not to come back.

Jessie caught me stealing that day. Until then I stole what I wanted and ran back to the crib. Climb then scaled, jumped over the neighbor's banister. I crawl back through the window and eat whatever I stole. I used to hit the Leather Lounge store too. It was a little harder to get away. I would run fast as I could there and back. It would take about five minutes. Thirty seconds there and thirty seconds, back. Hopefully, it was not a long line in the store. Mr. Santos sold candy next door to me. I'd hit him up when I had money.

Now why she took my comic books and locked them up I don't know? These are the things I used to read. If it gave me any enjoyment, I couldn't have it. The green skateboard I had, I couldn't ride it.

I had to have back up plans, if the plan went wrong. That's what I figured out while in solitary confinement. When caught red handed. I had some good reason why I was doing, the wrongdoing. I started having script ready just in case I was caught.

I had to think ahead and cover all basis or Moms was breaking me down and fucking me up. My lies were so concrete, because of the bashing I could get. One thing I always knew to tell her is what she already knew. The lie I got caught in would get me crucified.

It was always a reason why I hit dude in the eye or whatever I did wrong. If caught with the goods I had to tell her the real. I can't say it wasn't me when it was found in my pocket. Tell her what she knows, "Yeah it was me, Mom, but he cheated me out of my money earlier. He stole my stuff first so I got him back".

Her response, "I told you to tell me when someone does you wrong".

If my face could talk! This is what I would've said, "I ain't no snitch I'm just going to get even". That's even, if I wasn't lying. You can't come back with your momma and have any respect in the hood. Your respect is instantly gone soon as you bring mamma into it. For instance!

I am going to jump ahead one time to when I was about, fifteen. Mom was going to church. I had been selling weed good for a minute. I just copped a quarter pound Saturday night and was going to bag it up after she left. I grabbed my little yellow envelopes I got from Mary's record shop and my stapler.

She yells out, "okay I'm leaving for church".

I was laying down watching the Bears game. I jumped up and watched her walk to the car, while sitting on the porch. She pulls off and I go back in the house and locked the door.

I'm like bet I'm alone. I go back to my room close my door and open the window. I didn't want the smell going all through the house. I'm about to smoke some of this weed I just brought. I had to make sure it was fire.

The day before JB from off Halsted walked me around for two hours until I found some that day. I gave him two nick bags for his trouble. I met JB at the Robe he played on the football team.

JB looked and said this all you going to give me. JB was BD Folks from around Halsted.

I looked and said, "yeah what else do you want you didn't put any money on it". I smoke a couple of joints with him and broke camp back to the Met. That morning after Moms left I dump the weed on my dresser and starts bagging while watching the game. I have to see my money before I start smoking anything.

Mom surprises me and opens the door, and say. "I need you to..." and looks at the weed. Moms went off, "boy you got this pot in my house". I had a look of total disbelief.

She goes to reach for it while saying, "I am about to flush it down the toilet".

I think quick cause she going to flush it for real. I blurt out, "Mom it not mine I am just bagging up for some guys. They're going to pay me a few dollars".

Her response, "I don't care whose it is!"

I say looking worried, "you don't care?" They probably will kill me Mom, on the spot. I can't come back and tell them my Mom flush your weed". At that time she knew I was plugged, but didn't know I was plugged.

Her face was distorted with a disgruntled like look and says. "I don't care what they think they shouldn't have given it to you".

My answer to that was, "Mom nothing good is going to happen if you flush that weed. It's not that simple. All I got to do is just give them their weed back. They won't hurt me Mom, if I give it back".

Mom was so mad about the weed, but she knows it scandalous out here. She knows people get their head cracked out here for fucking up. Her friend and neighbor Mrs. Jackson's son got killed. He was mixed up in drugs and got murcked. It is conceivable so don't be naive. I'm shaking my head left to right with my eyebrows raised, while laying the script.

She thought about it then said. "You are making me late for church I want it out of here before I get back".

It wasn't any more whippings at that age. My preplanned lies rolled off so smooth.

I tell her, "I just need some money mom". She left and ended up scraping me something up later. She did not want me selling weed or dope.

Back to where I was before I jumped ahead. My momma was rough!

She told me plenty of times. "I will take a man down".

I was weary of that and never tested her. She was rough, but at the same time she could be so much fun. I know she don't quit and will keep coming at you. She was strong and would wrestle with us all the time when we were young.

She'd wrestle us into holes and we couldn't get out. Once there she would tickle us to death. She had fun with it though. She'll throw that left arm up and that muscle would pop up.

She'd then say, "I am strong".

She had a legitimate muscle for a woman. This would make me go work out. Her muscle was bigger than mine.

Other times Moms played like she was Dracula. She put us in a wrestling hole and would bite our necks like Dracula. We would be cracking up laughing. I'd be pinching my neck and shoulder together to stop her from getting to my neck. This had me so tickled. We would laugh and laugh trying to stop her.

She loved her some Muhammad Ali, Jackie Chan, Bruce Lee and Jim Kelly. She was into fighting. I remember when the Ali and Frazier fight came on ABC. We had our popcorn and blankets and watched the fight. I was literally scared of her cause I knew how strong she was.

I told my Mom when I was about fourteen. It was no more whippings at that time. I got brave or was high or something. I wasn't getting enough money and was frustrated. I basically told her if you not going to give me no money. I know how to get some.

She asks, "what do you mean by that?"

My reply, "rob, steal or whatever. I am tired of being broke".

She asked again, "what you say?"

I reiterated, "you heard me, I'm a get mines. Walley is always getting new stuff, skipping right over me. His stuff is new and my stuff is hand me downs. He got the brand new Green Machine. He gets rabbits, he gets this, and he gets that. I don't get anything. I wanted to be a boy scout. Here he is, with the boy-scout uniform on. Everything I wanted he's getting".

Two years earlier we just didn't have as much. It wasn't like that, but it felt like it. I was too old for a Green Machine.

She was doing other things for me. She squints her eye so I know it's coming. She swings I duck. She swings again and I block it.

She says, "you trying to hit me?"

I reply, "nope, but I am not going to let you hit me no more and broke out the door". I'd leave for a few days and she would come looking for me.

I'd pop up and people would say. "You know your mom was looking for you earlier. She says for you to come home".

It felt good to know she was looking for me. I wasn't taking any more ass whippings. That was over I don't care what I did.

I guess she had to be tough, raising three boys and a girl by herself. I guess you had to nip rebellion in the butt before it begins to up rise. Psychologically, she had me fuck up. My Mom hurts and whips me like a slave? A few minutes later loves me at the same time. When I get older and become a man. What compassion you think I am going to have for anybody?

Just think I can love you guy, but if you fuck up. I will hurt you. Yaweh knows I had rebellion in me, but this wasn't the way to handle it. She told me when I got older after her eyes were opened, to what she did. She apologized and told me not to repeat the cycle! Learn from her mistakes, with your kids. Take the good I gave you and spread it.

Believe me I know my mother loved me, but what that did to me at a young age. It killed the compassion later I would have for women. I later in life turned into a womanizer. My sister and mother had too much control over me. I couldn't speak my mind at all. I could never tell her what I wanted. She just told me what she wanted.

She always said, "Colo you are so bullheaded".

I still always tried to get my point across. I'd never want to relinquish control of what I wanted to do, for the rest of my life.

Don't get me wrong I treat woman great. She taught me what woman likes. They like you to give them gifts and to be nice and curtest. I had no opinion on my life though! It was all what she wanted all the time. The control and the fear that held me captive as a kid, was tremendous. I grew up from six to sixteen, which is the foundation for your life, wanting out.

The times I felt special. My mother always made me feel special. The times I'd have her total attention was the times I was sick. I was a sickly child. I broke out from eating things with acid. I couldn't eat ketchup chocolate or anything with acid. I would have super lumps all over when I ate too much acid. My hand, head and body would break out in hives. They weren't little bumps they were big as boulders.

When I went down with a cold, flu or the chicken pox. My mother made me feel so special. She was at my beck and call. She brought fruit, tea and babied on her baby. When I got better I always took an extra day of babying by faking, still sick. I would be sick all the time just for that attention, if it wasn't for the sickness part. One time I did catch a cold on purpose just for the attention. I played outside in the cold with no jacket on and caught a cold on purpose. I only did that once, fuck being sick.

As far as the discipline! I've often wondered did other kids have to go through this terror or was it just me? John it seemed like to me, you were living a childhood dream. I thought you did what you wanted to do, when you wanted and how you wanted it".

John shouts out, "Shiite come on man, my childhood wasn't all that".

A Misunderstanding

Listen Colo we all had our disciplines coming up. It's just mine didn't come from my mother. Oh, my childhood was anything but peaches and cream.

"*ding dong ding dong*" the bell rings. *John says,* "*t*hat must be Big Emus". Andrea goes to the door to open it, she opens the door and Emus and his buddy Tadpole walks through the door.

Emus looks at me smiles and shouts. "What's up my nigga?"

I smile look him over and answer, "I 'm all-good, Emus you are one massive nigga". We embrace and I give Tadpole some love. I shouted out Emus measurements, "Emus is 6'5" and 280 pounds with a bald head.

"Well you know a nigga got to get his grub on," Emus replies, "It must be nice to just jump on a plane and fly down and kick it".

Now you know Emus I prepared for this trip. The ticket only cost me $100 with advance notice. You remember the last time I was down here Southwest was giving out those free one-way tickets.

I planned 21 days in advance and got a round trip for only a100 bucks.

"That's my nigga always be planning some shit," Emus comments.

You know that's right. What's up Tadpole? How's that pretty little girl?" Last time I was down here he had just became a daddy.

Tadpole answers, "She's all good, getting big though huh huh", tadpole laughs after everything he says.

I asked him, "How old is she now?"

He pauses then answers, "she's four months now and eating everything in site huh huh".

Tadpole is Emus and John are college schoolmates. You know why we called him tadpole? He was tall skinny with a dark complexion and he laughed all the time.

Tadpole moved in with Emus, when John moved in with Andrea. They all went to HT. University and lived together on campus. The story on Tadpole and how they all, became cool at school.

One day Emus, John and Lil Rich were in the lunchroom chilling. Lil Rich is off the Met. He did a year at UT. He short brown complexion with a smart mouth. He used to dazzle everybody with his no hands backwards flips. He does them in front of everybody when it is a crowd.

When here comes this dude, with flowers and candy in his hand. Everybody stops eating and starts looking at this guy coming down through the lunchroom with flowers in his hand. Tadpole goes to the table where his girlfriend was sitting. He gets down on one-knee then looks her in the eyes. Gives her the flowers for Sweeties day and tells her, he loves her.

Everyone in the lunchroom falls out on the floor laughing uncontrollably. Look at the fool come in here with flowers in his hand. Right in front of everybody and give it to his sweetheart. At the time he was looking like a fool to us, but all the honeys were saying, "he's so sweet". They began knocking all on his door and writing him love letters. After a while all the honeys were on his tip.

In order to get close to the honeys in school we had to get close to Tadpole. After cooling out with him they found out he was cool as a fan!

"What's up for the day Colo?" Tadpole asked.

"Well I got a little jet lag and if it's cool with you guys. I feel like just cooling out today".

"I'll conjure up some appetizers before dinner while you and John finish the story" Andrea suggested.

Oh yeah Emus! John and I were just reminiscing on how it was coming up.

"Yeah Colo thinks I had it all gravy coming up" John reiterates.

Emus shake his head in agreement agreed and say. "Well John you wasn't hurting for too much coming up".

"There you go with that same shit," John responds we a look of, you don't understand.

"Well tell us John how hard did you have it?" Emus smirked and say with a crooked grin.

"I had a couple of dilemma's that made my childhood very hard to deal. At least you were accepted in the hood. I had to prove that I was black and find out why I was black. My Mom and I both had super light skin and could pass for white in today's society. The only thing is we are black. That's what we are and always will be. All throughout life I've been wearing the tag white boy or whitey. I also had to deal with alcoholism".

"Alc Alcoholism", I sputter's out.

"Yes alcoholism and I was fatherless. It was shit y'all didn't know about. I know what you are about to say, what about Jughead? Yeah! Jughead lived with us, but I knew he wasn't my father. He was more like an uncle to me. Now that I've gotten older I respect him as a father. Jughead was my mother man and they lived together throughout the time we were on, 169th. Come to think about it. I didn't know my real mother up until, about six years old".

"Listen my life wasn't as smooth as you think. Let's me start from the beginning of how it came about. My mother was in college at Tennessee State during the late 40's doing her freshmen year. That's when she decided to leave and become a dancer.

"I didn't know your mother was a dancer" Columbus comments.

John reiterates, "Yes she was a dancer. Since my mother was of fair skin. She had some opportunities come her way. She wouldn't have had those opportunities being of a darker color. Therefore, she was able to work with this show group called, "The Larry Steel Show". She got the chance to travel all over the country with this show group. She worked with the show for about four years. That's when she came to New York and met her first husband.

This is where my sister comes in the picture. My mother hooked up with this guy in New York. He was an Italian with Mob connections in Queens.

"Get the fuck out of here John, "Emus shouts".

John looks at Emus and says, "dude he was in the mob. At first he thought my mother was white. It's really vague to me how it all came about. One day I asked my mother why would you marry an Italian, in the mob?

She answers, "John he was a gentlemen very suave, he had lots of money. You can't help who you fall in love with John".

The only thing is my mother wasn't used to that type of lifestyle. My sister's father would leave and be gone for days at a time. My mother didn't know, if he was out killing somebody or he was dead himself.

My sister began to ask questions, "where's daddy and when is he coming back?"

Finally my mother realized she never could tell her for sure when he was coming back. This isn't the lifestyle she wanted for daughter and herself. She soon grew tired of this lifestyle and asked for a divorce.

"A divorce John come on, mob motherfuckas don't get divorced and she Catholic too," I states then asks. How can they just get a divorce during those times?

I went into his raspy mob voice, imitation. You know how those mob nigga's are. "You ain't going **no where no where**, I'll hunt you down, find you and I'll cut your throat myself, you fuckin bitch". Everyone starts to laugh.

"Yeah you would think so but he let her go," John assures us.

That's when my mother came back to Chicago. She moved in an apartment on Park Avenue. After she divorced my man Moms was living plush. She had jaguars, furs and bookoo dollars. Yet in still she got a job at Grand Crossing Hospital as a switch board operator".

"She soon grew bored with this lifestyle. Her passions and desires to be in the entertainment field began to brew inside her. Through her ties she'd developed in the past with the Larry Steel Show, she got an idea.

My mother knew a lot of stars back in the day. She knew stars that would play in her club, if she opened up a joint.

"I didn't know your mother had a club back then" I say.

John shakes his head yes, "yep, it was called the Pumpkin Room. It was located on 171st between Jeffrey and Commercial.

You mean on the strip?" I asked.

John replies "Yep, that's where I come in the picture. You see I was a mistake. At this time my mother was 38 years old. The doctors told her she could not have any more kids. My father,

Joseph Massy was the bartender at the Pumpkin Room. I guess one night after a show or something they got to fooling around and bam I hit the scene.

This was something unexpected for both of them. They wanted to do the right thing so they got a bigger apartment and moved to 169th & Paxton.

"John was your old man black?" Emus asked.

John answers, "yes he's black, but he was of light complexion too. I guess that's why I'm so light. Anyway, we live in a twelve bedroom, apartment".

"Get the fuck out of here nigga, twelve bedrooms," I yelled.

"I'm not bullshitting ask my mother. Nigga we were flexing. I had a nanny name Carmela that took care of me up until about three months.

They say my father wouldn't let me out of his sight. He often would take me for buggy rides and everything.

"Oh yeah, what happen?" I asked.

My mother knew this high-ranking political figure in Illinois. I think my Mom was involved with this guy back in the day.

My mother being in entertainment field probably met him at the club or a prestigious event.

"It sounds like, a lot of people were on your mother's tip," Emus comments.

Yes my mother was very attractive. She was not only attractive, but very classy. She attracts a crowd with her pizzazz and charisma. Not just anybody could be with her. You had to have class and a lot of paper.

Well my mother and this official continued to be friends even after I was born. They were cool.

"Your mother was kicking it with my man, after she had you?" I asked.

"I think so I believe her and my father had an agreement or something".

"She must didn't love your old man?" I say.

"John replies, "I don't think so, I think they did what they did, for me. I don't believe there was any love there!"

"Now, the reason why my old man took off, I don't know. All I know is this high-ranking official was going to help my father start a limousine business. He loaned my father a large sum of money to start him out. Well, my old man got slick on him and left town with the front money.

Dude put a hit out on my father with the connections he had in the state. If he ever showed up in Chicago again he would be assassinated.

"Wait a minute a politician was going to put a hit on somebody?" Emus asked.

John replies, "Nigga you know what's up with those motherfuckers". They're more crooked than the motherfuckers locked up.

After my old man did that, my Mom didn't want anything to do with him. He wasn't shit to her. Dude was helping them out and he fucked them off.

John you don't know where he's at now?" I asked.

John answers, "yeah, he's in Detroit with all my brothers and sisters".

I asked, "Have you been down there to see him?"

John quickly replies with a frown on his face. "No, never will I do that. He wasn't there when I needed him so fuck 'em".

This is where it all starts to turn around. Since my Mom was in the entertainment business. She didn't have the ample amount of time to take care of me. The time that a son needs when he's growing up. Carmela had left town unexpectedly and I needed another nanny. Due to the circumstances, I had to be taken care of by somebody she could trust.

My mother knew this lady named Shirley who bartended at her club. She knew what my mother was going through and the obligations she had. Well, Shirley's mother Mrs. Hall would baby-sit the kids while they went to work. My mother felt comfortable with Mrs. Hall after a few visits. That's where I would live the next few years of my life.

Mrs. Hall stayed on 169th & Michigan. Therefore, my mother had to move out of that big apartment. This is how we got to 169th & Calumet. That's about four blocks down the street. My mother wanted to be in an arm distant from me. From the age of three months to the time I would enter school. I lived on 169th & Michigan.

Life with Mrs. Hall was very structured. When we got up in the morning breakfast was on the table. You must eat everything on your plate. If you didn't we were going to get a whipping.

Mrs. Hall whipped you?" Emus asked.

John answers, "Oh hell yeah! Belts extension cords whatever she could grab. Bedtime was at a certain time every night. When I say bedtime I mean bedtime. Lights out and nothing else said or your ass was grass".

At night we'd put our pajamas on and say our prayers. I thought Mrs. Hall was my mother. She took care of me like only a mother would do. I must tell you I felt love inside and out in that household. She disciplined me, loved me, feed me and taught me everything. My mother only came and got me to hang out sometimes.

We went to church every Sunday. We practiced whatever was taught to us in Sunday school in the house. When my Mom would come and pick me up. I thought she was a friend or relative of the family. That's how close the Hall's were too me.

During the time I was at Mrs. Hall. My Mom was getting paid off of the Pumpkin Room. At that time it was one of the hottest clubs in Chicago. A lot of stars came up from playing at the Pumpkin Room.

Like who?" Emus asked.

Shaka Kahn used to sing their Larry Reico Freeman, Sencell Vaugh and Vaughn Freeman the great saxophonist. A whole lot of local talent used to play there, during that time. I used to think my mother was a movie star.

Everywhere we went people knew her. Everywhere we would go people would always be on her tip. No matter where we went someone would say, "Hey Katherine, Katherine. I used to wonder how she knew some many people.

As I got older I realize she had a popping ass club. This motherfucker was off the hook. Mom was chilling over there by the lake with a club.

"Was the club just for blacks?" I asked.

"Nope, it was for blacks & whites people of prestige, it was a classy joint. Jazz was the thing then and some of the greatest musicians played during that time. Since Chicago was known for Jazz. She had one of the hottest spots in Chicago. Mom became affiliated with lot of well-known people. She knew Ramsey Lewis... and a whole lot more...

All good things must come to an end. My mother had all these entertainers playing at her club for a very meager fee. These musicians would play for my mother during that time for a $100. These same musicians would go across town and play for the white people for $300. You know those whities didn't like that shit. Next thing you know they were trying to close them down.

The one thing my mother did wrong. She did not buy her own lounge. She was leasing from a Jew. She owned everything on the inside, but did not own the building. Well, I guess they put some pressure on the Jew who owned the place. The next thing you know they turned it into a bowling alley.

My mother tried to fight it. When her lease was up, she was out. I know depression had to sink into her. To be a successful club owner one year and the next year you're out of work. Her name was still heavy in the industry. For a while she went around managing popular clubs, bringing in a lot of talent.

I was about seven or eight when I came home to live with my mother. This was a very difficult time for me.

"Why John?" I asked.

"You see the first years of my life were very structured and exact. When I came home to live with my mother it was totally different. I came home to people I didn't know".

There was Jughead who became the male role model that was available to me. Yes, my mother was there, but it wasn't like Mrs. Hall. It wasn't how Mrs. Hall was teaching me. At night my mother managed clubs like Berries back in the day.

After doing that for a while it just wasn't the same. That's when she began to drink heavily. When she came in she would be drunk than a motherfucka. My mother would come in my room turn on my light and just shout out an array of derogatory names.

Starting from you stupid motherfucka to you ain't shit, to all sorts of indignations. I would wake up look in amazement and start to cry. I'd wonder who is lady coming home cursing me out and calling me names?

I believe my mother was depressed from losing her club. The pressure was getting to her and I was her release valve. A lot of frustration was released on me. It wasn't her. It was whatever monster came out of that bottle.

I got the nerve up and ran away back to Mrs. Hall. That's when I realized she was really my mother. I remember these words as if it was yesterday.

Mrs. Hall said, "John this isn't your home anymore and I am not your mother. I would love to keep you, but your parents want you to come home".

She said it in a very kind and sincere voice. I remember the feeling too, as if it was yesterday. I knew I had problems. I couldn't identify with anybody in my immediate family.

I had left a family I thought I knew, to be family. I enter a family that cusses me out. She used to come home so drunk that she couldn't get me ready for school. This is where Jughead came in; he used to get me ready for school. When my mother would be hung over, it was he. Other than that I stayed in my room playing with hot wheels all day by myself.

"Come on John you mean to tell me Jughead used to bathe you and feed you? This is while your mom was hung over?" I asked.

John answers, "yep! Jughead had his bad points. As far as looking after me and making sure I had something to eat, he did it. Jughead was the one who showed me how to take care of myself. He was the one who told me things that only a father could tell me. He'd pick up where my mom alcoholism prohibited her from doing her part.

Jughead was a goon back in those days.

Shit I remember back in the day Jughead had a sweet white Mercedes," Emus says. I know Jughead used to roll back in the day. Jughead was low-key on the down low with his game. Back then heroin was the drug back in the day".

John looks at Emus and says, "Jughead was the bodyguard for a lot of musicians". He toured around the world with a lot of jazz artist like Joe Morgan, the great triumph player, Charlie Parker, the great saxophonist".

I interrupt, "what the fuck did Jughead play?"

John answers, "he just was their bodyguard. Back then they used to have those parties. Whatever they were doing the bodyguard would do too".

You know back then heroine and tooting was going on and Jughead was doing em. He had a condo in Hyde Park over-looking Lake Michigan. Jughead was getting them their drugs, body guarding and partying all at the same time. He was a music jazz buff! He appreciated good music. I believe that's how he and my Mom hooked up. They both had a love for music".

"This is how I peeped Jughead. Well, when I was little, I would sneak down stairs to see what was happening. I'd see Jughead getting his groove on with the needle or sometimes it was the cocaine. My mother was an alcoholic and my fatherly role model was a drug attic and pusher. That's how Jugheads nose got fucked up. He tooted up so much cocaine that he burnt out the cartilage in his nose. There was no bone left in his nose cavity.

Jughead told Ted and I. Ted was like John cousin no blood. He wore glasses and was of light dark complexion.

Ted and I asked him, "how his nose get smooched in like that?"

He tells us, "I went to Africa and a bird flew onto his nose and bit it".

"Hell yeah, I remember you telling me that bullshit," Emus shouts.

"Man, hee hee hee", John laughs and begins to say, "that's what he told us, a bird bit him on the nose. Back then it seemed conceivable for a bird from Africa to bite you on the nose. As you can see, I had two different living life styles. Mrs. Hall and then there was my mother".

"For the first couple of months I felt no love in the household. My Mom didn't hug me and pick me up. She didn't kiss me like Mrs. Hall used too. She didn't say any prayers with us at night. She didn't do a lot of motherly things that Mrs. Hall used to do. The transitional part was devastating on me. I think what saved me is when I started to get friends.

Yeah man, I guess you can have a lot things, but if you are mentally fucked up, it doesn't mean shit," I uttered under my breath.

Things you didn't Know!

I didn't know that about you John. I do remember us going on Michigan playing tackle football with Chris in his yard. He couldn't come out the yard at first. John you went a little in depth with things we didn't know. Okay, let me tell you what was going on in my head. When I was on the block it's a lot y'all don't know, about me.

I kept a lot of things private. Emus and John went to Brownell.

No I went to Rock Manor, in the 7th & 8th", Emus declares.

"Well, I started off at Rock Manor Elementary School all by myself. Nobody from the hood went to Rock Manor.

By the time you made it to the Manor, Emus. I had it sewed up.

Let me tell you about Rock Manor. I have to start from the beginning I can't keep jumping around. Rock Manor elementary school prepared you for the world. It had all the elements: Smart people, funny people, bullies, not so smart people, criminals, thugs, gang bangers, players, comedians, thieves, artist, marks, geeks and gymnast, ballers, guys doing the rackets and con artist. I can go on and on. It was 1st thru eighth grade school. You could graduate from Rock Manor back then at fifteen going on sixteen in those years.

The girls were just as bad as the boys or as good as the boys. As I look back! The goons in the street now got their start at the Manor. They are the grown goons you see from around our area.

The scandalousness started at Rock Manor. Meneen too, but people went to Meneen after they left Brownell. Brownell highest grade was 6Th grade. Meneen Elementary School was on 170th &State. You finished at this school from our neighborhood for grammar school.

Rock Manor was on 171st & Rhodes. The distance between the two schools was a mile and a half. Rock Manor was like an introduction to thug life starting in the kindergarten. You had to fend for yourself in the schoolyard. At Rock Manor either you learned or you didn't graduate. It was no pass along to the next grade.

If you're grade point score wasn't at a certain level. You didn't move to the next grade. If you didn't pass that constitution you didn't graduate. This is okay, but in the long term. You have teenagers in the same class as middle school students. These cats got hair on their chin and the girls who didn't pass, were developed.

I could see if it was just one or two. Half of the room was supposed to in the next grade or in high school. This breeds turmoil in the class. Those people hated my soul, because I had the answers to the questions. I was some sort of pariah.

I used to think it was because I was poor and they were ragging on me. It wasn't just that, even though it did play a factor. They were mad, because I was smart. That's all I had back then, was to be smart. To be smart you had to be tough at that school. They're not going to like it and let me tell you why. It was rough from the start I'm a go back to the beginning.

Chapter II

First Fight

After graduating kindergarten I had Mrs. Bean for my first grade teacher. Gladiating started early in the first grade. John Strong and I got into it. John was short with freckles and red hair. John lived on 170th & Calumet. John wanted me to move or switch seats with him. I told him I was straight. I don't want to switch seats. John started pinching me.

At first I told him to stop, before I pinched him back. John kept pinching me just because I was sitting by him. I couldn't figure out why would he do that? I kept telling him to stop, but I didn't tell the teacher.

I was no snitch even back in the first grade. I wasn't going to move anyway, because he made me mad. He kept telling me to move and steady pinching me. I started pinching him back hard, but John was the antagonist.

I guess he wanted to sit next to the girl I was sitting by. It didn't dawn on me at the time. I wanted to sit next to her too, Michele Brown. Michele was Brown skinned with long hair down to the middle of her back. She wore glasses and braces but neither took away from her beauty. John kept on pinching me.

I told him, "I wasn't moving so stop pinching me". He then gave me the dreaded I'm a going to dot your eye move. By showing me his knuckles, close to his eye and saying. "3:15. 3:15".

This was the time we got out of school for the day. I'm like damn I got to fight my first fight.

I had the bubble guts, because John knew everybody. He was going around telling everybody what he was going to do to me. I was nervous than a motherfucka. Everyone in the classroom is looking and talking about me.

I hear the whispers, "John is about to beat Columbus ass".

My butterflies got to going and to tell to truth. I was scared a little bit.

I didn't know anybody in the class like John did. I wasn't any mark though! It seemed like 3:15 got there so quick. John gave me the, eye dot move. It was right after recess 10:45 in the morning.

We went to lunch and he tells more people. He's going to dot my eye after school. I am getting my lunch from the counter and hear the whispers. My stomach started to bubbling. It seemed like 3:15 came in a matter of minutes. We started lining up to leave. I couldn't believe how quick 3:15 came. On a regular day it would move slow as hell.

I didn't know what I was going to do. What I did just came natural. He walked outside and was waiting for me at the front door. He was slapping his fist into his palm. He got his boys out there routing him on! "Fuck em up John".

I didn't say nothing and just step down the stairs. Once I got within three feet I just stopped there and swung. I hit him dead in the nose, bammm. His nose spewed blood all over his face.

He looked at me and said, "you bust my nose".

I replied, "I know I bust your nose. Stop messing with me". He was holding his nose and went and told on me. No, he might didn't tell, but Mrs. Griffin seen his shit bleeding.

She told me to come here and she ushered me to the office. Mrs. Griffin watched all the kids leave or arrive before and after the bell. She was about thirty-five and a little heavyset. Only reason, I got in trouble is because I busted his nose.

All that pinching shit he did, didn't matter. What matter was his nose was bleeding and I had hit him. Mrs. Griffin grabs me. That was just in case his buddies were ready to jump me. She saw them gathering after I hit him. My mother comes and I told her the story. "He was pinching me in class and waiting on me after school. I hit him before he hit me".

My Mom asked, "why didn't you tell the teacher?"

I look at her if my face could talk, I ain't no snitch. I got to figure this out myself. To be a snitch, meant I wouldn't be in on anything. When I walk down the hallway they would be like.

"Here comes the tattle tale. Don't say nothing while he's around".

Now John had uncles and shit that was holding the neighborhood down. They were first generation Folks. Folks were an organization a lot a teens joined in the middle 70s. His uncles were in high school or gone to Vietnam.

Lil Gooch and John were saying they were cousins at the time. Gooch & his brother Rob stayed a couple of doors down from John. Gooch was known as the terror dome and he was only in the second grade. Gooch and a guy named Curt were already known to jump on people. That's what I was worried about, the smashing.

Nothing developed after the fight though and we became cool. When we were in the second grade we used to go to his crib for lunch. He'd take me in the basement and show me all these assault rifles and guns. His uncles had brought them home from the war.

He knew how to work them and everything. This is the first time I saw real heat. I thought they were play rifles, until I picked rifles up. I felt how heavy they were. I said with amazement. "John this shit is real and it's just laying here on the floor".

Yeah, John was my first fight in a long line of them. Corey was next, I did the same thing to him. He called me out and I busted his nose. This time it was at the park. It was all in growing up.

This gives you prime example of after the fight is over, we are friends. Reason being, we know where each other stand. They know I ain't no hoe and I don't bother people. Leave me alone or I'll fuck you up.

You call me out and I'm going to bust you in the nose. I don't know why I aimed for the nose. Every time I fought I hit you in your nose. These fights built character. These fights made us into the men we are now. Once the fight over, right or wrong, if you lost or won the fight. You had to address and think about why did it happen?

Rock Manor was the gladiator school. I had a lot of fights in grammar school. Come to think of it I never started one of them. Reason why! By the second grade my back up was gone and it wasn't in my nature. My sister graduated and went to Darobe high school in 1976.

My click was John Strong, Fester Delldow, Ronald Goodwin, James Wisher, Anthony Combs and Jeffrey Robinson, Reginald Allen, Hubert Berry, Chris Hill, Buster Ford, Roddell Ward, Eric Dickerson, Tallie Weaver, Steve Flowers and Marcus Thomas. Academically and sports wise we covered all basis

We used to go head to head. The challenge was to see who was the best, in athletics and academics. We went head to head for the smartest in the class. We would race to get our work done. The competition didn't stop in the school. The schoolyard was a battleground for sports. Fester, Marcus, Chris and I ruled the front yard.

Hill dill started off as a race. The last three in the race has to catch and tag everybody else. We ran to one side of gate to the other side of the schoolyards gate. Once everyone is caught you start over! You have to tag with both hands squarely on the back at the same time. If you tag with one hand it didn't count.

This is where you get your football moves. After a while everybody is trying to catch just a few people left. This is when it's fun. When everybody is chasing you and you're putting on your best moves. Cutting and turning on and off the speed.

Marcus was the sweetest at hill dill. He was short, skinny and wore his hair short. Dude was fast. This was a fun game, if you were the one everybody was after. In the wintertime when the snow hit the ground it was tackle hill dill.

The game was 'Off the wall' in the summer and fall. Everybody came with their baseball gloves. We threw the rubber ball off the side of the school building. We threw it in an angle where it came high off the wall. It would be ten or fifteen of us trying to catch the ball. If you caught the ball you were the one throwing the ball off the wall.

If it wasn't off the wall it was Frisbee. It would be a gang of us throwing the shit out of a Frisbee. We'd be catching it all type of ways. We'd sling it all type of ways. We'd catch it between the teeth, while running after it. We played teams to set each other back. That's another game we played, set back. The object was to run you out the yard. I guess you would call it field position.

We played, 'Your It', in the cage. This was the most fun, because you had to jump in and out the cage. The person who is 'it, is trying to catch you running around the cage. The chaser would be trying to jump in or out the cage to get you. The gate was seven feet high. You had to jump over the gate or climb the pillars.

The pillar was an easier way of getting out. You had to climb the two big cement pillars, one on each side. You had to jump the gate or climb the pillar in order to get out the pit. This was a fun game at lunchtime.

We took it to academics. We wanted to be the smartest. Most days I would get them in the flash cards math game. The math game was fun, because I won all the time. The way it went is you stand next to each person in the class and work your way around the room.

The teacher stands in the front of the room with the flash cards. When she turns it over the first one with the answer continues. If it was close the classroom will say who answered first. I was quick I didn't even have to think I saw the numbers and I'd rattle of the answer. I was quick with the multiplication and division.

Coming up my Mom used to buy these math records when we were little. They had a nice beat to it. While the beat was going a man would go through the timetables. (1*1 = 1 all the way up to 12*12 =144).

All I had to do was glimpse at the equation. Now in the addition and subtraction that was another story. Jewell Rolling was the best at those addition and subtraction cards. They used to get me on those, but most of the time. We played multiplication and division cards.

When we used to have writing assignments John was the fastest in the writing assignments. John used to write with his left hand and his paper would be turned completely upside down.

You couldn't understand a word he wrote it was so sloppy. I used to tell him you might have finished before me, but it's scribble scrabble. He could understand it though and after he read it back I could make it out.

Our lives were parallel. What happened to me academically happened to them. All the way up until we graduated. Jeffrey Robinson left in the fifth grade he was a hanging buddy. It was Fester, Jeff and I that were crazy about those comic books. We hunted them down and traded with each other.

Jeff lived across the street from the school. He moved in the fifth grade. He was skinny with a narrow head. He was up to date with his gear. He stayed at Rock Manor until the end of the year he moved.

Fester and I went on an adventure to his house. I think Jeffrey moved somewhere on 79[Th] and Fester knew the way. We caught the bus over there and had a day of fun at his house. He stayed on the first floor of one of the colt way buildings. We rang the bell and he came to the door.

This was my first adventure on the bus by myself. We played in his room with all his toys. He had a lot of toys. He had these boxing gloves I always wanted. We played darts and cards. We ate some sandwiches and cooled out. This was the last day I saw Jeff. I remember that adventure was fun.

Anthony Combs left in the sixth grade. He was a short guy with a nerdy look to him, but he could play some baseball. His grade point average was like a 10.1 in the sixth grade. He was my academic competition. This guy was smart and didn't have to work at it. I knew I was smart, but I was working hard at it. He came back for the eight grade and graduated with us.

In athletics Chris Hill was the second fastest in the class and Marcus Thomas was first and I was third. Chris would edge me out by a nose every time we raced. We all wrestled, body punched, slapped boxed, arm-wrestled. Anything physical we did. We all were the top athletes in baseball, jumping, hill dill, football off the wall and running bases.

While we were playing sports or whatever, the girls would be jumping double dutch rope or something. They were on the swings or playing on the monkey bars. The game we played with the girls was, catch a girl and freak a girl. The girls knew when they got caught we could freak their booty, leg back or whatever we could freak. You could freak them a good ten seconds before they got mad. Some girls didn't play! You knew who they were, because they didn't run and dared you to touch them.

Fester was my hommie until he played me on his birthday, one year. His mother came to class with treats for Fester's birthday. Fester's mother didn't bring enough for everybody. Fester had to choose who wanted to have some. I knew I was straight because Fester and I hung all the time. We did everything together. When I got to school I would stop at his house early so we could play football.

He lived across the street from the school in the colt way building too. I went to his house for his birthday and got him. I already saw the treat I wanted and was going to pick it. I knew I was going to get it, because I know he's going to stop at me first.

Fester started handing out to the girls first. Okay I can feel that, give the girls some first. That's player style can't hate that! He was getting down to the end though. He had about four treats left.

His Mom said, "okay give some of the boys a treat".

Fester paused and looked around. He looked me in the eyes and right over my head. He gave the treats to the guys we weren't even cool with. When he gave the last one out he cracked my face open. I look at him in bewilderment. He was leaving school with his mother that day too. His mother looked and knows I was disappointed, cause I come over all the time.

I didn't say anything about it! I just knew he wasn't my best friend anymore. We still had fun and played ball, still. I knew he did that shit on purpose though! We kicked it every day how could he play me like that! I knew she was coming to get him. I knew about the treats before she came. He told me the deal. He hurt my feelings that day. I didn't go over there as much anymore. I always wonder why did he do that to me?

James Wisher and I were best friend's one year. We called him Cubby. He transferred in the third grade, but came back. He transferred again in the sixth grade. James Wisher was a straight up clown. He clowned all the time. I remember he was left-handed too when he threw the football.

James Wisher would have names for everybody. He called me Frankie baby off the Flintstone cereal commercial. The one he gave the most grief was Jewell Rollings. Jewell had some pretty big ears on her. He used to hit her with the baby New Years joke. In the animation cartoon 'Baby New Year' hid his ear under a hat. When he took his hat off everybody would laugh at his ears.

James would say it over and over again. "Ears ears ears earrry earrry earrrry earrry earrrry".

I never cracked on her, but James rode her like a pony. Jewell didn't take any shit, she'd give it right back to him. She'd crack back on him, but he'd drown her out with the earrry song.

James and I were going to the store right next to the school. We let the bell catch us so everybody had made it in the school already. We were walking down that alley going back to the school. We were going to use the entrance to the gate by the parking lot. We notice this bum walking in front of us. He was a dark skin bearded man with gray sprinkled throughout. His hair was medium length and kinky. He was wearing a funky dirty holey coat.

James started fucking with the man a little bit. James walked up to him making faces and noises. When he got close enough, dude grabbed James hand and put it on his private area. James snatched away and got his distance. We both look at the man, while backing up. I told James, "let's go dude some type of freak".

James face was cracked as he backed up. I'll never forget the look on his face. The guy didn't chase him or nothing. We went in the school and dude walked away hurriedly. I used to see the guy all the time, but after that he didn't come around anymore.

I was the best at fighting in the class at the time. Chris was next, but we were cool. Chris was stronger he'd beat me at arm wrestling, but we never fought. Marcus and John were the tumblers. I think both of them got on the Jessie White tumbling team. These two boys could flip their ass off. Arabian knights, backward no hands, 50 of them in a row. They were doing twisting shit all in the air and coming down on their feet, on concrete.

The girls in the class were Theresa Williams, Angel Ford, Tamara Ross, Lida Hyde, Teresa Miller, Karen Franklin, Barbara Penn, Pamela Thomas, Yavonna Hodge, Sharon Jackson, Laverne Cosby, Cessela Jones, Monica Burch, Jewell Rollings, Michele Brown, Kim, Veronica, Nichelle, Darshone Goshae and Gwenivere.

I wasn't cool with the girls at the time. Well, I was cool, but not cool enough for a girlfriend. I was too black and black was not in at the time. I liked them all I just couldn't get a girlfriend.

The girls liked the light complexion guys. If you weren't light skinned, you at least, had to have good hair. Dark skin was the same thing as ugly back in those days. Jordan made it cool to be dark again. I wasn't getting any airplay from the girls. If I did score it was for only one day. For instance, I'd send the note, will you be my girl friend? Check yes or no!

Yavonna and Kim gave me a yes at different times. Both of them marked yes and I walked them home that same day. This was too totally different times of course I wasn't macking, yet. They told their friends the next day and they gave me the thumbs down. Once they found out they both quit me the next day. No luck with the girls!

The only girl I did have a little luck with was April Flowers. She stayed next to Brain and Willie Weeks. Willie Weeks and my brother were good friends. She stayed on 169th & King Drive. I got a kiss from her one time in the back of her house. She stayed about a block away from me. She moved and transferred at the end of the fifth grade. So no luck with the girls!

The girls fought too in grammar school. The first time I saw a real tittie was Karen Franklin and Barbara's catfight. I should know Barbara Penn, because I had a crush on her too. She's light skin and was developed up top to be in the sixth grade. Anyway Karen and Barbara went at it. Karen was a strong girl. She was developed also. The girls were on Karen, because of her big lips and her teeth were bucked.

I guess Barbara made fun of her. Barbara was strong willed. She would fight a boy too. Karen was no joke I'd seen her fight before in earlier grades. They both squared off right in front of the schoolyard. They met in the middle of 171st.

Barbara said, "come on bitch what you going to do?"

Karen replied, "I'm going to beat your ass bitch".

They were swinging like guys, but then Karen put Barbara in a headlock. She worked out on Barbara once in the headlock. We started trying to pull them apart and they started ripping clothes off each other.

They both got good blows in on each other. It looked like Karen came out on top. The fight was good and both were torn out of their shirts. Karen was in her bra, but Barbara's tittie came out.

I was like, "oooh weee you see that". Her nipple is pink with a brown circle around the point". They were fighting with titties hang out. She popped it back in her bra, but it was too late. I saw it.

Karen was torn out her shirt. She was walking around after the fight in just her bra. That was until she found something to cover herself up. Every time I seen Barbara after that I would visualize how that tittie looked hanging out.

This was the best times of my young life. On activity day we would play chess, checkers, Uno, Monopoly, Battleship, Hot Hands, Knuckles, Backgammon and a lot more. Fester was good at chess. I thought it was boring. It was fun being a kid, when I was with my age group. Being a nerd brought an end to that. This is how things went up until about the 1st through fifth grade.

Ever since the 2nd grade, after we took those test to see how we placed. They always moved Fester, John, Anthony and I up a class up. It was no use of us being in that class when our scores showed we already knew the material.

I went to the second floor for second grade. Mrs. Sterling's was one of the teachers who taught second grade. She was an older white Jewish teacher who was very mean. She never smiled or had something good to say. Mrs. Sterling had a constant frown on her face. It was a look like, she just didn't want to be there or you smelled.

She was strict and she never said my name right. I would pronounce it correctly, "my name is Columbus" and she would still, fuck it up royally.

She'd called my name in roll call "Colo Columbeez Colo. That's all I got is my name and she was fucking it up. I don't need any more reasons for the class to crack up on me. When she called attendance I kept telling her over and over again, how to pronounce it. I left it alone, because the more I tried to correct her, the more she savaged it.

I really thought she did that shit on purpose. I was the blackest something in class. I think this was my first form of racism. Our test scores came back. After coming back they moved me to Mrs. Buckley, which was a third grade class. Mrs. Buckley was the other side of the coin.

How I hated Mrs. Sterling is how I loved Mrs. Buckley. She's of dark complexion heavy and wore glasses around her neck. I was so happy to leave this teacher, Mrs. Sterling. I was only in her class, about two months and hated every fucking minute. This was one thing good about being smart. I moved out of her class.

This was my main problem or dilemma in school. I was smart and couldn't stay in the class with my age group. Therefore, I am always in a class with people older than I. In my age group I was one of the strongest and one of the fastest. Every time the school moved me up after the fifth grade. I had to deal with something else. I was not one of the strongest in the upper grade. I was not one of the fastest. I was in over my head with these guys. The feelings of the older people in the class were resentment! This was a little later though before I started moving up a class. I had a life-changing event.

The Hawk

Something happened that would have a life-long effect on me. At the end of my third grade I had mental and physical traumas. William Hawkins transferred into Rock Manor. He stayed in the colt way buildings across the street from the school. Dude came from the projects. He was dark with a whole lot of little scares all over his face and body.

Dude just looked tough and rough. He was bigger and had muscles in the third grade. You know the guys from the projects. They had an automatic tough reputation that came with em.

Anyway, he transferred into my class for a little while, but left. He was a straight really aggressive. He started extorting some of the students he'd picked out. I was one of them. He wouldn't beat your ass, as long as you brought him fifty cents or a dollar. Instead of fighting him, all you had to do was give him fifty cents. A lot of us chose that route. Dude is controlling the rackets at Manor in the third grade.

Here's the catch once you gave him the money.

He would say, "let's go to the store".

Once at the store he would split half the money with you. We could get all kinds of penny candy and cookies back in the day for a dollar. I guess he did that so I wouldn't tell a teacher or a parent.

After we got the candy and ate it. We played basketball at the school for a while laughing and joking. It was time to go home cause it was getting late. I said to myself, "dude is okay, he ain't that bad". I was out of breath from running around playing and I said. "All right, I got to get home".

He replied, "Okay! Before walking away he said, bring me a dollar tomorrow and I want beat your ass". While saying it he gave me the, I'm not bullshitting look. My mouth dropped and I was astonished.

This stunned me, because I thought we were cool now. I looked at him crazily like, I thought you were my boy, look.

He looked back at me and said, "bring the dollar and I won't beat your ass", while bucking his eyes.

He said it slowly so I could understand. Every time I brought the money he upped it the next day. Again, I wasn't the only one he was beasting. He had his days for different people to bring him money. We weren't up on this game.

William brought the extortion game straight from the projects. Now this went on until I got to two dollars. Dude was making me steal or whatever I had to do to get him that money and I was stressed. I was getting the money from my mother's purse. I knew I would get caught, if I took that much. I also couldn't tell her somebody was punking me out.

Next day, I didn't come with the money. That's the day he started pummeling me. He started going off in my shit, because I didn't have the money. Bam bam bam! I didn't swing back. My little brother was with me.

Walley was telling him, "leave my brother alone".

He was trying to fight dude, but of course he was too small.

I told Walley, "come on Walley" and told William, "I got you tomorrow. I'll have it tomorrow". This is while I was holding my nose and walking away.

William replied, "Yeah you better or I am fucking you up".

This situation was enveloping me. Here it is, I can fight, but scared to throw a punch. Dude was intimidating me on a high level.

It got so, some of the teacher aids or play leaders that knew he was messing with me. They used to see me running from him. I still wouldn't tell the teacher. I told the play leaders not to say anything.

The play leaders would give me a head start. I would run home. What was fucking me up was I had to locate my brother first. He was in the first grade. I had to get him first then make an escape. I would have never got caught, if I didn't have to wait on Walley. What had me scared more than William, is my mother. I bet not come home without my brother.

This one time Hawk was on me after school. I don't know why I wouldn't fight him back. I was a good fighter, but the project shit, had me spooked. Those niggas from the projects fight coming out the womb. He was from the Robert Taylor's homes.

That project was across the street from the church I attended on 51st & State. I guess I thought, if I fought back, it would make it worst. Anyway, he was chasing me home everyday like clockwork. Hawk was actually on my heels, chasing me down after school. Hawk was fast and you sure can't fight while you're running.

When he did catch me he'd hit me a couple of times and bust my nose. My nose was easy to bleed at the time. My little brother is in kindergarten jumped in the middle. He was trying to keep Hawk from doing me real bad. For some reason he never touched my little brother. Most of the time I left him with a good head start. Hawk would usually run after me a couple of blocks trying to catch me then stop.

After he caught me the first time and blew my shit out. He would have a run for his money next time. I was burning rubber on his ass. If, he couldn't catch me after a couple of blocks, he would turn around.

I knew he wasn't messing with my brother so I would break out.

Hawk would yell at me, "I'm a catch you tomorrow and I am busting your shit". Once he stopped I would wait on my brother to come.

He'd catch up and say, "you need to tell momma".

I told him don't say nothing. I didn't want her to know I was scared.

William got tired of me losing him and giving him no money. He chased me all the way home this one day. It's five blocks from my school to my house, the short cut route. This time he didn't stop running. I wasn't going to let him catch me, anymore. I put on the afterburners and kept a good distance. Every time he stopped for rest, I stopped for rest.

I left my brother this time, but he knew the way home. I'm coming through snake alley and he was still on me. I cross King Drive he was still behind me. I get to Zells cleaners, which is right across the street from my house. He is still chasing me.

My mother just happened to be on the porch sweeping it down. She's watching me running and then looking back at Hawk chasing me. That's when William stopped, because he seen the lady's concern. Now the Hawk, knew where I lived. Something I was trying to avoid. I was going to duck in a gangway and lose him once I got around the crib.

My mother saw the fear in my face. She saw me running frantically looking back at the Hawk. Her face just tore up into little pieces. She didn't say a word. She just looked at Hawk. Moms squinted one of her eyes leaving one eye open. She had a mean ass scowl on her face.

William looked at her and said to my mother, "he was messing with his little brother".

I told my momma, "I wasn't messing with his brother," but his words calmed my mother down. Dude was crafty like and had everything planned out. He had what he was going to say, if caught. He retreated back to the school and had to wait another day.

My Mom told me to come inside the house. I come over and she grabbed then snatched me in the hallway of our house.

Mom collard me up, while looking dead in my eyes and said. "If I ever, see you running from anybody I'm going beat your butt. You are running from that little boy. Who you rather see him or me?"

After she said that, she starts to slams me repeatedly. She swung me side-to-side slamming me on both of the hallway, walls. Boom, boom, boom, was the sound I was making bouncing up off the walls. She stops and looks me in the eyes.

I said, "momma I'm not going to run anymore". I rather see him anytime, before I have to deal with my mother. She basically was calling me a wuss. I rather holler at him then have to see my mother. It was something that happened when she looked in my eyes. She went down to my core to see what was there on the inside. She uncovered my weakness and went straight at it.

Here comes my little brother through the door. He was trailing me, but couldn't keep up cause I was burning rubber. He hears what momma was so worked up about, me running from Hawk.

Here he goes, "he beats Colo up all the time Mom and makes him bring him money".

I looked at my little brother and was shocked. Up until that point, he never said anything about Hawk. I begged him not too. After hearing that, my mother got on him about the situation.

She told my little brother, "don't let nobody mess with your brother".

Those words hurt more than Hawk whipping my ass after school. I am the biggest and the oldest. She's telling him to help me. This broke the hold he had on me. I wasn't going to be a punk,

Here's where one of the Larry's rules come into fruition.

Mom said, "If you have to, both of you jump on him. If he's too big, pick something up and bust his head. Why should you be the one hurt? You start running now. You'll be running the rest of your life. Deal with it right then and don't let it linger".

I know y'all wondering why I didn't tell, if that's all you needed to do. That's one thing I never did was tell. Only punks go running to the teacher or to their mothers so I thought. I had to figure this out myself. I had pride even in the second and third grade. I can't have my momma up at the school, trying to defend me.

I can see her saying, "leave my son alone".

Naw, I would get teased to the end of life. I rather take the smashing from Hawk. I said to myself that day, "this is going to stop". The humiliation I felt from my mother seeing me running was too much.

See it was the end of school year. I guess William had to get his last little money, before the school summer break. He never chased me that far. He usually would just chase me a block then it was two blocks. Now he's chasing me all the way home. Now he knows where I live. I knew myself this had to stop. This nigga will probably get up early and be waiting on me to come to school.

Nobody's going to help you, if you don't help yourself. A lot of times people would just stand around being amused at my terror. They weren't thinking about breaking it up.

Hawk was on me the next day. Dude didn't give a fuck about shit. Crying didn't help and telling him to stop didn't help. Giving him the money is the only thing that cooled him down, until the next day. Hawk had me not even wanting to come to school.

I see him in the school hallway the next day.

He asked, "you got my money Columbus?" Hawk asked.

I frown and reply firmly, "I ain't got shit for you".

"His retort, "oh you tough today I am going to catch you today".

I reply, "I ain't running".

He then says, "Oh you a bad motherfucka we will see".

I know what y'all-saying Tadpole. Colo wasn't cussing like that at that age. By the third grade I was cussing like a sailor. I practiced cursing in the mirror while making mean faces. All of us were cussing by that time.

After school he came at me. I am still scared ass hell. I believe I started tearing up. I wasn't crying like a pussy, I was crying mad. He swung and missed then I swung back and gave him a two-piece combo. The fight is on! I can fight this nigga. I was just scared to fight. I hit him in the chest and at the bottom of his neck.

Hawk looked at me and I guess, he knew, the gig was up.

He just said, "gone head man," then turned around and walked away.

I was glad he walked away, but I should have beaten his ass, still. I was amazed though! I said to myself as I walked home, "is that all it took, was for me to make a stand". The Hawk never fucked with me again. I think he transferred the next year anyway.

One thing I am glad about. He transferred after I found my balls. What, if he'd transferred before I found my balls? It would be somebody out here that had power over me. That pussy shit could've set in me. I had to settle something with myself. Don't be scared of anybody. I don't care how mean, big or ugly they looked.

The projects he was from along with the Hawk had me petrified. The reputation on those guys is tough, starving and scandalous. That right there, is just a front, if you are a punk, you will get punked. William Hawkins taught me one of the most valuable lessons in life. People will do to you, what you let them do to you.

My little brother though would tease me to death about William Hawkins. He was only in the 1st grade, but he never forgot.

Anytime he could jab me with it he would say. "Remember when William used to chase you home?" Remember he busted your nose and you took off running? Walley would laugh and laugh about it. He'd hit me low at will with William Hawkins, while signifying or cracking jokes".

I'd talk about him, but that would just make me shut the fuck up. It was like revisiting the trauma when he said it. All I could say was, "he won't do it any more".

My brother would laugh and say, "but it happened though Colo. Heee haa ha hha haa".

He had me on that one. He'd show how my face would be looking while running. He'd do the reenactment of William hitting me in the jaw. Where's the money, bink bam, scram and you running, in the wind. He knew how to cut me, because it happened just like that!

It wasn't too many people who knew Hawk was on my head. Everything always happened after school off the school premises. He didn't want too many people seeing what he was doing. Dude was slick as hell and knew how to do strong arm shit, but that's over now.

It seemed as, if the new students who came to the school had a target on me. In the fourth grade it was another stud trying to punk me. Here we go again, dude is fucking with me. His name was James Tate I think. He had transferred in and I'd already had the reputation for fighting. I handle the business.

Mrs. Owens's taught our fourth grade. She was a white young teacher. I thought she was beautiful. She was tall with long legs. After Mrs. Buckley, she was the nicest teacher in the school. She drove a 1979 Pontiac Firebird. It had the big bird on the hood that look so sweet to me. It sat outside the side of the school every day.

That year we had the worst winter of my life. We had a snowstorm and got like 30 inches of snow. The cars were covered with snow from the ground to the top of the hood. We opened our door to the house and we had to dig our way out the house.

The snow was taller than I was at the time. We still had to go to school after the first few days. It took me an hour walking through the snow to get to school. We just dressed warm with boots gloves and coats. I say coats because you needed two of them. One coat didn't keep you warm. We'd wear two pair of gloves and four pair of socks. We still went to school after the snow hit. Rock Manor rarely closed for school in the winter.

The fourth grade was cool before James Tate transferred to Rock Manor. He was brown complexion, tall with a fro. He was trying to act cool in front of the girls. He had gotten cool with Fester, when he first came.

That was Fester hommie. He didn't like me from the start, because I had the props in all areas, but the girls. My gear wasn't tight and of course the stigma of my skin color. This is what had my esteem low with the girls. I was the guy, in the areas that counted: Fighting, sports and being smart in class.

James stayed fresh and just didn't like my swagger. Other than sports I didn't fit in the group. Everybody else wasn't or seemed like they weren't hurting like me.

He comes at me, "Columbus ain't shit, black ugly motherfucker and I'll prove it. Look at his clothes he's a bum".

I was like, "man I got no beef with you". Dude was about three inches taller than me. The girls liked him so I guess he was going to show off for them. I guess he didn't like how smart I was in class.

He was going to make his come up off of me. He gave me the 3:15 sign. At this time we were in the fourth grade. I didn't want to fight, for what I never said a bad thing about the dude. All while he was calling me out like a pussy I didn't say anything.

I just told him, "I don't have no beef". Now when leaving for the day we went out the side doors of the building. I was hoping it would be a teacher out there or something that would stop it. Usually Mrs. Griffin would stop all the fights she could get to after school. I peered out the door. No bet!

I honestly had butterflies in my stomach. The flies were going crazy in my stomach. Dude was talking mad shit about what he was going to do to me. No big sister to back me up or save me. See that's the move for the aggressor. You hurry up and go outside, stand there with the mob. The mob is the people wanting to see the fight. Now the one who gets outside first or the one who is starting the fight is waiting.

They make sure you don't get away by waiting at the entrance. He is waiting on me to come out.

He was like, "yeah Columbus"! Looking mean and slapping and holding his fist tight by his side. It something that happens at the point of confrontation I noticed. Anything I was scared of immediately goes away when you step in my face. The only time it failed is with Hawk.

I came down the steps and didn't say a word. The crowd circled around us.

He said, "what's up now?" then flinch like he was going to steal. Wrong answer! I gave him a two-piece real quick and fast. Smack smack, jaw then the nose. He wasn't ready, he was new at the school, and we bang at Rock Manor.

This is the Manor we ain't bullshitting over here at this school. What the fuck is all this flinching for? You get stole on over here at the Manor. At this school we are straight gladiators.

Tate held his nose and looked at the scowl I had on my face. The scowl I got from my Mom. No words from me I'm ready. I just looked him dead in his eyes like, what's up, come on.

Someone in the crowd said, "he don't know about Columbus". I began to think once hearing that that the class wanted me to beat his ass. It's like they showed their loyalty to me, because I was there before him.

He kept it moving. He threw his hands up and said he was straight. I was learning right there to go for what you know. There's no use of being scared. Even if you are, don't let it stop you for moving. The worst thing you can do, is not address your fears.

William Hawkins taught me that, a third grader. They say the youngest kid can teach you something. Well the Hawk taught me a lesson that has lasted a lifetime. That was the first and last time I ever got punked!

Creativity

We had a few other interests in school. I was very creative and like to draw. I finished my work quickly so I could draw. I had gotten pretty good, the older I got. I drew every super hero that I liked: Iron man, The Incredible Hulk, Thor, The Fantastic Four and Spiderman. I would draw them and put them on my bedroom wall. I picked it up from my older brother.

I made my own gun with the tools in the basement. Since Mom wouldn't buy me in toy guns. I made a gun that shot screws. I had a handle and place to put the screws. How I shot it was sling it in the direction I wanted the small screws to go.

I made zip guns that shot pull rings off the pop cans. I made paper airplanes that were state of the art. You had to come to school with a sweet paper airplane that could fly. I spent time on making a plane that could ride the wind. You had the sweetest plane, if it would stay in the air. Everything was a competition. You had to be creative because you would go crazy while on solitary confinement. I had a lot of time to visit my own world.

Set up for Failure

Moving up without stability stopped my progress. This I believe set me up for failure and then mediocrity in life. They should have had some place or somewhere we could go.

They put us in a class with distraught thug motherfuckas. The girls were okay, but the guys didn't like it at all. How about a ten year older, making you feel like an idiot or ignorant. There wasn't anywhere to go and the faculty should have known that! They should have had an advance class for us separately. They have a class for the kids with a learning disability.

I slowed down and didn't study as much. I was a geek and geeks got fucked with all the time. I didn't look like a geek, but I love to read. I loved math. I didn't have the pocket protector or the glasses, but I was a nerd.

I would do math problems on my own. Fester and Anthony look like geeks for real. Socially this was a disaster. Being thrown in with those older kids lowered my esteem even more.

Like I said they should have had other programs. The Rock needed programs where only the smart kids are in a room. It could be a room with eight students in it. Like the classes they had for the kids who couldn't keep up. It was a room for the learning disability that had eight to ten students in it.

Rock Manor inability to separate the young smart guys from the older thugs was disastrous. This would start a downward spiral from me not wanting to be the smartest one. They should have had an accelerated class. This is where Mr. Fody or Mr. Pimmerman was the two principals, failed us.

The Adventurer

Around the crib I was an adventurer. It was times when I weren't on punishment. I would get all my work done the night before. Get up and be gone early Saturday morning. I was on punishment so much that I would plan what I would do. When I got out on my release date I had fun. I would kind of take on life, like the comic books I read.

I call myself, "kid make it". In order for kid make it to get out of the house. I had to do my housework first. I always got up real early on Saturdays to watch cartoons. They came on around 6 am. Hung Kung Phooey, Scooby Doo and Jabba Jaws were my favorites. If I get up early I can get outside and go on an adventure.

I kept a ball, glove, football or basketball. When my work was done I went where I wanted to go. There was no telephone and no pager. There was no communication when I hit the streets. Moms had to wait until I got home to see where I've been. She told us to keep telephone fare. That was a dime at the time in case of emergency, call home immediately. I could play around the crib, but a lot of times. I would go kick it with my schoolmates from the 4th grade until about the 6Th grade.

I would go to their house and sit on the porch until they got their work done. I always came to your house to challenge you to a game of ball. I would come to your house to trade comic books. I didn't have a bike so I walked everywhere. I'd hit Iron Park and play baseball. I'd play all day and then before dark come home. Every time I got out I made the most of that day.

The first time I ran away from home. I ran away to Fester's house. I did what I normally did played all day. When it was time to go home I told Mrs. Delldow, I wasn't going. I had gotten into trouble and I had a whipping coming. I told her the deal. "I left home Mrs. Delldow before I could get whipped or put on punishment".

I took me a few clothes and I wasn't going back. This is how Mrs. Delldow found out. It started getting darker and darker. Mrs. Delldow knew I usually had to be gone by that time. Fester and I worked it out. He was going to sneak me in his room after things calmed down. I was going to spend the night over Fester's house without anybody knowing.

Fester must have told his mother. I begged him not too, but he did. He had to what was he going to say in the morning?

Mrs. Delldow asked me, "why don't I want to go home?"

I answered, "I messed up and my mother is going to kill me". Mrs. Delldow knew my mother and had her phone number.

She said, "I'm a call your mother, because I know she's worried about you".

I damn near started shaking in my boots right before her face. She saw the terror in my eyes when she said it. She told Fester and I to go on the porch. She would speak to my Mom in private. You know the grownup didn't talk about anything in front of the kids.

I get on the porch and said, "damn Fester you had to tell".

He said, "yeah I had to tell".

After a few minutes later she comes on the porch and says, "it's okay to go home".

I was like, "I'm not going home I don't want too".

She said, "it okay Colo you're not going to get a whipping".

I responded, "you don't know my mother".

Mrs. Delldow reassured me, "go ahead home she's really worried about you".

Mrs. Delldow didn't have a car neither did my mother. They had to hope that I came home. Fester lived on 172nd and Vernon at the time.

I began to walk home scared than a motherfucka. My Mom didn't whip me when I got home though! She gave me that look, but I didn't get a whipping. I didn't get on punishment either. I don't know what she said, but I wished Mrs. Delldow were around all the time. I was petrified of my mother when it was whipping time.

The last time I got a whipping, she let me think everything was cool. I forgot what I was supposed to get a whipping for it was so long. She told me to take a bath. I am like bet she let me ride.

I get in the water and about five minutes later her she comes. She got this big ass belt that had two holes all the way down the leather. Now my skin is wet. Here's my Mom calling out the shit that I did wrong and swinging. I am butt naked and wet so I can't do shit.

No matter where she hit me, it was damage done. Those holes in the belt were sucking up on my skin when it landed. Leaving my skin raised in little round circles wherever I got hit. All I could do was beg her to stop. I couldn't get away so I didn't try. Wherever she hit me it hurt equally. I'd be screaming, "sttoooooppppp momma please please sttoooooppppp momma please".

These whipping would have a lasting effect on me. This is how I would treat other people with no mercy later in life. My mother beats me like a slave. Who knows about going to school in the summer wearing long sleeve shirts? The shirt would burn my whips on my body while in school. The long sleeve shirt was to hide those whip marks all over my body. I still have some of the scars till this day.

How can I express love to someone else? This is why I could flip my switch in the street. I could be pleasant, but if ticked off. I could go to the highest degree of pisstivity.

I could hurt you and have love for you at the same time. I was mentally fucked up and thought this is how it works. The funny thing about it! I thought I was by myself with this torture. I found out later. It was a lot of kids being abused just like I was. Nobody said anything about it until they got older.

My mother used to be like, "call the police. I'll give you the dime to do it".

One time I did think about calling them, but didn't do it. I came to the conclusion that this is how it is and this how it going to be! It's nowhere else to go I got no family like that! How could I tell on my momma?

No Chips

The no money was a huge factor in my criminal development as a kid. I got a lot of whippings for the things I did for money. Let me tell you how tight it was coming up. We used to have those bake sells at the school. I rarely had money for bake sells. We were on assistance for a couple of years and money was scarce. As long as we paid the bills and shopped for the month. Everything else was a luxury.

This is how economics play on you and your development into criminal life. This is how you know you are poor. You don't know at first. You don't know when you are a kid until you want something. No disrespect intended but when it was time for bake sells the teacher would say.

"If you had money, line up and get ready to go to the bake sale".

They would let us know two weeks prior to bake sales. Taffy apple day came. I am the only one, with no taffy apple. The teachers weren't even coming off any money, if you didn't have any. It must have been against the rules for teachers to give us money. This though would separate the people with money and the people who didn't have money.

Nothing could show this anymore better. Here it is most of the time I'm sitting by myself looking at everybody eat. There would be maybe one other kid with no money. Everybody else is lining up to go get goodies. My favorite line was I forgot to tell my mother, about the bake sell. What they should've said was anybody going to the bake sell, line up.

Everybody won't know that I'm broke. They just know I'm not going to the bake sell. I could say, I wish I could, but I'm allergic to some things. I can't take a chance on eating the wrong thing. This was true I used to break out in super lumps when I ate too much acid. When I had a reaction, all over my hands and body, were lumps. I didn't want that to happen for sure!

After they came back from the bake sell. They would eat the pastries or whatever in our face. They wouldn't share or nothing. That's why when they left I tore off everybody I could. I went in the teacher's desk and stole the candy prizes for the math games. I stole their writing paper out of their desk.

For some reason I had a fetish for clean, crisp, writing paper. I would steal a little bit out of everybody desk. Any gum or candy in your desk, it's mine. I could get away with that, because we weren't supposed to have candy in the classroom. Not unless the teacher gave it to us, for excellence.

When I did have money when I got to the bake sell they didn't have shit. I got to pick over leftovers, because the goodies were gone about time we got down stairs. Taffy apple day was around Halloween. Sometimes I did get taffy apples on that date. When I did get me one I would eat it so slow. I wanted it to last forever. I wanted everybody to see me eating a taffy apple.

Most low-income families didn't have the best of clothes. We didn't have candy money at lunchtime, to get the extras. John Strong dressed like me, but always had money. He got hand me down from his uncles. He always wore drag alongs.

We called them drag alongs, because he always walked on the back of his pants. He always had strings on the bottom of the back of his pants that hung off. He had short ones, long ones and medium size ones. John just didn't give a fuck about clothes. We would walk behind John while talking about his pants. I think he could have gotten whatever he wanted when we were shorties. It wasn't his priority

Most of the students in the, in crowd, went out for lunch anyway. John always had money to buy things. They had spots all up and down 171st street to get something to eat. They had these French fries that were boss pimp. You get a bag of fries with the mile sauce that cost thirty-five cents.

John would say, "come on man with me to the fish joint. I got you then he would share with me or buy me something.

John had all the little video games soon as they came out. We used to go over John house, because he knew what he was getting. That Coleco hand held football game with the sticks as the players. John couldn't play a lick of sports, but he did that extreme shit.

He used to know how to ice skate. He was skating at the ice rink in the wintertime at Iron Park. The way he could flip, amazed me. He was the mascot for the Rock Manor Stallions. I used to always kid him by saying, "John you are a cheerleader. Who do that?" He was getting out of class going to the game for free. Everybody else had to pay a dollar or something. Marcus and John would come out at half time and put on an aerial flip show. John showed Lil Rich and Rob how to flip on the Met.

Break-dancing came out in the early eighties. After that movie Breaking and Beat Street came out. John was at the forefront. He could spin on his neck. He had all the poses after doing some cold shit.

John would walk around the neighborhood with the cardboard in his hand. He would do his spin moves for the crowd or anybody who wanted to see. Y'all know John was the most entertaining person in the hood. He was kind of a show off, but I would too. He did everything, but play sports. John could throw the football just as good with both hands. The only thing is he couldn't throw with either one.

He had an older half brother or brother in law. He used to come and spend some nights over on the Met. His name was Steve and he was a Black Disciple off of 161st. Dude was cool. John has a sister I used to like, named Sherise. I love when she came to the door.

I think a lot of times I stopped there for her, but played like I wanted to see John. She would come out on the porch, if John wasn't home and wait with me until he showed up.

We spent a lot of time at John house when we were shorties. He had all the gadgets to have fun. As a matter of fact both John house's used to be the spot where everybody cooled out. Your house John and John's house was the stoop. We always sat on John Strong's porch.

Back in school, ohh I couldn't wait until it was time to sell those candies and cookies. You know when you get a prize, for selling a lot. You can get a radio, skates the highest prize used to be, a ten-speed bike. Money would be coming through my hand. That means I am in control of some cash.

I would keep a third of the money and turn the rest in to the sponsors. I didn't get greedy. When you greedy, you get caught. If caught doing a little, you could play it off. Somebody stole the money. I forgot where I put it. I had it in my coat and it's not there anymore.

Students used to leave money in their pocket in the coatroom. You used to have to stand in the coat-room when you were bad. I would steal anything in their pockets so money came up missing.

I did want my prize so I turned most of it into the teacher. That meant some people weren't going to get candy. This happened every year. I never got close to winning the top prize. It was people who were selling 900 and 1000 dollars worth of candy. The one who sold the most got the ten-speed bike. I guess so if you sold a 1000 dollars worth of candy back in the day.

The Jacket

Yeah it's tight for everybody, but not this tight. It some things in life that happen that are pivotal. This incident amplified my hustle game. I'm a hustler because of this situation, still till this day. I needed to make money. I would never wait for somebody to give me something. I would go house to house trying to see if someone needed help. In the winter I went out and shoveled snow in the neighborhood. I would hustle bottles or whatever I could do for the extras. In those days money was tight for the five of us.

As a matter of fact for a few years we didn't have new clothes. There was no such thing as new clothes. Everything was thrift or hand me downs. We had hand me downs from somebody else's families, hand me downs. After the hand me downs makes it through their family. The hand me downs made it through our family too. Christmas time not all, but sometimes we got somebody else's toys, from the previous year. Toy dog would be missing an ear. My bike might be missing a pedal.

This often had me embarrassed as far back as I can remember. It was so tight my mother made our gloves, hats, scarf's and pants, if she could. My mother loved to sew so she rather buys some clothing patterns and sew us something together. Now that's love but in school, that's not what's going on!

I remember washing those items in the bathtub. We used a washboard the old fashion way. Sometime we didn't have money for the laundry matt.

My mother always said, "if there's a will there's a way".

When for most families the washboard was obsolete. I just couldn't realize then the love she had for us. She did all those things for our survival. She was doing this without degrading herself. This gave me a perfect example of perseverance.

I can remember her putting tissue paper in our shoes so they could fit. They could be up to two sizes too big, but never too small. Whatever season was coming she prepared for them before they seasons hit, getting on her hustle. She was hitting thrift stores, checking the church, schools, and lost and found whatever it took to survive.

Mom brought me home this sweet jeans vest jacket. She brought it home from the lost and found at my school. She got the jacket at the end of the school year. Well, I loved that jacket. I wore it all summer that year, like I was the Fonz on Happy Days. It was a vest so I could wear it with no shirt on or with a shirt. It had a wad of gum in the corner of the pocket. I couldn't get it out so I couldn't use one of the pockets.

Well, in the fall of the next year. I wore the jacket to school not knowing that's where she got the jacket. In those days if no one claimed the lost clothes by the end of the year. They gave the things away that the kids lost. At the end of the year they would discard the things anyway. They invited people to get what they wanted, before they dumped it out. She would bring things home and whoever could fit it, it was theirs.

This confrontation was ingrained in my head. We were in school, in the hallway, lining up to be dismissed for the day. I was in the fourth grade. This guy named Curt came walking by me looking at my jacket.

Curt was couple of years older than us. He had muscles and was on the school basketball team at the time.

He came out and asked, "where'd you get that jacket from?"

I replied, "what's it to you?"

He answered, "because that's my jacket"

I replied, "you are a damn lie, my mama gave me this jacket". I thought he was just trying to strong-arm me for my shit. I stood firm and said, "this is my motherfucking jacket". Everybody's in the line was now looking at the situation. The people in the line were wondering whose jacket is it? I got it on, but that's what everyone was wondering. I'm putting up a strong front.

He looked at me frustrated while thinking then said, "I bet you I can prove it".

I said, "prove it".

He said, "it's some gum stuck in the pocket and you can't put nothing in it.

I knew he was right as soon as he said it. If my face looked the way I felt on the inside. It's in the eyes; my eyes were distant and small. Everybody in that line knew it was his jacket. Curt then reached at the pocket, turned it inside out and he showed everybody.

Shouting, "see, see, see, take off my jacket".

Curt then started tugging and pulling the jacket off me. Everyone was looking at me to see what I was going to do. I felt so low that I just conceded the jacket. I left school feeling lower than an ant. It was his jacket what could I do?

I was so embarrassed. I didn't tell my Mom about the incident. She was doing the best she could without degrading herself. I can say, we were clean clothe and had a roof over our head. We ate three meals a day. When she didn't eat, she made sure we did. Later on my sister would tell me. Mom went to bed some nights only drinking water.

My mother showed me how to be rock strong. She did it by never compromising her morals, values and spiritual beliefs for monetary gain.

A night of enjoyment for my Mom was to watch the Jefferson, Maude, Archie Bunker, Carol Barnett, Good Times and the Dukes of Hazzards to name a few. These are shows that made her laugh and she sure loved laughing. Her laugh was very distinctive just like her singing. Whenever she did either one you knew it was her immediately. My mother sung in highest soprano.

One of her favorite actors was Sidney Portiere. She loved the way he talked and expressed himself. How well groomed he was portrayed. I didn't like his movies. It seemed to me, he was trying to play a white man. I wanted to where a fro and his hair was short. He dressed like a white man. I couldn't identify with that, even as a shortie.

She loved her daytime stories and I couldn't stand them: General Hospital, As the world Turns and The Guiding Light. All these stories were about white people who were rich. The stories were about people who backstabbed each other constantly.

We watched the Cosby show and Different Strokes. You know this is fantasy. This is a well off white man who takes in two black boys. It was a funny show, but not realistic. A white man comes in and save the day and adopts two black kids. Come on man this is what you have to offer? You see what happened to them in real life.

The Cosby show was funny, but I grew disinterested in it. It wasn't a realistic show in my world. It was like a cartoon or comic book like, his show. Bill Cosby Fat Albert show was bullshit. The Fat Albert show, demeaned black people visually, even though it had a positive premise. It was a show to teach black people how to act even though we were heathens. Another reason I didn't like it they called me Rudy one of the characters on the show. I didn't like that shit, because I had big lips with dark skin.

As far as the Cosby show. I never met a family like that in all my years on earth. This is a black family with parents who worked as a doctor and a lawyer in the same household. Just having one parent in a high-powered profession, was extraordinary.

They never showed the struggle of how did they get to that position. How did they come from descendants of slaves and get to this position? My mother liked shows like that! It was a funny show, but not realistic to me.

It was just like one of those comic books I used to collect, all fantasy. This was something for my amusement at the time. Other than that she would be on the phone with my Godmother or Mrs. Helen. She'd be sewing or setting up one of her patterns. We were literally her whole world, except for church.

Shocked by the Truth

Yes, we were coming up, on our knuckles. Alex Haley, movie Roots, came on TV for the time in the 70s. My mother called us in the room, to watch the series together. This series was mind blowing. I watched those slaves get on and off that ship, naked.

They were shackled and looking desperate. Once on the ship the women and men were stacked like lunchmeat. Our ancestors were stored underneath the deck shackled to one another. This just blew me away. I couldn't believe what I was seeing

Some tried to escape and swim back, half way into the ocean. The ones that died and couldn't finish the trip were feed to the sharks. The sharks followed the ships, because they could smell the food. I was shocked appalled and awakened all at the same time. Our ancestors were chased down, caught or was sold into slavery by the Portuguese and Spaniards. This is how we got to America, ain't that a bitch.

This movie was self-explanatory I had no questions. That's why my mother thought it was important for us to see it. She was strong and literally just carried us on her back, all four of us. I guess that's why I developed those hustling characteristics.

Mom could make something out of literally nothing. When I was eleven we finally got a car. We would be driving along and she spotted a rusted old cabinet. She would get out take a look at it. Tell us boys to get out and get the rope. She'd grab a blanket out the trunk and put in on top of the car. Strapped the cabinet down and off we goes with this rusted out cabinet.

This was unbearable for me. People were looking at us picking through the garbage. Worse getting home and my friends see me dragging this rusty cabinet in the house. I would pray nobody be on the block when we were bringing garbage in the house.

I always wished I were rich so I could take my mama away from this type of living. This didn't bother her a bit. She would get it in, on the cabinet. Start to sand it down, then get some paint and paint it and before you know it, it look like new.

Now, she was doing this for her kids so it didn't bother her one bit. She stood proud no matter what the situation was like. Here's when I knew that I wanted to make it to another level in life. I wanted my mother to have better things in life. I had to practice my sports so I can take her away from this life. I can't stand being poor. Why should I be poor when you could do something about it?

After seeing Roots I was flabbergasted. I understand at this point we are sub servant. We lived in Chicago we didn't see prejudice. No wonder I felt lost it was because I was lost. The city was segregated you didn't see white people for miles. Now if you don't have a car and you don't leave the neighborhood. You'd be shock to see that it was so many white people. I thought Chicago was mostly black at first.

Chapter III

Barbara

My childhood with my brothers and my sister Barbara was normal. I didn't get along with my sister. She was in charge of me and could discipline or punish me as she saw fit. Whoever heard of your sister with the power, to punish you. It seemed to me that she had it in for me. I felt that I was the last on the totem pole as far as her brother's favorability, in her eyes. When there was work to be done. She would always assign me the hardest task in the house.

When we signified on each other she would often tell me to shut up. This is while the rest of them sing songs about my big lips.

She would sing that dreadful song, "rubber lips".

She would have my brother's join in and sing it, over and over again. She used to have me on the verge of crying. My sister had me prepared, for the signifying we did in school.

The song went like this, "rubber lips, dun dun dun, dun dun dun, rubber lips, dun dun dun". She had a nice little tune for the song.

Here she goes, "come on Samson and Walley, rubber lips dun dun dun dun". Anytime I got on her nerves she would sing the song. She kept me in check with that song I would do anything not to hear it.

My siblings would make gestures by pulling their lips to spring backwards and forwards. Giving the rubber effect, bong, bong, bong. They would be walking around me in a circle like a band while doing it. Out of everybody in the house who got on me or whoever called me names. My sister words hurt the most, because I thought she was super girl.

One thing about my sister is that she was very head strong and protective. When in school, if there was someone messing with us, she had our back. She would turn aggressive and go to bat for her brothers.

She look at whoever messing with us and say, "You better leave my brother's alone before you have to mess with me," was her favorite words.

Most of the times, ending our squabbles with very little force.

She was years older than the people trying to mess with me. She was my play leader when I was in kindergarten. Once she graduated and went to Darobe, after my second grade year.

My brother and I had to fend for ourselves at school. I had to protect Larry if he had problems too. John and Alberta wasn't in school yet.

I felt a security blanket then like somebody had my back. She always made sure we ate and often bought us treats with her own money. She made these homemade pizzas I used to love when she was making them up. She made everything from scratch. She made the dough and the meatballs and sauce.

After putting it in the oven all four of us used to be waiting patiently. Once ready we would bust it down. She never was funny about sharing with her brothers. She would bring us home those Jew Town polishes and fries. I can remember her being very creative.

She would write and have us act out her plays when we were young. Everybody had his part. I was a pimp. I always had shades on trying to act cool and say my lines. You know back in the day all those black exploitation films were out. The pimp was the main character. I was a cool as pimp with a cape. She had the basement section off with blankets so we had different sets.

The little plays were cool but repetition became unbearable. We'd rehearsed our lines so much I probably can recall them now. She would make us practice over and over again. She had little tolerance for us messing up.

She'd say, "we're going to do this play for Mom and dad. We got to do it right. I had an unpronounced drive to act. I never thought about it. All I know is I can do it, it's in me and she brought it out. I was only seven or eight. I don't remember ever doing this play for my Mom. We did others plays, but we didn't do that play.

She had me playing a pimp talking real slick. Mom wasn't on board with me even acting like a pimp. I know that was my sister's secret play. I think I still got that swag from acting like a pimp, in my subconscious.

She monitored our development closely. One time I thought it would be funny. I dressed up like Geraldine on the Flip Wilson Show. My Mom used to crack up when she saw him playing that roll.

I put on my Mom heels and her wig and made a stance like he did. My mother looked played it off and got close enough. When she got close enough she slapped me out the heels and the wig with one slap. I was slapped into another world.

Before I came down out the air I hear, "don't you ever put on any women clothes", and was about to take it to the next level. I convinced her I understood, but didn't.

I said, "I was trying to make you laugh like on Flip Wilson Mom. Every time you watched Flip Wilson it made you laugh". That's all I was trying to do was make her laugh. She said acting or no acting you are not suppose to put on women cloths. I never tried that again.

Barbara could be mean just like her and sic my Mom on me. One time we was playing doctor and she was the patient. My sister played like she was dead and that wasn't the game. I was supposed to operate on her make her better then she'd get up. She used to do it before, but this time she played dead. I was poking her doing all types of shit to her.

I had a fork looking in her mouth messing with her teeth. She did not move at all. I was a shortie so I started to get worried. She was not responding after an hour. I had to be about eight years old. I panic and called my momma at work. I tell her I can't get Barbara up. She is not responding. My Mom hangs up the phone and says she's on her way.

No sooner than when I hang up the phone. My sister comes out of the coma.

She asked, "why was you putting that fork in my mouth?"

My eyes bucked out of my head in amazement. This is devious, because she knew exactly what I did. I had just crucified myself. I called momma home from work and nothing is wrong with you.

I looked bewildered and said, "I told her you were dead!" This is not good for me I got immediately nervous to the bone. My Mom comes in and sees her walking around. First I knew it was relief to her then she was mad as hell. She went to work on me for the bogus call. Barbara got in trouble too and she knew what I was doing. What was I supposed to do?

One thing I didn't realize until later on! My sister had to give up her childhood. Mom was at work and she was her replacement. She couldn't do things that other girls were doing. After school she had to take care of her brothers.

She had a lot of responsibility when we were coming up, being the oldest. We took the place of her friends. That is something that I grew to appreciate, as I got older. When my nephew Deshaun hit the set I knew how to play him. She taught us by taking care of us.

Samson

My brother Samson was another story he was four years older. It was something about my brother I didn't understand when I was young. He always went to different schools than we did. He could not talk as fluently as we did. He didn't play sports to the level that me and my younger brother did. He wasn't as active like we were. I would later use his inability to converse as an advantage. When something got broke I would blame it on him and beg him to take the blame. Oh I loved my brother and he was autistic. I didn't know what that meant.

My Mom used to tell me he was autistic. I thought she was saying he was an artist. He could draw and was smart as hell. It was nothing he didn't try to do. He wasn't retarded. He joined the basketball team at his school. He couldn't play like them, but he played better than some people and he was, autistic.

We used to go up to the park and play. He had moves they just were slow, but they were moves. I know he can beat Matt Loukas. That's one of my buddies who couldn't do anything athletic but run. Samson had a shot and everything. After graduating he went to the military. My mother and brother tried their best to be as normal as possible.

This wouldn't last. The world would not let him be normal. He was doing something with his school one time. He did not come home and we were waiting up for him. Samson knows how to get around anywhere, so we were worried. He should've been home around seven o'clock. I was worried, where is my brother? I couldn't sleep I stayed up under the covers waiting for him to come home

Around 11:30 pm the police had him and called. He knows everything about numbers so he knows his phone number. The police knocked on our door a few minutes later. My mother answers it.

They ask her, "is that her son in the back seat, in a blanket?"

She looks and says, "yes what happened?"

They said some kids probably played a prank on him and took his clothes. I was upstairs, but I was at the door listening. I heard that and I wanted to do something, but I couldn't. I was only ten years old at the time. It was nobody I could tell. It was nobody to go get, to get revenge for fucking with my brother. Why would you do him like that? From that point on I knew I had to be the protector. I can't have anybody, fucking with my family, especially my big brother. He didn't bother anybody.

Everything he did I wanted to do. Later I understood he had communication problems. My mother asked him what happened, but he wouldn't tell her. My brother was still trying to be a regular teenager. He didn't want to snitch on nobody. My mother knew and I knew. He couldn't function out here, by himself. Someone's going to take advantage.

My brother had special abilities he could memorize maps from anywhere in the world. He had all the highways of the United States in his head. He had maps from everywhere. He could tell you how to get anywhere in the world. He didn't have to look he knew exactly how to get to any place.

When my Mom needed to go somewhere Samson was her GPS. He would give her directions to anywhere in the city, right to the front door. He'd tell her what L what bus and how far you had to walk. He was amazing.

Remember the movie rain man. He wasn't like the actor portrayed, but he could do shit like that! He could draw his ass off. He was the reason why I started drawing. He used to draw cartoon baseball players that fascinated me.

My brother was so smart he had a computer for a brain. I would have a calculator and give him a problem. I would give him division problems, multiplication fractions and percentages.

I say, "Samson while I'm just punching in numbers. What is 67,987.333* 333339005688?" He would rattle off the answer in seconds down to the last decimal. I'd look at the calculator and buck my eyes in amazement. I wanted to be smart just like him. I couldn't come close he was just too smart.

Samson never told on me, when I was a kid. He knew I was treacherous.

He would often warn me before I did the mischievous, "if Mom was here, she would tell you to stop".

I would tell him to be cool and if something went haywire. He would have my back.

When I was doing something wrong he gives me the heads up, "Mom is coming chill out". He wouldn't let me get caught, unlike my sister.

One time Emus and I were throwing snowballs at the bus, from the gangway on 169th. We were right by Mrs. Elizabeth house, with the dogs. Mrs. Elizabeth was cool she gave me something for my birthdays and Christmases every year. Emus and I did this every year the first good snowfall.

When the snow stuck together good enough to throw like baseballs. We would get our artillery together. We'd be making and lining up snowballs in the gangway. We would have about ten snowballs ready to go.

We'd pop out of nowhere and bomb the CTA buses or cars with snowballs. After bombing the bus we'd disappear through the gangways and get away.

We never got caught doing it before. You couldn't see us in the cut and the snowballs came out of nowhere. Just like usual we bombed the bus from the gangway with snowballs. I shake loose and shoot through the gangway. Emus went his way and I went mine. I come back through the backdoor of my house to escape and disappear into the house. Emus shot another way; we always split up when running. I'd come back through the front door, once the bus was gone. I wasn't even worried about getting caught.

It was a man looking and saw what we did. He laid back and waited to see where we had gone. He saw me coming back through my front door. He saw where I lived.

The man confronts me and says. "You know you're not supposed to be throwing snowballs at the bus.

I look at him and said, "yeah you right".

I am stuck. I couldn't say anything, but yeah you're right.

He said, "I am going to tell your folks what you are doing".

He walked on my porch and rang the bell and was going to tell my momma.

I am like to myself, "oh shit! No don't tell her I was throwing snowballs at the bus". That's thirty days solitary confinement. My momma was upstairs sleep tired from work too.

Samson came to the door. The man gives my brother the lowdown.

My brother had to be about sixteen, but looked older.

Samson looked at me and said, "you know better than that Colo. I'll let his mother know".

He sounded like a grown up. He talked plain and used very little slang to the man.

The man said, "okay" and left.

The man walked away after Samson said, "he'd let her know".

I was like, "good one Samson".

Samson was like, "he thinks I am a snitch and laughed. Samson wouldn't tell. He was no snitch.

I responded, "You no snitch Samson what he thought" and we both laugh at dude while he was walking away.

It was like we got one over on him together. My brother Samson had my back.

One thing my brothers and I loved doing. We loved watching the Three Stooges together. This gave my big brother uncontrollable laughter. I never saw him happier then when we used to watch, the Three Stooges.

We'd be in the house straight up poking each other in the eyes. We had to straight put the hand up perpendicular to the nose. This is to split the fingers so that you won't get poked in your eyes. Oh! When Moe hits his fist with Larry fist downward then he'd come over the top with the fist and hit you on the top of your head. We used to make the sound effects and everything. Bong Bonk!

It was a couple times my brother took the weight for me. I had done something and mother didn't know whom. When she didn't know who, everybody was getting a whipping anyway. It was warpath time.

I'd be like, "Samson I can't take it. Tell Mom it was you, you can take it".

I wasn't going to say it was I anyway. We all were going to get whipped. She was about to go on a warpath unless someone spoke up. My brother could take it. She would whip my brother and he would not cry. This would amaze me how he could take it. I would bust into to tears, while she was just gathering the whipping material, for me.

He loves baseball. My brother and I went to Wrigley Field on the train together. My big brother was the first one who took me to a Cubs game. We sat in the bleachers like bleacher bums. My mother would let us travel. We traveled all the way to the North Side, to the game by ourselves. He knew how to get anywhere.

This was the only professional game of any kind that I seen as a kid. My big brother took me to that game. I never knew anybody in the hood that went to any games. Basketball, baseball or football everybody watched it on TV. It was free on TV. The bleachers were like a couple of dollars. I remember that one time I was a bleacher bum and at a real Cubs game. My big brother was my real life hero! He was like a super hero with super abilities.

Walley

My brother Walley was another story. He was the baby boy. It seemed to me that he was the odds on favorite to my mother. She says she didn't have any favorites, but I couldn't tell. My brother and I had a strange relationship we loved to play together. I was only two years older than him. When you are young that is a whole two grades though!

The only thing about him when we would be playing and it started to get serious or something. He would always do his little part and then go run to mother. If he's running to mother than you know he's crumb snatching.

My mother seemed to take his side 95% of the time. She didn't even know the situation.

She would shout from the other room, "stop messing with your little brother".

I would say, "he started it".

Our lick passing continue, cause that's what we were doing. Backwards and forwards he taps me, I tap him. He wouldn't let me get the last lick and I would let him have it. As long as I touch him with the tip of my finger I got the last lick. It was the same for him. This could go on a couple of hours until you got pissed off.

Moms would come in from the other room and give me a couple of smacks.

After that tell me, "if he bothers you, I'll take care of him. You're the oldest so you come to me".

Well being a little boy those words didn't rest easy with me. He could do what he wanted and I have to tell like a punk.

One time I did what she said, I tried it! I told on him and his punishment was light, verbal only. Therefore, if he got out of pocket with me I'd handle it. I would bash him and take the consequences later, when he told on me. My mother would always take care of her business. I didn't care, because he can do what he wants, all he gets, is a verbal. I get a smashing across the head when I am on him, okay. I would just dish out punishment and take the consequences.

Walley knew how to get under my skin. He was playing with my food one time. Now he ate his hotdogs and now he's acting like he going to eat mine.

I told him, "don't mess with my hotdog".

Do you know he picked my hotdog up out the pot of water, with his bare hands? He was holding my hotdog in his hand while I watching him my blood pressure shot through the ceiling.

Then he asked, "you still want it?" then he started to laugh.

I walked over to him and said, "nigga…"

He knew it was coming. He called out, "momma".

I swung hard as hell with evil intentions. I would have knocked his teeth out, if it could've landed. He ducked and my hand goes right through the glass pane in the door, shatters it. You know we got that wood door, but it has like 12 separate glass windows in it.

My hand goes right through one of those windows, crasshH. I looked at my and notice the blood, swung and missed again. This nigga was ducking and he was only nine. I looked to see what happened to my hotdog. The hotdog is all smooched between his fingers. He clutched the hotdog so hard that it was oozing between his fingers.

Most kids when they see blood they stop immediately. I hear my momma coming down the stairs fast. I looked and see the gash on my knuckle and got even madder. I was about to swing again. By that time the O G was downstairs with whipping material.

She looks at the busted glass and asked, "who bust the window?"

Walley pointed and said, "Colo, he tried to hit me".

I explain my case, "he took my food momma look and it's smooched between his fingers".

Didn't matter she ran through me for busting the glass and fighting my brother. It didn't matter I was dripping blood all over the place. The G was banging me; look here it is right here. I still have the mark on my hand. She took me to the doctor after I got my ass beat. I got some stitches.

He got his back though! Even though! I couldn't laugh, not one bit at this one and never did. He took an ugly. We were playing in my mother's room. My mother room set up like the dresser is on the wall the bed in the middle the floor model TV sits in front of the bed in the middle by the window.

She has her sewing machine and patterns with material on the other wall. My mother always tell us don't play in her room. Now she always had her water for her coffee sitting on the dresser. She was downstairs in the kitchen cooking and we were supposed to be watching TV. You know we get to playing and throwing each other in the bed. I grabbed him and throw him on the edge of the bed.

Dude bounced off the edge of the bed hit the dresser. When he hit the dresser the water that was heating up for mother's coffee spilled all over his back and arms, spashhHH.

Once the water attached to his skin he was up like a rocket.

He got up screaming a blood-curdling scream, "aahhhhHHHHHHgg".

He ran immediately through the hallway upstairs, schroOOM schroOOM schroOOM schroOOM. He ran backwards and forwards in the hallway trying to cool himself off. He ran so fast that he burnt a path in the carpet. Smoke was coming up off the boy, literally. I am shhhhhooooshing him and telling him to be quiet.

I know I am going to get beat to death.

I hear my mother coming histerically while asking us, "what's wrong, what's wrong Walley and running up the stairs fast?

All my brother could say was, "It's burning its burrrrnnning it's burrrrnnnning". The words came from the pit of his stomach. Oh I felt so bad. By the time my mother gets upstairs he had bubbles of water forming on the top layer of his skin.

Thank Yaweh we had a car at the time.

Mom looks and then gasps loudly, "auuuuhhhhh Jesus" then says, "what happened?"

I told her the truth the water on the dresser spilled on him while we were playing. She immediately put her clothes on and was out the door with Walley. She got to the hospital in a matter of fifteen minutes.

When Mom was putting on her clothes he was still running.

He never stopped saying, "it's burning it's burning".

I was wishing he'd stop screaming. I felt so helpless I couldn't do anything to help him. I had to cover my ears so I couldn't hear his pain. It was my fault and it was killing me internally to hear him. After Mom put her clothes on and getting him to the hospital.

He had 2nd and some 3rd degree burns. I just knew when she got home she was going to kill me. I was on pins and needles so much I couldn't eat the rest of the day and night.

To my surprise she didn't say anything about us playing.

She came home and said, "it was my fault that he got burnt".

She said whether we were playing or not she forgot to turn the water off. She couldn't make me believe it wasn't my fault.

It was good to hear her take responsibility that was big. I finally exhaled! I was glad I didn't get a whipping, but I felt terrible about him being burnt. I felt responsible. He came home after a couple of weeks rapped in gauze. My mother changed the gauze regularly like the doctor's said.

The first time she took the gauze off I was shocked. I almost fell out or fainted or something. He was all pink, no skin and the meat left looked like fried bacon. I never laughed or talk about his burns in a joking way ever. It was nothing funny about that day or the consequences of that day. Mother nursed him back to health and babied on him for months.

Other than that day! My brother used my momma to his advantage, uncannily when we were young. It was the same for my sister. When I messed with him, they messed with me.

I can still see his face standing behind my mother or my sister smiling. When they punished me for messing with him or was telling me to leave him alone. I always felt coming up that I was loved the least. I had to be the black sheep in the family. It wasn't because I was the least loved. It was because where I fell in line, in the family.

My sister was the oldest so I had to listen to her. My older brother never really did anything wrong. He was very obedient. I on the other hand was very mischievous and thought I was slick. I was always trying to cut a corner. Mother had to make an example out of me. My younger brother didn't make the same mistakes I did. My mother would bash me so Walley knew to be cool. I know without a doubt I got the most whippings coming up.

Walley and I had to do almost everything together in our early years. For years before we could go outside. We stayed in the window playing that's my car. We didn't have a car so we'd sit there for hours. Just looking out the window playing, that's my car.

The way it went you wait until you see the sweetest car and that's your car. Only thing it always seemed as, if the next car was sweeter. He gets a turn I get a turn. You had ten seconds to pick your car. When you ran out of seconds you had to pick something and it could be raggedy. That where the laughing part came in, you are riding in a bucket.

We played fast pitch strikeout in the basement. I think that's how I developed my eye. Momma shades were beat up from the paper balls we used to shoot in them. We'd throw the football in the house like it was a Nerf ball. We got many whippings for tearing down and breaking things in the house. We couldn't go outside. We had too, too much energy, to be in the house.

While we were inside the house he was cool. On the outside of the house we feuded. I had to make sure he was cool or I'd be in trouble. This was a hindrance to me. I had to walk him to school. Hold his hand everywhere while crossing streets.

If he fought, I fought. This guy had to fight all the time. Walley wore those bifocals back in the day. He took a ribbing for those glasses.

I got on him remember Emus and the nigga tried to take my head off with a brick. I told him to go home or something and pushed him in that direction. He got a few paces and picked the brick up and threw it. I just got my head out the way. I chased the shit out of him and he could run.

It was two things you couldn't say to my brother or it would set him off. Say something about his momma or talked about his glasses. He heard either of the two and it was automatic. No matter how big or small you were he was going to steal on you.

You didn't have to say anything else but, your momma. You know your momma could mean anything. Your momma is a whore or your momma ugly. Saying your momma got your ass kicked, if you said it to my brother

I couldn't shake him.

When I wanted to go to the store, my Mom would shout, "take your brother".

When I wanted go and play, "take your brother," was mother stipulation.

After I got to a certain age I didn't want him to go anywhere with me. I don't know why I always wanted to be in the streets without him. Maybe, because if something went bad. It was I who had take the fall and I certainly didn't want him to tell on me.

We got a chance to play in the backyard sometimes. We would play kickball or baseball with a can. Most times we didn't have a ball. We'd play right in the confines of our small backyard.

Sometimes my older brother would play. Most of the time, it was just Walley and I playing together.

He was my audience during my magic tricks. I had the disappearing pin trick. The pin was connected to a rubber band. I wanted to be a magician like on Mickey Mouse. I went to the library and got the books and demonstrated the trick. I had him amazed. He really didn't know where the pin went. I grew disinterested once I found out it was illusion and not magic.

Deacon Williams from church used to bring fish by the house that he had caught while fishing. Some of them were still alive and some dead. I would chase my brother around the house with the dead fish and he would go crazy. He would damn near shit his pants. He was scared of the dead fish.

He would cry and say, "I'm telling momma when she gets home".

I'd say, "what you going to tell her I did not do anything. During those days mother would not let us go outside. Not until I was about ten, at least not by ourselves. We lived a very secluded life up until that point. We had lived over there for three years and we didn't have any friends. My mother was very protective back in those days.

We were not to let anybody in the house when she was gone. That meant nobody she didn't care who was at the door. Do not open that door when she's gone and don't go outside. That goes from Walley all the way up to Barbara. Mom made sure her orders were clear all the way up to the top, nobody excluded.

"If president Nixon comes, tell him you can't open the door", she would always say.

A lot of people were on that heroin back in the 70s. We would be sleep and couldn't see what went on after 8 o'clock. We lived right by the alley on 169th St. They attics used that alley to shoot up or make transactions in the alley.

Mom used to come out in the alley first and check for needles on the ground and then let us play.

Mom would warn us if we seen any needles to tell her. She would put gloves on grab some paper towels. Pick them up and then throw them away. I believe they used to discard them without realizing kids would be playing in that alley. We didn't know what was going on as kids. We just wanted to go out and play.

Freedom

My world opened up just a little bit. I guess that was around the time I met John for the first time. I had to be about ten. Well I used to see him in the hood, but we never played together.

John had this wooden skateboard he used to let me ride after we met. That's how John and I became cool. I didn't have one and he let me ride his skateboard up and down 169th St.

John was the sweetest in the hood with the skateboard shit. He used to tic tack his ass off. The moves were pretty basic at the time. I was right behind him, cause I learned fast. For my tenth or eleventh birthday my father bought me a green precision skateboard with red wheels. This was the best present I had gotten in my brief life.

I finally got something I wanted. I was playing with John outside.

My father got out his car and yelled, "Hollering Jack".

I looked and saw he had a green precision skateboard in his hand. It had the red wheels and the platform was made out of some durable plastic. Up until that time most of the skateboards were wooden. It had the grip on the platform so your feet wouldn't slip off. It also had a aerial dynamic fin on the back.

My dad had a smile on his face and said, "happy birthday Hollering Jack".

My dad seemed just as happy as I was. I was in awe. I couldn't believe it I had a smile on my face that would light up midnight sky. It was more than I wanted. It's what I asked for, but I didn't even know they made them like that.

At the time I had the sweetest skateboard in the hood. I finally had something that nobody had before I did. Before the skateboard I had those hand me down skates. I used to zip around the hood in those boys. I got those from Derek. Dad went and talked to my mother and I put mad work on the skateboard immediately.

Now during this time skateboards had just became popular. Oh yeah! John had a pink skateboard later.

"Joe bought me that skateboard," John replied.

"Joe, gay Joe?" Emus asked.

Yep. John answers.

Emus say, "No wonder you got the pink skateboard, John". Everybody laughs!

Joe was a long time friend of John's family. He was a person that used to do things for John when he was coming up. At this time I was able to ride to the end of the block and back and John lived right on the corner. I lived down by the alley on 169th.

John lived at 16855 Calumet it faced horizontally on 169th street corner.

"Yep" John says, "I could sit on my back porch and see everything that happen on 169th". "I also could sit on the front porch and see everything that happened on Calumet," John comments.

I couldn't go in the street or around that corner. It was no use in conferring with him at first. The skateboard plugged us though, because I asked him for that ride. After I got my skateboard I didn't have to ask him for any more rides.

When I first got the skateboard John came over and asked for a ride.

I told him, "no my Mom said I had to ask and not to give out any rides".

My mother was in fear that someone would take my skateboard. Stealing bikes were rampant in the hood. I never heard anybody going out stealing skateboards. Anyway, I wasn't allowed to give out rides unless she knew about it. John looked at me like, man fuck you.

John snickers, "Hee hee,"

I felt funny inside, because I didn't really mind him riding on my skateboard. I actually wanted to give him a ride. Especially, since he used to give me rides on his skateboard. John broke his wooden board and was riding that pink one. Even, back then I didn't want to ride nothing pink so I had to get my own.

The problem was my mother had lookouts when she wasn't looking. Once she heard I disobeyed. First my mother would have told me to come inside. Next, she probably would have taken the skateboard and locked it up in a closet. At least for a couple of weeks for disobeying! I couldn't have that I knew the consequences. So, I looked back at him the same way, fuck you too nigga!

After mom came in that evening I asked my mother. Can I let John have a ride, because he had asked? Mom didn't mind as long as we stayed out front. Instead of me risking punishment to sneak him a ride. I waited and asked and it was okay. The next day I couldn't wait to see him so I could give him a ride.

"I thought he didn't give me a ride, because he thought I was white". John comments.

I reply, "Come on John why did you think that?" John you used to let me come over and play with your hot wheels on the porch.

Check it out Colo, "Back then my skin tone was quite a problem for me". Not just me everybody else. I used to get chased home every day when I was in school, because they thought I was white.

I agreed, "yeah come to think about it. That's when you came to the door to see if I could play.

My sister used to be like, "the little white boy is at the door for you".

My sister would say it with sass. "Why you got this white boy knocking on the door?"

I did think you were white or didn't care. Unless somebody teaches you, you don't know anything about racism.

I answered her, "he's cool though you wouldn't even think he was white, if you talk to him, Barbara".

Here's John, "I used to be the fastest little white motherfucker you knew. I was running for my life! It got so bad the teachers used to let me leave five minutes earlier everyday".

"That's how I met Emus and Lamont. Just like clockwork I was getting chased home from school that day. For some reason they got on me a little closer this time. I remember running, heart beating fast.

It seems as if they were going to track me down this time. I ran through the Prairie building gangway. This is one block over and a block down from where I lived on Calumet. It also was about two blocks away from Brownell Elementary School. I was caught in the middle too far from both places to get away from the mob.

Lamont and Emus were walking down the Prairie and Calumet alley. This is a short cut to Lamont crib when they saw me running. They knew I stayed on the block and stop the guys from chasing me. Back then Lamont was towering over everybody. Emus was big himself so they backed off.

Emus and Lamont both told them, "get up off him, he's off the Met".

After that day, I seemed to always walk home with Lamont and Emus. That's how we became cool they were my protection.

I commented, "they saved your ass that day". That's one thing about the Met you could not mess with anybody off the Met, Tadpole. I can remember that from my earliest years of kicking it. Now we might get into it with each other, but if you we're off the Met. Adrian, we got your back.

Grench Snatch

Come to think of it John, Emus was the next person I met too. I met him and he was eating a Suzy q and some chips.

"Yeah right," Emus reply while laughing.

Emus every time I saw you, you had something to eat. You made that Suzy Q look so good while eating it. You would eat it slow and lick the sides of Q's cream filling. The cream filling was on the side of your mouth. You kept the goodies. I used to sneak up on you and say cobs once we were cool.

Adrian, you had to say no cobs, in order not to share. As soon as you seen one of your guys. No cobs on this, no cobs on that, when you had snacks! You had to specify what you had no cobs on. You might want to share the chips, but not the Suzy Q.

Now, when you were eating something you had to constantly look around. To make sure one of your buddies didn't sneak up and say cobs first. You'll be looking all over your shoulders and down the street all while your eating.

"Hell yeah! Emus reply's, I used to always say to myself, "Colo motherfucking ass always catches me".

The next level of that game was the 'Grench Snatch' game. The snatch game was scandalous. I mean we were out to get you in the worst way. This game tore at your soul, because its nothing you could do. When you're playing the game, you're playing. It's cool if your doing the snatching, but if you're the snatchee. You're about to address some emotions. You can have five dollar worth of goodies. All your shit can be snatched. I saw somebody get all their shit snatched one day. First you're mad and sick to the stomach.

When you're not playing you got to let it be known, but we all played. You were out when you were ready to fight about getting your food snatched. You were out the game once you couldn't control your emotions.

I think I was one of the coldest at that game. They always had money to buy goodies at the store. I had to scope out my snacks. I was like an animal predator looking for his next meal.

You see Colo was good at shit like that, go ahead though," Emus comments.

Cobs was a more civilized game. When you got caught playing Cobs you just gave him some of your hookup. You gave him how much you want to give em. You could give him one chip.

The Grench Snatch game, you grab as much as you could, scandalously. I used to get Emus so much that he quit playing all the games. I made him quit playing Cobs and Grench Snatch.

I get him good! Emus had a cheeseburger and fries. He was walking down the street by himself. I see him busting down his fries. He's really enjoying his snack he doesn't have a care in the world. He was about a block away before you get to Calumet.

I figured he would stop on John's porch. Like we usually do and bust the sandwich and fries all the way down. I hid on the porch behind the concrete railing, where you couldn't see me. I was in front of John's door, but crouched down. The railing divided the two dwellings. John stayed on the inside. The deaf ladies house was on the corner.

She would always come out and jester. Get off my porch or come out there with some hot water in a pot. She would threaten to throw it on us. She signed that she was going to call the police all the time. We used to trip on that, cause I know the police can't hear her, if she called.

Anyway, Emus must have eaten all the fries while he was walking down the street. That's what I would've grenched snatched. He didn't have any more fries, because I was scoping for them. I'm peeking over the railing and I saw he had unwrapped the paper around his burger.

I sprang from behind the concrete barrier. I startled him at first, because he peered through the glasses with the widest eyes.

I shouted, "grench snatch nigga".

Whatever you touched was yours. I had about half his burger in my hand. I snatched what I wanted so quick and stuff it in my mouth. His sandwich didn't even look right any more. I had snatched a massive hole in his sandwich.

Emus was looking at me and then the sandwich, me, then the sandwich. I burst into laughter because of his face. Hee hee, I couldn't hold back my laugh. While laughing, I take a breath and continue the story. I stuffed the burger in my mouth laughing and eating it at the same time. I probably could've killed myself.

I barely could eat it, because I was laughing so hard. Damn near choked, cause I had to stop and get it together, before I did choke. I started coughing up the burger. After clearing my throat I kept looking back at Emus face.

He made me laugh more and more I couldn't stop. You seen one pissed off nigga with some big ass glasses on, looking the meanest. He didn't say a word he just looked at me. He was addressing his emotions. I fell on the ground laughing more and more. My brain was hurting from the overload of the laughter.

Emus looked like he damn near wanted to fight. I never saw him look at me like that before. He had the, I could fuck you up face on. Emus could've choked the shit out of me.

After he took in what just happened to his burger. He sat there I mean literally stone-faced for about 45 to 60 straight seconds. Emus face was so blank while watching me eat and laugh at the same time. I couldn't even enjoy the food. His face said it all. He was going through some thoughts, but he didn't say shit, he just looked.

He probably was thinking about fucking me up or this nigga got me good, which one I don't know. He kept looking at his mangled burger and then me.

Emus cut in, "the nigga scared me half to death and then half of my burger is gone. That's what the look, looked liked.

"I just kept on laughing", I couldn't help it".

E yelled at me, "That's it Colo don't snatch no more of my shit" and threw the rest of the burger on the ground.

I asked, "Emus you quit, you not playing no more".

He responded, "Man, don't snatch no more of my shit. I'm not playing cobs, grench snatch or no of that shit" and walked away.

I think he went and bought another burger and fries. He dared me to fuck with it without saying anything. Emus didn't fuck with me for a couple of days after that either. That was the end of that game. That game got shelved.

The Met

Who were the Original families on the Met back in the 70s? John, I know you knew everybody before I did. I couldn't come around the corner at first.

John thinks and then said. "First person I knew around there was Gina Marie and Linda House.

Gina stayed right next door to me at 16854 and Linda stayed in 16834. The reason why I knew them was, because they used to walk me to school back in the day.

Colo interrupts John and says, "Emus you should know the people who all stayed on the Met back in the day".

Emus ponder and then said, "Let me see, Gina Marie stayed next to John. The Stable sat at 6846 and their people used to stay up stairs. Robert and Chucky, they had about two sisters.

Kenny and his brothers and sister Toni stay under us at 16840. Next to us were the Houses then it was Darkness and his little brother Daryl.

Oh yeah! Daryl, how old was he when he got killed? I asked,

"He was about 10 or 11," Emus replies.

Was he that old? How did you feel when Daryl died? Colo asked.

"I think this was the first tragedy for us as shorties". John responds, "At the time I was mad. Daryl had stolen some of my Hot Wheel cars and I was mad at him.

Linda House, was sitting on her porch. She was telling me while I was riding my bike.

She said, "John they found Daryl and he's was dead. He was cut in half, on the train tracks. I said, "that's good for him".

At the time I guess death didn't hit me as finality. I can still remember the look she gave me when I said it, but I didn't mean it. He just stole my hot wheels and I knew I wasn't getting them back.

John I remember coming over playing with your hot wheels all the time.

It hit me kind of harder, because Daryl and I were cool. I can remember not wanting to go close to any train tracks," Emus comments.

Colo agrees, "yeah that's who you were hanging out with at first, Emus. Y'all stayed three doors down from each other.

One day Daryl ran away from the crib and never came back home. His mother knew Daryl was very mischievous. She worked all the time. She couldn't give him the time he needed and put food on the table. Daryl didn't have a father figure in the household either.

He had his big brother Darkness, but Darkness was a teenager doing his thang. When Moms went to work, Daryl did what he wanted to do. Back in the day I can remember going to see if Daryl could come out.

We used to throw the football around. You know how I would come to your house to get you to play. I would hear him in their being chastised, for his mischievous actions while she was gone.

Daryl wasn't well liked in the hood, because he was kind of a bully. He took what he wanted and didn't have respect for other people things. He pushed me off my skateboard and wanted to fight. I don't even remember why. We used to throw the football all the time. I did not fight him, but after that! He wasn't one of my favorite people.

John cuts back in, "One day he went into the Leather Lounge and stole a fifth of liquor and was drinking it" He asked me did he want some and I he said no. Anyway not too much later he disappeared. This wasn't unusual for Daryl to run away. Whenever he knew he was going to get a whipping he would run away. This time he did come back. They said Daryl must have been playing on the train tracks and were run over by a train. He had disobeyed for the last time. Rest in peace!"

"John continues, "After Daryl crib it was Bruce the story teller". Bruce will tell you a story that was so wild it was crazy. He would have the whole porch cracking up.

The Small's stayed at 16848 Calumet it was about eight of them.

A couple of doors down lived Darrin Wesley, we called him Big D.

He was always ways doing something not well thought out. Like when he got that tattoo with the dollar sign and the pitchforks. He did it himself and did a good job. It was a big $ that took up the middle part of his arm. He had a big ass bicep and triceps. At each end of the dollar sign he had two pitchforks pointing horizontal in each direction. It was sweet and it went with his arm, big as hell. The only thing was the S on the dollar sign, was backwards.

On the other side of the block was Big Mike who stayed by the sandlot at 16740 Calumet.

Andrea, all this reminiscing got me hungry. You have any quick chips or something over there," Emus shouts.

The food is almost ready. You can come and grab what you want in a few minutes. Everybody just be calm", as Andrea stirs the dip sauce.

"Same old Emus, always wanting something to eat. Shit ain't change, just the scenery change". Go ahead John!

"Then it was Otis and Bluski who were foster children. Back then we didn't know what foster kids were. Otis was real light skin and Bluski was dark as Colo. Next to him it was Half-and-Half.

"Who name was Half and Half?" Andrea asks.

John answers, "Half & Half was a this girl could do just about whatever the guys could do. She could play basketball, climb trees and played catch just as good as the boys in the hood. That's why the called her Half- &-Half. She could do things as well as guys could. We had no idea about homosexuality or gay tendencies for girls.

She stayed at 16755 Calumet. Corky stayed at 16847 Calumet. She was one of those girls who looked good. She went outside the neighborhood to get her boy friends. Don't forget about Alisha. Next, it was the Paxons. It was Raymond we called him Fat Cat and his family. Then it was the Bilkins. Oh don't forget about Mr. Glassmen and Elroy.

"On 169th, 170th & Calumet, it was Robert Jackson and his family. In the building on 16960, Calumet was Brandon and Kevin Stroles,

Benita and Regina, there was Danny and his big brother that knew Tae Kwon Doe. John Strong and his sister Sherise Major. You know it was Lil Gouch, Rob, Lil Rich and his family.

I cut in, "I knew Diago Jake and his family because they stayed behind us on 314 E 170TH street. Jake used to walk the shit out of a Swinn. He would take the wheel off the front and go for his. On King Drive it was the Big, Jake & Stanley. Paul and Evette Racks were on the Westside of the street.

On the other side of King Drive were Roddell, Chris and their older brother Carlos the Ward family stayed on the other side of the street.

Emus grandmother on King Drive. Those four blocks was our first exposure to the inner city of Chicago street life.

Back then it was so cool. Everything back then evolved around competition, having fun and fighting. We used to line up and race down the block at least five times a day. We would start at the beginning of 168[Th] & Calumet. The finish line would be Lamont house.

Big D, Freddie and Lil Todd were the fastest, but Otis used to motor. Otis was always locked up for some reason.

I don't care what sport or what game it was we were playing, it was competitive. You might have a fight here or there, but that was competitive too. You never wanted be branded a punk on the strip. When we were coming up it was we, on 168Th & Calumet playing some sort of sports. As long as we were playing somewhere in the street or in the alley we were cool. The only person who used to be after us was Mr. Glassmen, Elroy's father".

Mr. Glassmen was our nemesis back in the day. When we were playing any kind of game and the ball happened to go across his yard.

He'd chase us off and shout and say, "stay off my property!"

You couldn't play running bases in front of his house. When we were playing football and the football hit his car. He would come out and try to take the football.

Mr. Glassmen got so fed up with us that he came out with a pistol. He was threatening all of us with it.

He started waving the gun around and saying. "Get away from my house and car", Mr. Glassmen shouted.

At first everybody went for cover. I know I was ducking behind a car. When all of a sudden the gun fell apart and he was left standing with a handle in his hand.

The whole neighborhood fell out with laughter while shouting, "go back in the house old man".

He picked up the pieces of the gun that fell and went in the house. We thought back then, that Mr. Glassmen just didn't want us to have no fun. He just was trying to take care of his property. Now that I have property I know why. Mr. Glassman was a year round Ebenezer Scrooge, Baaa humbug.

Getting P's in the Hood

Andrea, the main thing was holding yours down, physically and mentally. I got my P's on the block the first fight I had. I had to be about eleven. I was over by Todd Stable's house, in the vacant lot.

Robert and I were out with the baseball gloves playing catch. Robert went in to get some water. I waited on him so we could finish playing catch. While waiting Mark was on the porch. All of a sudden Mark started throwing rocks at me and telling me to get away. Mark is Todd's little brother.

Mark had something afflicted with his arm and was a little slow. He was mean though! I let him get away with a couple, but he wouldn't stop throwing the rocks. I tried to tell him to cool out. He kept telling me to leave. Anyway, he was throwing rocks at me so I start throwing them back. I wasn't throwing them hard though!

It was the principal you throw rocks. You get rocks thrown back at you. Here's Robert, coming down from upstairs from getting the water. He saw what was happening and he started protecting Mark by checking me.

He frowned and said, "don't throw no more rocks at Mark".

I responded, "then you need to tell him to stop throwing at me". It seemed like a good trade off.

Instead of him telling Mark to stop throwing rocks. He told Mark to throw another one.

Robert then looked at me and said, "you bet not throw one back. Mark did as he said and threw another one. I didn't move; I let it hit me. I threw one and hit him right in the back. It was on, like Donkey Kong. He came running down the steps so fast to get at me. He was swinging and I was swinging back.

Robert and I were out there trying to kill each other. I remember him slamming my head on Emus's building. I remembered me beating my fist, on his face. We went from the front to the back of Todd's yard. It wasn't fenced in at the time. It was a vacant lot in between Blues and the Stables.

We fought in the street, on the Met, back in the yard again. He'd backup from my blows and I would back up, when he came hard.

First, it was just Robert and I out there fighting and Mark was watching. We fought so long and hard everybody on the block got a chance to watch the fight. Bang #*@# boom, bang, boom, **@# boom. Wrestle for a minute, fall down, get up and fight some more.

People had time to go get, other people. They'd come back and still see a decent part of the fight. At first we were outside by ourselves, but after ten minutes went by. We had the whole neighborhood watching.

That was good I needed people to see how cold I was at fighting anyway. Robert was tough, he and Chucky; his older brother must have fought all the time. He did not give, but he thought I was soft and he was wrong.

People came from everywhere and we didn't disappoint them. Bang, boom, ugh backwards and forwards. The fight had to last at least thirty minutes. We would rest a few seconds catch our breath and go back at it.

Neither him nor I shed a tear, from the fight. It seems as if, he was determined not to lose, but I was determined not to lose too. It was like Ali and Frazier. I could see it in his eyes he wanted to fuck me up, but I wouldn't let him. I was banging his ass.

If I didn't win it had to be a tie, because I know I didn't lose. He had home field advantage. I was in his yard. I wasn't giving and we both were bloody. I remember having a scratch on my chest after the fight. That day I found out I had pit bull in my blood. Finally, I think Dave Bilkens broke up the fight.

Dave said, "that's enough go home Colo".

We looked at each other. He walked toward his porch and I went on home. I went home, looked in the mirror and said to myself, "You are a beast".

Will, Lil Todd's older brother came and saw me the next day. You know you had to see the back up, if they felt he lost. Will was too far out of my age range to fight. He had to be about sixteen. He asked me what happened? I told him about the rock thing and I had to go for mine. Robert tried to play me like a punk.

Will said, "all right, but don't throw no more rocks at my brother".

I replied, "I ain't going to start as long he doesn't throw none at me".

Robert used to let me ride his bike, if I paid him a quarter. I didn't have a bike and he used to get all the sweet shit. I learned how to ride a bike with his bike. It was worth it because I was fucking his bike up, trying to learn. After that I never bought another ride.

People in the neighborhood talked about that fight we had for years. Word was they never seen two shorties who wouldn't give. We were cool after that altercation. We had a mutual respect for each other. In the hood, if you were a hoe, you were going to get fucked with no doubt. After the fight not only Robert, but everybody else knew I was no hoe. Meaning, don't fuck with me like that.

My Dog Tiger

After that Todd would ride by my house and throw rocks at my dog Tiger. He would do it right in my face. I'd tell him, "you better stop throwing them. My dog is going to bite you, if he gets the chance".

Todd's retort was, "shut the fuck up that dog ain't going to do shit, fucking mutt".

My dog Tiger I had him ever since he was a puppy. The breed was a mix of Colley and German Shepherd so Todd wasn't lying. The dog was black with a white chest. White fur ran down the nose with the brown trimming and black ears.

I was responsible for feeding and cleaning after the dog. I had to use my own money to buy dog food. That being said, sometimes you could see my dog ribs. Until I felt bad and I'd fatten him up.

When he was a puppy he went through hell. My brother and I would think of terrible things to do. The dog wasn't that big, but we rode him like a pony. I used to tie a sack around my dog's neck and push him down the stairs. The stairs had carpet on them though!

Everyday Todd would walk or ride by on his bike and throw rocks at him.

Todd was just trying to get back at me for his brother Mark.

Whenever Tiger saw Todd he would run for cover. He was tired of trying to dodge the rocks he threw. This one time Todd was coming through the alley riding his bike. He was eating an ice-cream cone he had gotten from Mrs. Howard. He was riding through zig zagging on his bike while eating his ice cream.

Tiger saw him and I thought he was going for cover. Now the gate had a chain on it so the dog couldn't get out. Tiger knew he could get out though, but I didn't know. This time he wasn't bothering Tiger. Tiger saw Todd and he hit the gate, slid through the gap and charged Todd.

Todd sees the dog charging and barking so he tried to speed up. It was too late. Tiger growled dove at him and bit him right on the ass, chomMMP!

Todd screamed, "get your dog".

His ice cream flew up in the air and landed on the ground. I watched the ice cream in the air a long time. It was like in slow motion before it landed. I called Tiger back and he came and shot in the house. His ice-cream was toppled over and the cone was up side down in the middle of the alley.

Todd ran in the crib, holding his ass. I was laughing at him low-key, because I told him. He left his bike in the middle of the alley and ran and told his mother.

I ran in the house and told my mother.

She said, "boy that dog is going to get us in trouble".

Mrs. Stables comes around to our house. She wanted to find out, if our dog had his shots. My mother assures her and shows her Tiger's shot record.

This gave me a chance to talk to Mrs. Stables. I told Mrs. Stables. "Todd keeps throwing rocks at Tiger that's why he attacked. Everybody knows my dog. I walk him with no lease. Mrs. Stables knows my dog is not dangerous.

She told my mother and I not to worry about it. She's going to take him to the doctor. She told Todd to stop throwing rocks and they got in the car and left.

Will came back the next day with King their big German Shepherd.

He asked me, "why don't you let Tiger out so they could fight?"

I told him, "it won't be a fight".

I never fought my dog. It was good for Todd. He used to fuck my dog up and I couldn't do anything. He was too old to fight at the time.

Lamont

I had a fight with Lamont not a real fight, but a real fight. Lamont was cool, but he picked on you.

I used to get tired of Lamont cause he had those jokes that cut. His laugh was so bold; it hurt worst than the Joke. He couldn't really cap, but he said hurtful things.

He used to say shit like, "get off my porch, you look like you stank. Just looking at you and I know you stank".

I be like, "fuck you Lamont".

Lamont was big to me, but we were the same age at the time. I couldn't really get on Lamont he had the whole hook up. He had the nicest parents and they had a car. His sister name was Mary Jane. I loved to be over there, just to see her. She'd walk down the stairs in her PJ's and speak.

"Hi Colo!"

Mary Jane didn't hang in the hood at all. She was sophisticated to me. She was brown skin with a nice shape. She kept her hair looking nice and wore glasses some times.

There family had the first computer I saw in the hood.

I am over there kicking it and he told me, "get the fuck away with your stanking ass".

I wouldn't leave and started talking shit back. "Fuck you with your big goofy ass Lamont". He said, "oh yeah"

He walked over and started hitting me in the chest.

I was like, "Lamont cool out, because he had mean intentions".

I was passive all this time so he thought I was scared. I was just trying to be cool.

He hit me again and we got to real body punching. We didn't hit each other in the face, but we were real body punching. I showed him what I was made of that day. Once he saw that I could go. Lamont didn't fuck with me like that, but he still picked on other folks. I learned that from him I cut people up with the shock joke.

Lamont was cool, but he could be mean, if he doesn't like your ass. You'd go over his house. He'd feed you and let you play his games. You had to be cool with Lamont he had all the gadgets and sports equipment.

That reminds me of the time. We were in Lamont backyard playing tackle football. Lamont had a pretty big backyard. This is one of our major shortcuts to the block from Prairie to Calumet and vice-versa.

It was Big Darrin, Slick Freddie, Lamont, Emus and I. Emus was the artificial quarterback. Freddie saw us throwing the ball. He was already playing for Darobe High School at the corner position. He was of average height brown complexion and ripped up. He had something different about him. His eyes were hazel brown and green. His eyes changed colors when the seasons change.

Big D was on my side. We were having a good game, until Emus threw the pass to Freddie. Freddie caught it and started running and Big D ran him down by the gate. Caught him and picked Freddie up in the air and body slammed him. Just like he was rag doll right by the fenced gate.

Now Freddie is four years older than Big D. Big D is big as hell and didn't know his own strength. I could tell by his face, Freddie felt disrespected. He shook it off went and picked up a brick. Ran over and hit Big D in the head three times. I mean slamming the brick against his head, cause I heard the thudd sound bam, bam, bam!

Big D went down to ground clutching his head and asked. "Why you do that Freddie?"

Freddie shouts at him, "What the fuck! What you pick me up like that for and slammed me like that?"

Big D started crying and went home.

We like, "damn Freddie that shit wasn't right".

He looked and said, "y'all better shut the fuck up. Before I hit y'all little niggas in the head too". After Freddie said that, he started walking home.

Mrs. Jackson came out and caught Freddie on the front and asked Freddie before he left. She heard the commotion and seen our concern for Big D.

What did you do to Darrin Freddie?

He answers, "Big D was playing dirty so I hit him with the brick".

She told Freddie, "that wasn't right," while Freddie walked toward home. I've been talking about fights since I've been here. Somebody change the story cause I can go on and on!"

Andrea asked, "so y'all like football cause I love football. What other games did y'all playing coming up?"

Emus reply's, "I like all three, basketball, baseball and football. Which one did you like the most? All the sports were cool. It really depended on what we were doing.

If everybody is out there playing baseball we played, like my older brother or his friends.

We would be like, "let's go play some baseball. When we felt like shooting. Let's go shoot. I think its whatever we saw on TV. That could have played a part in what sport we played.

"In the summer it was baseball and basketball. In the winter it was winter games like football and tackle hill dill and we went sledding on the hill. Remember the hill we used to come down.

Yep, "I remember because my little brother and I had the only sleds in the hood".

"We also used to use card board too on the mountain when we didn't have sleds". John comments.

Chapter IV

Strike Out

"**I** think our main sport we played. When we were shorties, shorties, baseball was the sport. We all had gloves and bats. I remember us hustling up on balls by taking bottles to the store. The rubber balls we played with cost 59 cents. We got the balls from Mike's on King Drive. Him and his cousins were the first Arabs store in the hood.

At first black owned the gas stations and the stores. The Arabs started moving in after that and you know the rest! He took over the store on 169th & King Drive from Jessie. If Mike were out of balls we'd walk up to Michigan. Michigan was about four blocks away to get balls.

"I think baseball was my best sport". John brags as he stands up and gets into a batting stance.

"I was too little to play football and too short to play basketball. Even though, I played both of the other sports. I loved and played baseball the most.

Colo intercedes, "You had to play baseball the most, because I had you pitching all day. I used to rock John shit playing strikeout. Strikeout was a game where you can play baseball one on one, Tadpole. Chicago is the only place I've seen strikeout boxes.

It was graffiti everywhere else. It was a place to play for Chicagoans' kids without leaving the area. We sprayed painted the box on a perfectly clean wall. When we played strikeout it was usually no more than three players on each team.

The pitcher, middle infielder and the outfielder were the defense. You mostly seen strike out boxes on the sides of buildings. You had them on the skyways, schools and parks. Anywhere there was a lot of space on the other side of the box.

The box was about three feet wide and three feet tall. The box was usually sprayed with spray paint, crayon or chalk. Andrea, it had an X from your knees up to your chest with a square box around the X. In the middle of the X was a circle. This is a target for the pitcher to aim the ball. Anywhere inside the box is a strike when the ball lands in it.

John became very formidable, but I would get him. John used to get a running start and pitch the ball. Say like if the mound is here. He would step behind the spot about six feet then run up to the spot and pitch.

He was trying to throw heat, Andrea. His shit sizzled too coming of his small frame. It sizzled coming off my bat too, zzzzzzzzzzzz PowWW.

It was a trip we stood on the little grassy sidewalk to bat. We're pitching from across the street into the box for the batter to hit. We had to stop when cars came by. It was a slow street though!

John pitched straight fastballs that didn't move. All I had to do was time it. I must say I was the ultimate athlete, Tadpole, in the hood. I played them all at a high level. I had aspirations on playing pro. I knew I was going pro, Tadpole. I had to get my mother out the hood.

When Emus and I played one on one I used to have Emus out there so long pitching. We only would play two innings when we used to be at the skyway. Emus had this little curve I used to bang. Once I got too many hits in the inning. Emus wouldn't even go retrieve the ball after a hit.

He'd looked at me and says nonchalant, "game over Colo you win".

I'd say, "go get the ball it's still my bat," while laughing. I got two more outs.

He'd say, "Colo I ain't going to get no more balls".

I'd say, fuck it! I had to go get the ball, throw it to him, then pick up the bat. I get back in my stance and swing. The same exact thing happened. I'd smack it and have to retrieve it, with his lazy ass. I was playing offense and defense.

I used to laugh and laugh because I would get Emus so frustrated. My defense was so hellva I would chase a pop up, down. Emus would think it was going to fall. Nope I dig it out running fast as I could. When you got it on one hop it was an out.

This is how you beat me, Tadpole. I couldn't pitch. I would lose control sometimes and couldn't find the box. I'd walk the hell out of you. I get two strikes and the next four pitches weren't close to the box sometimes. If you had an eye you could wait on a walk after two strikes. Yeah baseball was my first love too. Didn't too many people get me at strike out.

I played against Paul and Fonz all the time. 'Pauly' was brown and skinny and the neighborhood thief. He always talked to you like you weren't shit. Fonz was light skin with a long fro and wore braids all time.

I hated playing Pauly, because he would lob the ball when he was pitching. He would lob it high in the air and when it came down you had to time it. I would be so anxious that I swung and missed it half the time.

When I did make contact it was a feeble hit. You couldn't hit the ball as hard neither when you are pitching lob balls. Pauly could hit too. He used to be knocking the ball deep into the vacant lot or alley.

When I played Fonz, one on one, he used to come with heat. He didn't give up. We played until the ball was minced meat. Fonz was good competition. He didn't have trick pitches, but he had an eye.

He'd beat me a couple of times cause I was all over the place with my pitching. The worst thing is when we fouled tipped the ball back on the skyway. Game was over! It was no way to get up there unless you went up over by Big Mike house. That was like a two-mile adventure to retrieve the ball back and forth. The skyway wall was about twenty feet high.

Fonz and I would just go down to the basketball rim in the dungeon. We would play two out of three or three out of five games. He was high energy like me. After winning we'd sit down for a second.

Fonz would be upset, because he almost won, but blew the layup to win the game. I grabbed the rebound and goes out shake and bake him and hit my lay up game over!

He just kept saying, "damn," and got up and walked over to the mattress the Houses' left in the alley.

He took his lighter out his pocket and was lighting the cotton and then put it out. He was just fucking around. I as watching him put it out to make sure. He lit it again and then let it go just a little too long.

You couldn't really see the flame you just saw the cotton turn black. When he tried to put it out it was too late. He pulls the mattress in the middle of the alley and we both tried to stomp it out. It was too late we had to break the mattress was in full blaze.

Somebody called the fire department and they put it out. I'm like, "damn Fonz"

He just laughed and said, "you see that was an accident".

I say, "Fonz we got the fire department in the dungeon cause of you".

Meeting my Match

I met my match one-day I ran into Jeffrey Hudson. He was in my class, but a couple years older than I. He played all three, football, basketball and baseball. I knew he could play football, because he used to quarterback during lunchtime. He was sweet at basketball too.

Really that the only reason we were even playing baseball. One day after school he popped me playing basketball. He was on the Rock Manor Stallion basketball team.

Jeff went to work on me with the jumper and then the drive game. He was shaking me up, but I played hard.

I said after he won, "you got me in basketball". At the time basketball was my weakest sport.

I then said, "play me in my sport"

Jeff said, "what's your sport nigga?"

I answered, "play me in some baseball.

Jeff replied, "you really don't want to play me in no baseball. I kill you in some baseball".

I was like, "yeah right while we were just shooting around".

He kept talking shit like he could beat me in baseball. I finally put him on the list.

I ask him, "okay where you live? On the weekend I'm going to come see you". This was one of the times I wasn't on punishment. I had a paper route at the time. After I do my paper route I was going to his house.

This would be one of my adventures. Go to Jeffrey Hudson house and beat his ass in baseball. He told me where he lived. The very next weekend I go to his house and get him. I got two brand new rubber balls, a bat and my baseball glove. I walked from my crib to his crib, which was about a mile.

I had four more blocks to walk after I'd walked past the school. I get to his house and rang his bell.

He came to the door and said, "he had to finish his chores".

I waited about thirty minutes outside his crib until he finished his chores. While waiting I was in the alley next to his crib throwing the ball off the wall and catching it. I was thinking about my strategy for the game. After he finished his chores. He came out and we walked back up to Rock Manor to play.

I gave him first bat. I was confident that I was going to win. He could bat first, that means I get last bat. When playing strikeout you played up to six innings. I go to the line to pitch.

He look and said, "you too close".

He comes and shows me where to pitch the ball. He goes back to the area where the big fellas pitched. This where we are pitching from, it was three feet further back.

I said, "ain't no big thing," and began to pitch.

Tadpole, I think I was pitching the first inning about an hour.

Tadpole laughs, "Huh huh huh huh"

Jeff was tearing the lining out the ball. When he hit the ball it sounded like when the grownups hit the ball, Yaaakkk. I was throwing curve balls and fastballs. I don't think I got one strike past him.

Anything close to the box Jeff was sending my shit over the outfield gate. I'd pitch the ball and next thing you know I'm looking deep in the outfield to see where did he hit it.

I was like damn dude is no joke. He had two homers in the first inning. The only reason I got out the inning was because of defense. I chased down his fly balls in the middle of the outfield.

It was six to zero before I could even come up to bat. I get up to bat. We had to start with a new ball, because he ripped the first one already. I look at the first ball like, damn.

We usually go three innings before the ball rips up. Only the big fellas rip the ball in one inning. The big fellas played strike out with five or six rubber balls to get through a game.

Jeff spotted himself six points. My strategy to get back in the game was to have a good eye. I was going to take a few pitches and try to get bases loaded. After I got the bases loaded I was going to catch up with a homer. I hit a grand slam the score would be six to four.

Jeff warmed up and I was impressed. I get in the box and stand and wait on the pitch. I was trying to locate it coming out of his hand. No bet! Jeff would wind up and next thing you know! The ball would be bouncing back off the wall, back to him.

I looked and knew right then this motherfucka is a beast. Jeff wasn't that big. As a matter of fact! He was skinny and wore glasses. I swear dude had to be throwing 90 miles per hour.

All I could do was hear it at first. It sizzling loudly and hit the wall like fireworks, powwww. His shit was moving and it didn't come in straight.

He was throwing strikes too. I was whiffing and foul tipping his shit. Strike one, strike two then strike three, I'm out. I'd take a pitch and it was hitting dead in middle of the circle. I couldn't wait on shit.

He'd asked me, "can you see it little nigga?"

When I swung I was late on everything. I couldn't pick the ball up. I had to swing when Jeff was in his wind up or it was too late. Next thing you know I was back in the field.

I struck out three times in a row. Jeff wore glasses and looked like he could be a nerd. He was no nerd he was a straight athlete. I go back to the field and say to myself.

"I ain't never struck out all three times without getting a man on base".

His next at bat, my first pitch I threw. He swung and fouled the second ball back on the roof of Rock Manor. Game over!

He said, "you're lucky I was going to kill you".

It was clear to see he was a lot more talented than I was at baseball. I tell him good game I got to get back. He gives me dap and I walk home disgusted. It was hard to comprehend. I didn't like the feeling of losing while I was walking home.

I sucked it up, but told myself I would be prepared next time. I walked home that day slowly thinking about the loss. Jeff had me practicing everything relentlessly. I practice basketball, baseball and football. This is what's was going through my head.

My momma used to say, "It always somebody out here better than you".

I bought the balls and traveled knowing I was going to kick his ass. My walk home I had a chance to investigate losing.

Jeff made running through me look easy in two sports. He was laughing at me while he was at bat like I do other people. Now I know how y'all felt. I practice for our next encounter, but it was the last encounter. We never played again. When I transferred to Communication Metro high school he played on their baseball team.

The last time I saw him though I worked at The Inter-Continental Hotel on Michigan Ave. I was a valet, parking attendant for Standard Parking. He walked by every once in a while on the way to his job.

Dude was big as hell. He had muscles coming from everywhere.

I'm like, "damn Jeff you've changed you've got muscles on top of muscles".

He told me what gym he went to, but we never exchanged information. Anyway Jeff had me really practicing. I really practice basketball. It was the only sport I could practice by myself.

Dungeon

It was always a rim up in the alley. We just couldn't play on it all the time. Emus states.

Colo agrees and says, "Yep, because when the older kids were playing we could not play. When we were playing and they started to come out, getting in the game. They would gradually put us off the court. I believe that's why they played elimination so much.

All we did though was, pick up our bats and gloves. We'd walk down to the skyway and play baseball. Emus pointed out. All the equipment was lying down by Todd's gate when we played. That's why we played so much baseball.

That's a trip we played on that rim in the alley for years. We called it the Dungeon back there in the alley. It was a rim on a light pole with a night-light on it. You could have day and night game because of the light.

It was located in the back of the church adjacent from Todd's crib. Sometime we would get too loud during Sunday service.

The reverend would come out and say, "calm down were in service".

He never told us to stop playing though. A couple of times the reverend came out and played with us. He could play too, to be a pastor.

Right behind the pole was a fence that surrounded the churchyard. The pole was about 1&1/2 feet away from the churches' gate. The gate was about 15 feet high. The rim was about 11 feet high to discourage people from dunking. Had it not been for that I would've been dunking, but I didn't even try it was too high.

The boundaries for the basketball court in the dungeon's alley were. Mr. Henderson old school car he worked on sometimes. The Stables gate was a boundary it that sat adjacent to the pole.

There was Mrs. Lane's gate, which was, preceded by rocks and gravel pit.

"Y'all play basketball in the alley?" Andrea asked.

I answered, "I know right, coming in I rolled by about fifty basketball courts in Austin. In Chicago we played in the alley. I am a legend in the alley on 169th.

How many years was the rim up there?" Andrea asked.

The basketball rim was put up every year. Somebody in the hood would ante up on a rim. First the rim was in Todd's yard. After Robert and I fought the gate went up. I don't know if that was the reason why, but shortly after the fight they had a gate put up. Everybody would pitch in each summer to put a rim and a net up. Todd and I put the rim up about three times by ourselves a couple of years.

People in the hood don't have fun like we used to, when we were kids. We played all types of games to hold our attention. Baseball, football and basketball were the basics that we played.

We also played Simon says, hide and go seek, softball, Frisbee, two square, racing, skateboarding, skating, four square, pitching baseball with pennies and the whole block played.

A homer was when your penny landed in the line. Four fingers was an out. You measured by fingers between the penny and the line. A triple was one finger from the line. A double was two and a single, was three fingers, from the line. We played baseball on the lines to past time, but we were getting good.

In the winter we had sleds. We'd hit the hill at the end of the block. "If you couldn't play sports when we were coming up. You didn't hang out. Reason was, because we didn't like to lose and at any given time. Someone could challenge us on the Met. When you couldn't play, didn't hustle and you, caused us to lose.

The probability of you playing with us again was bleak. Not just that we would talk about you, not only about ball. Anything that we could talk about would be fair game. The only thing off limits was saying, "your momma".

That was another thing the whole area was competitive. After a while we started playing against people out the neighborhood. We played Michigan in football all the time.

We would walk over to Walter Readus or Tookies house and play football in the front yard. Walter Readus was light complexion and mild mannered. That means he was cool. It was his squad against any squad we brought. We had some good games playing in the snow.

Another event we always watched first and played coming up was in the Wine Bowl. Every Thanksgiving day the Old G's & BD's and the up and coming BD's & GD have played football. We would play against each other in football at the park on 171st & King Drive at Iron Park. The Brothers were welcomed to play on that day. This is a day it would be no drama!

I was a shortie, shortie going up to the park just to watch until I got old enough and the courage enough to play. It used to be no joke playing in that game. You could be easily carried away from an elbow to the chops or a clothesline. People used to get bones broke and teeth broken.

Around the house it was different brackets. The hood was basically divided into three groups. The older teenagers which was: Steve Bilkins, Maurice, Freddie, Dave Bilkins, Jason, Lando, Will Stables, Stag who where about 18 or 19.

The next group were the younger teenagers: Lace Bilkins, Todd Stables, Bluski, Big, DarrinWestly, and Rodney Henderson AKA Big. Freddie Large and your brother Cool Blue was about 13 and 14. Slick Freddie was sixteen and kind of fit in the middle.

The last group was Emus, John, Robert, Lamont Paxton and Daryl before he died. My little brother Walley I had to drag with me. Alisha, Penny on King Drive, Theresa and Kendal were the girls on the block our age.

Working Started Young

Once I got a chance to know everybody on the block. I started noticing the things that they had and the things I didn't have. Before I got my paper route I had to wait until momma gave me some money. Sometimes she didn't have money to give. I realized at a young age that in order to get some of those extras that other kids had. I had to get a job.

On some Saturdays I'd go with my sister's father Curtis Felton, to deliver steaks. This means on that Saturday, I wouldn't be watching cartoons nor could I go on an adventure.

I had to make a decision cartoons and adventure or money. I had to get up and go to work I needed those scribbles. He had a van and was delivering steaks out of the van. He had a built in freezer in the van and it used to be packed full of meat. He had NY stripes, Porterhouses and T-bones. He'd also have chicken among other things.

He'd come about six in the morning and grab me up. We would stop and grabs some breakfast before we started. We'd eat at one of his favorite restaurants; boy did they have good food. After eating we hit the road. He used to drive the hell out of that van.

We called him daddy Curtis. Daddy Curtis would be on the expressway bumper to bumper. He used to be flying. He kept me on pins and needles in my seat. I would put my seat belt on and people didn't where seat belts back in the day.

We'd go to a lot of ladies who bought meat from him. They would be in their gowns, early. I would get a peek at a nipple through the nigh gown. We were early when we came to their house. We went to all type of businesses to drop off meat. He had a nice hustle.

By the time we finished every box of meat was gone. He had orders and everything was accountable. He would keep the dollars and throw the change on the floor of the van.

You know I had to scarf at least two or three dollars. He knew it too, because one day he counted down before he dropped me off this one time. He usually just dropped me off after a day of delivering. This taught me about math and how you catch a thief. Numbers don't lie!

He counted everything we sold. I received the money so I was responsible. This man taught me business at eleven years old. He always checked behind me to make sure I didn't cheat anybody. Worst I cheated myself.

He soon saw that I could count, add and subtract. Anyway he started counting down. I did my usual and took about three dollars of change extra for the arcade. He counts the dollars and then the change. The change is short. He looks around looks at me and counted it again.

Now I know I got the change in my pocket. He didn't say anything though he just looked at me! It was just he and I and I had to have the money. I knew what he was doing and I was caught. I didn't even think he was paying attention, to the change. In business everything must add up. Change adds up.

He would pay me ten dollars for the whole Saturday. I didn't think it was enough so I got me some extra for the games. I was busted though! I guess he was waiting on me to come clean.

I wouldn't have taken it, if I were going to come clean. I just looked at him and hunched my shoulders like I don't know. That was my first job working with my sister's father. I went out with him a couple of months.

I don't remember him picking me up anymore or I faded one of the two. I didn't think ten dollars was worth my whole Saturday. I hit the game room and I could blow that in two three hours tops.

The Neighborhood Paper Boy

My second job was at the age of eleven too. There was this guy who ran a paper branch on 169ᵗʰ & Prairie. Emus and John knows him. They probably worked for him too. He's name was Denis. Denis used to have this 1975 white Rivera with the white seats and it was cold as hell. It had the bubble windows and sweet red leather seats.

He was all I had to go on at the time as far as a hood role model. He had his own business and a sweet ass car. Denis also had a nice looking woman too; her name is Denise, Freddie older sister. Denis was one of those guys who drank beer and smoked cigarettes all day. He had real big, super big lips.

He had the biggest lips I ever saw. I got really big lips and after seeing his lips I was cool. If, you think my lips are big. Put my lips up against his. You would think my lips were from a Caucasian decent, the thin ones.

His lips were 3 &1/2 times my size and I'm not exaggerating. He literally had booty lips. It was two half bubble moons with a split deep in the middle of his lips. When he had been drinking beer and he'd talk to you. His lips used to shake twice every time he said one word. They were spring loaded. He didn't have to be drunk, come to think about it. I'd look and you know my dumb ass. I'd have to keep from laughing. I'd have to turn away from him.

It was just like one of those Chinese karate movies translated in English. Emus knows it, he used to work for him.

"Yeah his lips were pretty big," Emus agrees.

It was like, if he said, come here. At the end of "here" his lips would move twice more on a bounce. It would be quite hilarious to me. I would conceal my laugh and not laugh in his face until I got used them bouncing.

Well, I told my mother I wanted a paper route. Six months had past and she wouldn't let me. I didn't know why, because a lot of kids had paper routes. I would have been the youngest one, because most paperboys were at least thirteen or fourteen. I was about eleven at the time. At this time Lacey and Emus' brother Coole already had paper routes.

The reason why Moms didn't want me down there is, because she checked it out. She found out that Denis was drinking heavily over there after hours. She finally gave in and took me down to Denis. She called him and told him that I wanted a paper route. She told him she'd bring me down later. I remembered it as if, it was yesterday.

Denis knew my mother, because we got the paper everyday. Sometimes we were late on a payment for the paper. She would call down there and tell him when she could make a payment.

My mother and him had a cordial relationship. She always said Denis was a nice man. We walked in the paper branch.

Denis sees my mother and says, "how are you doing Mrs. George?"
Denis was real polite and courteous. Denis talks to all the customers with respect.

Mom replies, "fine and how are you?"

"fine" he replied.

I was so eager for a job, it was a shame, because I wanted money. I was sort of scared to ask for fear he would say no.

My mother said, "if you have a moment my son would like to ask you something?"

Denis said, "Yeah! I know your son he always playing strike out behind the laundry matt".

My mother urges me to go ahead and ask.

I asked him, "Denis do you have any paper routes open because I need a job?"

Denis replied, "Not right now, but maybe in a couple of weeks something might be open. If there is you are the first person I will call".

I said gleefully, "thanks let me know cause I'm ready," but was still disappointed, because I wanted one right at the moment.

I can remember waiting up to a point till where I said forget it. My mother talked to Denis and told him, if I was to be hired. My route had to be close to the crib. That meant either King Drive or Calumet.

I think Bluski had King Drive. I was hired, because Bluski had got fired and I got the Job. Coole Blue had Calumet. Lacey had route, 7 and 8, which was both 168th, 169th & Prairie. Donnie and Paul Venebal were the older guys who had the rest of the money routes.

Denis never drank around us much. The next morning you can find three or four bags of beer cans. We could have just cleaned the paper branch up the day before and the next day it would be filled again. It was full of empty beer cans liked they partied every night.

Denis used to get so drunk sometimes. We had to go to his house to wake him up. He had to open the branch, but wouldn't show up for work. We would be standing outside the branch with the bundles of papers sitting outside.

They'd drop the bundle off at 4:30 of 5 am opened or closed. We used to ride over to his house on Perry with Stagg. Stagg had this sweet 1980 Cadillac. He was one of the go-getters in the neighborhood.

He'd ring the bell and bang on the window for about ten minutes. Stagg was the branch supervisor. He was the one who opened the door for thievery.

Before I got the job I collected those beer cans. I would just take them to the crib and crush them. Denis was always a good spot for aluminum cans. Once I got enough I'd take them to the aluminum yard and get me a few more scribbles.

The money was straight but I needed more. I had been working for a while and one of the most dependable paperboys. Mom would get me up every morning around five o'clock so I never missed work.

Chicago Slick

After working a while I picked up the game. I sat back and watched how everybody got down. I already had my own customers on my route and everything. I'd make my receipt up from the empty customer slips he had around. Of course you're not supposed to have your own customers. After a few months of doing this, this is how I got caught.

You have to be there every day because, if the paper is not delivered. When your customer didn't get his paper they'd call the branch number. It's located on the bottom of the collection receipt.

When you missed work you would want to at least drop that paper off to your customer. You might have to buy it from the paper stand. I made up their tag and receipt and was clearing an extra 40 bucks on collect day plus my tips.

My man Stag showed me the whole game about getting extras. Stag was the one who showed me my first route. I saw him selling papers. He told me to take somebody a paper and I got the money from it. He gives me the game.

Now I got money coming in the house. Every morning rain, sleet or snow the paper comes every day. You don't get a day off, if you are a paperboy. It was my dog Tiger and I.

Sometimes I would take Siltec the branch dog. This was a stray that everybody would take on the route. I had my own dog. My dog came with me most mornings on my route.

Tiger dog would follow me wherever I went. He used to chase the cats early in the morning. I used to like him chasing cats, because those cats were acrobatics.

They look so sweet trying to get away. I never wanted my dog to catch them. I just wanted to see the cat run.

One time this cat was jumping from one porch ledge to the next porch ledge. The cat looked like it could fly while jumping. When the cat jumped, it was at least 15 feet to the next porch.

On the last porch the cat jumped and soared sweetly in the air. The cat measured it about three inches too short. Bam, hit its head on the porch and slid down to the ground. It was some Tom and Jerry shit.

Tiger was on the cat's trail, but I called him back. The cat shook it off and kept it moving. Siltecs would have killed the cat that's why I didn't take him. Siltecs was white gold & brown and was battle ridden. You can tell by all the fight marks all over him.

Anyway I had been delivering to this one customer for about two months. He hadn't paid so he owed for two months. It was time to get paid. That was a good fifteen dollars for my pockets. I go over there to collect and dude pays me in a check.

I wanted to say, "this shit ain't any good", I need money, but I couldn't. I grabbed the check from him and had to figure it out. I didn't figure on that! Now where am I going to cash this check? It was about a fifteen dollars check.

After my route was done and right before school. I stop at the currency exchange on 169th & King Drive.

I said to myself, "I'll try to cash it here". I see my Mom always cashing checks here. I used to always wait in the line with her when she cashed them.

I've forgotten the lady name, but she knew my mother. Here I am eleven years old trying to cash this check.

It was a football that had my name on it in the sport store window. My plan was to cash the check and then go buy this football. The sports store was next door to currency exchange. I walked by the sports store everyday wishing I had that football. This check was going to get me that football.

I went in and hand the check to the lady behind the bulletproof glass.

She looks at me and said, "hold on honey, step to the side I got to wait a few minutes on checks".

I'm stepping to aside while she handles other customers. I am waiting and waiting. The lady took a while and now it was no more customers in the place. It's time for me to be in school.

I'm waiting for that money cause she says it almost ready. I'm really trying to make morning football before school. I had to buy the ball and play with the new ball this morning. Next thing I know my mother is walking through the door. My face cracks open and my mouth drops to the floor.

I looked back at the lady and said to myself, "she set me out".

My mother comes in talks to the lady.

The lady says, "yeah I know this is your son and gives her the check".

The check did have my name on it.

Mom asked me, "who's writing you checks?"

I answered, "I got this off the route. They gave me this as a tip".

She frowned and said, "A fifteen-dollar tip,"

She couldn't believe it.

She gave me a look and said, "go to school and she would see me when she got home".

What did my mother do? She goes to the paper branch. Takes the check to Denis to see what was up. Denis checked his sheet and tells her he doesn't even deliver to that address. This must be his customer. He is not supposed to have his own customers.

My Mom gives him the check. Denis didn't fire me, but he gave me an ear full when I came to work.

He ended the conversation like, "you slick motherfucka, you're fired, if I catch you again".

Hey, I did get him another customer. He's got fifteen dollars too. My mother was so honest it was unbelievable. She gave me up and was surprised to see how slick I am. Being smart works both ways in life. She'd call me in the room and talk to me about righteousness.

Of course I didn't stop. He wasn't my only customer. I was only making ten to fifteen dollars a week working my route. I can blow that with a few comic books and a hour in the game room. Sunday was payday for us. I snuck in real early.

I had to change the collect money sheets, because I was short on collection day. I was short the whole hookup. Whatever I collected, I spent. I couldn't sleep because I had to get there before everybody.

I had to get there before Denis for sure. Denis came in on Sundays late 95 percent of the time. He partied on Saturday nights. I had to change the sheets without anybody seeing me. I dragged behind and the early guys left the branch and I made my move.

Denis kept the books in the front draw of his desk. He had this funny kind of writing that I had to mimic. I was in big trouble. I had never fucked the money up like that. If I was short it was no more than a dollar or two. That's one thing I was a good paperboy. I made sure everybody got his or her paper and Denis got his money. They used to rob the paperboys on collect day. I never got robbed.

This particular week I was balling out. I bought a bike from my man Marcus from school. I paid fifteen dollars for it. I also spent about twenty dollars on video games. Mr. Reef's game room on 169th & King Drive got some. They had a game room on 171st. I spent a lot of time in that one on collect day. Let alone the candy I had bought. I was collecting the money on the route and took a break. I was intending on just playing one game and finish the collecting. Next thing you know I was spending the collect money like it was mine.

I figured I was at least 75$ dollars in the hole with the collect money. The only way out was to change the collect sheet. This was a sheet of entries for how much we paper boys collected on Fridays and Saturdays.

Sundays we got paid. He kept the sheet in the draw. Again he had this funny kind of style of writing his numbers. I was an artist though and drew all the time. I had to change the numbers and changed them without him knowing. That it's not his writing.

I got there before Denis came in and fudged the sheets. I figured it wasn't going to work and this could be my last day. He already knows I'm slick, but let's see. I just did like everybody else.

I would take about 20 extra papers and sell them to whoever asked for one that Sunday. That would get me about 12 extra dollars on my last day. The Sunday paper hit for 60 cents. I did my route and turned in my collect book. It was time to get paid and we do the numbers.

I am shaking in my boots, because I just know he's about to bust me out. He gets to me and adds the numbers. He squinted and turned his head sideways at the numbers, but kept on going.

Denis wasn't dumb he was on his square. Only thing is he drank and it affected him. He kept looking sideways at the numbers.

I said to myself, "I am busted," but played it off by not looking in his face.

After he did the figures. He paid me my week's pay. I was over five dollars so I got extra's that week. I got away Scott free. I believe he was on to my game though, because the next week. He sent Stag after me, on my route the next Sunday. Of course he caught me selling papers. I was in the middle of the street hustling papers like a motherfucka. I would hug that middle lane and cash in on the people in the cars who wanted papers.

I didn't know Stag pussy ass was following me. When I got back to the branch Denis busted me out.

He asked with his eyes bucked. "You're selling papers aren't you?"

I looked at him funny and said, "naw, I'm not selling papers".

He tells me to pull my pockets out and there was nothing. I saw him do somebody else like that! He fired him once he seen the money.

I said, "I ain't got nothing in my pockets". I wasn't going to get caught like that!

Here comes Stagelee busting me out. "Yes he is Denis, I saw him".

I 'm looking at Stag crazily cause he trained me. Who you think I got it from?

Stagg spilled the beans, "yeah Denis look up under his hat".

"Oh my God," I said to myself.

Stag comes over and knock my hat off. All the dollar bills came down, like I made it rain on myself.

Denis looks and shouts, "you thieving motherfucker, you are fired!

He picked up the money and said, "here is your weeks pay and I will holler at you".

The money I hustled already was my pay. Well that was the end of that for a while. I got fired for selling papers.

I went to the store on the corner of 169th & got me a job. This was the first Arabic store in the neighborhood. This was before Mike who got it now had it. His cousin had it first. I worked for about six days after school.

I worked about four hours after school. I was cleaning and getting up all types of nasty shit up. I'm washing walls and climbing ladders and guesses what my man gives me?

Emus answers, "15 bucks".

Nope dude gave me six dollars. I asked him, "this all I get paid".

He said, "what, you did not do nothing much".

I'm not the smartest guy, but that's a dollar a day.

I said, "okay" and never came back. Every time from then on I went in that store and raped him. I stole everything that wasn't tied down.

I got my job back later on at the paper branch. I couldn't believe Stag tricked on me. I could've been like, "Stag showed me how, I got it from Stag".

My momma always said, "two wrongs, don't make a right".

I couldn't be a hoe, cause he was a hoe. He taught me the game. What had me tripping is that I never saw him peeping at me, on the route. I slept, so this put me up on game.

"Don't think you're that slick to not watch your back. Somebody is watching you for sure".

I should've known he would send someone behind me. I got caught with the check plus the sheet change. One more thing, someone got to be the fall guy. He was stealing and I was stealing along with everybody else. Everybody took their extra's to sell. I had to take the fall on that one. Even Denis sold papers.

Like I said Denis hired me again. After Lacey and Mike quit he needed somebody who could bang. He saw me one day and told me to come in and do route 7 and 8. I still took extra's, but I got the job done. I would deliver Prairie and Michigan both blocks got those four story colt way buildings with all these floors. At first I used to walk up all those steps.

I began throwing the paper on the second and third floors. I busted a couple of windows. I keep it moving and get back to the branch they'd be done called. You have to pay for all your busted windows.

I already paid for one on King Drive. I only busted a couple though! I was fast and efficient. I had a way of folding and throwing the paper where it landed right on your doormat. You open the door and bam you could read the headlines when you picked the paper up.

I rarely missed a day of work. He needed me especially since we always had extra papers left over. What were they going to do with yesterday paper? Let me get that! Denis started getting there early counting all our papers before we left. When all routes were done they would be bundles left over sometimes. I figured that money should be mines, it's left over.

You delivered the daily papers every morning all year round. The little extra he knew I was getting, wasn't bothering him. He needed somebody to deliver the papers every day. Most times when people didn't come in Denis delivered the route.

All while attending school I used to deliver my route. I was trying to deliver my paper early and fast. Early enough to play that morning football game we had at school. We played football before school and at lunchtime. Sometimes after school we played football for a while. I had my paper route in the 5Th, 6Th & 7Th grade.

I had to leave the basket for the papers in a spot until after school. Usually I would put it in the back of Charles Jennings building across the street from the school. I've known Charles ever since the first grade. I had three or four routes at this time. I didn't have enough time to make it back with the buggy. Denis made it so I delivered around the Rock Manor area last.

Denis would have me delivering other people routes. When they didn't come in Denis used to come out while I was on a route. Ride up in his car and drop me papers for another route. When he thought my buggy was empty he'd ride up with another load.

I could fit one hundred and fifty papers rolled up in one load Monday thru Thursday. I was a hustler and took whatever I could handle. I was the branch as far as getting the job done. I needed that money.

My only problem is that I had to make Tiger go home. He didn't want to leave me and sometimes would be waiting for me after school. I had to throw rocks at him before he got the message. He would tuck his tail and go home.

My dog loved my ass. He would act like he was going home. I'd go in the school after he got a couple blocks away. I get in the class and I'd see him walking up and down the street chilling along side the school. Sometimes my dog would wait all day until I got out of school. I can't take Tiger with me anymore on my route.

Ronald Bronson

Enter Big Ronald Bronson and Billy Daymond. They both transferred into Rock Manor in the fifth grade. Ronald did the Hawk to a lot of people. He wasn't extorting, but he would just bully you for no reason. His people had money, because he came with fresh shit to school.

When you came to school fresh you had money. He fucked with everybody else, but he did not fuck with me at first. My reputation preceded me. He stayed about a block away from the 171st park.

When he transferred in he was bigger than everybody else. Billy Daymond and Ronald were straight Bully's. Ronald was the real bully, because he tried you, if you could fight or not. Billy just messed with the peons. How I plugged into those guys.

I used to go over Billy's house all the time to trade comic books. He had the old comic books I was trying to get. Billy would try to steal mine and I would try to steal his. Billy was the one who put me up on stealing comic books. At first I had no idea to take the books, when trading.

When you went to trade comic books, stealing was rampant. You always have to check dude comic books before leaving a trade. Billy was slick he would put my comic book inside his comic book. I would check his books before he took his back in the house.

I counted mine and checked his. Usually you would just scan through the top left-hand corner of all the books. Make sure none of yours are in his stack.

You can't just trade obliviously you have to count too. The only way you don't get, got. You got to count your books before leaving someone's house. Once you leave the trade is done.

I kept counting mine though and I was short.

I look and said to Billy, "I came with 30 comic books and I only have 28". I knew what I had, so he had to have them. I am sitting in this hallway and they couldn't have disappeared, Billy".

Mr. Curtis taught me you can't get around math. Now I would do a two for one, if he had something old I wanted.

I'll give you the two newer comic books. I could get those two back with no problems through trades. Billy wouldn't trade his older comic books unless they were reprints.

I don't want any reprints, because they were worthless. I had to get loud and said; "I did not do no two for ones, Nigga. Give me my motherfucking comic books in his hallway".

He saw I was getting upset, but tried to still play me.

"I ain't got your books what are you talking about ssshhhh?"

He's trying to Shoosh me. He starts pointing inside while saying, "my grandmother," in a low tone.

He was still looking all astonished and trying to play it. I started getting louder so his grandmother could here.

I got amped up, "where's my shit? I can count Billy, I can count". I was putting emphases on each phrase.

Billy finally said hold on then he went in and got em. After he came back out with them and gave them back. I still was wondered how he did it? I was on him. The only way I caught him is, because I was short. I went through all of his and I didn't see any of mine in his. I didn't do any two for ones. I should still have 30 comic books. I started with 30 so I should still have 30.

After he gave em back, he showed me how he did it. He kept me busy and talking while he kept showing me other comic books.

While I'm busy saying, "Ooh, you got this, you got that". Billy is duffing my comic books inside one of his comic books.

Billy Daymond was smart. He scored high on the reading test too. Billy wasn't thinking about trying me physically. He bullied everyone who would let em. He was a mild mannered William Hawkins all over again. We got into a verbal before in the front schoolyard.

For some reason he tried me that day. I guess he was mad I made him give my comic books back. He did the bully stance pushed and grimed me. I instantly stole on him. I hit him dead in his nose.

Billy grabbed his nose and looked. It happened so quick that I didn't know I hit him. He knew what was up after that.

He said, "damn man I'm straight," then started checking for blood. By feeling around his nose and then looking at his hand. After seeing it was no blood and me looking grim.

He said, "I was just playing Columbus".

He was trying to feel me out. I knew what he was doing and gave him his answer. We were in a playground full of kids and nobody knew it happened but Billy and I.

Those comic books had us captivated when we were shorties. I used to get them from Luke's paper stand on the corner of 169th & King Drive.

Old Luke was cool he always tried to get the comic books I collected. I did what Billy Daymond showed me to do. Old Luke would turn his head I'd duff the books inside each other. I didn't like doing Luke, but I rather kept the money for the books.

He caught me one time like, "oh what this inside here". Luke pulled the extra comic book out the comic book I was buying and looked at me.

I looked back and said, "it must have been stuck in their Luke, on the stand".

When I started buying comic books they were 35 cents. I was making money from my route so I bought me favorites, when they came out.

When Luke didn't have the comic books I needed. I would walk to the 171st & King Drive paper stand. It was a stand also on 175th & 179th St. These were the paper stands that sold comic books.

When they didn't have it I would get on the bus and ride to 195th & State where they had all the comic books. Now if 195th St. didn't have the ones you wanted. You have to go downtown to get a specific issue. I did that a few times too. I was a real comic book collector. I had the plastic over the top of them and everything.

Oh no! You don't quit looking for your books, because they didn't have it at the local paper stand. You wanted to get every issue as soon as it came out. I collected Avengers Xmen, Spiderman, Fantastic Four, Luke Cage, Hulk, Silver Surfer and host of other Marvel comics.

I only collected Marvel comics. My first comic book I bought was Jug head from DC. As a matter of fact my first six comic books were DC. When I bought my first Marvel Spiderman I didn't think about DC anymore.

Billy and Big Ronald were cool and hung together at first. The day big Ronald became my nemesis I didn't even know. We were all getting out of school and we walked up to the park. Everybody went up to the park for some reason I can't remember. When we get up there, it was two sets of boxing gloves up at the park. Big Ronald was boxing with somebody else when we got to the park.

He was putting the uglies down on him and then they broke it up. Everybody in school knows me for boxing so you know what happened next.

Everybody said, "go with Columbus, you want do that to Columbus ".

I remember Fester, Danny and Deonte saying it, because I wanted them to shut up.

I'm like damn to myself, "can't back down", never could. I knew sooner or later Ronald and I was going to get into it anyway.

He's started shouting at me, "Put them on Columbus I'll smash him too. Put the gloves on nigga". He's doing this while slapping the glove together and scowling.

Boomph, there's those butterflies start popping off. Everybody got faith in me. My man who was boxing him, takes the gloves off and gives them to me. Fester was trying to help me get the gloves on! I started to put them on and Ronald tries to steal. He tried to steal before I even get the gloves on, dirty motherfucka.

"Let me get the gloves on Ronald," I shout.

This right here was a moment of truth. The whole fifth and sixth grade was at the park. Along with some grown-ups, they were being the referees. People were tired of Ronald. He had been strong arming people, because of his size. I get the gloves on and somebody said ding.

Ronald swung twice trying to take my head off. I ducked and backed up trying to get comfortable. He came at me thinking I was going to keep backing up. I stop and two piece him bing, bam stops him in his tracks.

The whole park was like, "whoooo damn he hit big Ronald".

Ronald got mad and came at me hard again swinging. I ducked, but this time I stuck in there like Ali and countered, bam bam. Knocked him off stride and he almost went down. The crowd was going crazy. I let him recover.

After recovering Ronald rushed me and knocked me off balance somehow. He didn't hit me though! I had gone down to my right knee. I had my right foot digging into the grass keeping me up though! Ronald got himself together first and didn't let me get up. Ronald ran and swung at me doing both, simultaneously.

I saw him coming. I ducked up under the swing while getting up at the same time. He was off balance falling in the direction he swung and missed. He dug in and tried to hit me with the other hand and I was on him. Bam bam, I connected with a two-piece. I spinned Ronald around and he hit the ground.

The park exploded, "Columbus just knocked out big Ronald". They picked me up like at the fight and carried me out the park.

Shouting, "Columbus is the Champion over and over again. He knocked out Big Ronald".

This was one of the best days, of my young life. This was the first time everybody wanted me to win. The champ crosses all the lines.

The Cardinals

Now Ronald and I played baseball that summer together for Mr. Wilson Cardinals at Iron Park. Mr. Wilson was in his forties and stayed across the street from the park.

Mr. Wilson Cardinal was known throughout the whole city. I never thought anything else about Ronald and I boxing in the park. We had the gloves on and it was a set environment. It was all in fun. Really, I had forgotten about it. I was putting in work, without the gloves.

At this time I stayed at the park. I was on the court, on the baseball field and the football field. Ronald was good at all that shit. He was above the rim dunking. He was throwing no hitters in little league.

When it's his turn to bat he's hitting home runs. I don't remember him playing too much football. He was a beast at baseball and basketball. I liked Ronald cause he could play. I didn't have anything against him. It seemed we were cool, because we played strikeout a lot together.

I always started sports teams late. My mother wouldn't let me go to the park by myself. I had to be about eleven when she relinquished her grip. I was already working so I was already in the streets. I can work, but I can't play. That's when I joined the team it was my last year to play little league.

I didn't get any time even though and I was cold as hell. I could hit and I could field. I spent years in my basement throwing that ball off the brick wall. I'd throw it in all type of angles high and low. I'd bounce throw it off the wall, out of reach so I would have to dive to scoop it up. I had this sweet blue glove my God-mother, Mrs. Carmelita bought me for my birthday.

I was sweet, but I started too late. I was supposed to start playing when I'm eight or nine. Mr. Wilson was just using me as a backup. He already had kids he had been working with for a couple of summers.

When I came for tryouts I did impress him. You had to be sweet to be on the Cardinals. We had those green yellow and white uniforms. My family wasn't into things like that so they didn't come to the games.

My little brother played for the Jay Hawks. This was the Evening Star church baseball team. I should've played with them. At least I would have got some time. Mr. Wilson Cardinals were the shit though.

He always had good teams and I wanted to play on the best teams. I used to go watch cause Blue, Lace and Bluski played for the Cardinals. Blue was sweet with the baseball glove at first base, gobbling the ball up.

It was an adventure though! Mr. Wilson would take us on the West side to play. He would load us kids up in a station wagon truck and we were out. It would be about three or four carloads of us. I would've played, but some of the pony league players somehow got to play.

We played all over the city and it was fun just to go along for the ride. Dave and I were the same age, but his birthday was after September. He got to play another year of little league.

We were one of the best teams in the city Curt Hill, Lil Tyrone Hill, Jeffrey Pettway, Kevin Stroless, Maurice Valenzuela, Kevin Dougall and Shaun Jackson.

Anyway, some days Ronald and I could share a meal. Some days he couldn't stand my black ass. He would get to talking shit. I was right there to talk shit back. I didn't know why dude always wanted to get into it with me. He already knew I could fight. It's like he had something to prove. Why would he keep trying me? He knows I am a beast!

The Agony of Defeat

One day Emus and I were in the Mr. Reefs game room on 169th. We were leaving the game room and saw Ronald walking by himself.

Ronald started shouting at me, "I'll fuck you up Columbus, you a pussy".

Emus was with me, right. He couldn't believe that Ronald is talking to me like that!

Emus says, "is Ronald talking to you Colo, what wrong with him?"

Emus and Ronald were cool at school. This was after Emus transferred in the school. I think they were in the same classroom.

I replied in a smooth voice, "Ronald you know me better than anybody and you coming at me. We go to the same school. We played ball together on the same team. I just couldn't figure Ronald out.

We make it back to the game room somehow. Ronald is still talking shit in the game room.

I gets fed up and said, "fuck it lets go in the alley". It was winter and we got coats on and the snow is up past our ankles, midway to our knees. We go in the alley across the street from my house. We bend the corner so we were in the back of Mr. Zells cleaners.

"What's with it Ronald," I asked.

He said, "I am fucking you up".

I said, "okay," faced up and it was on!

Ronald couldn't fuck with me with the boxing. He swung first then I gave him a couple of shots and then rushed me. I gave him a couple of more shots while backing up with the counter. I could see the frustration in his face. He charges me again I upper cut him. Grab him then slung him down and was on top of him.

I didn't smash him because I knew him. While on top though!

I looked him in his eyes and said, "Ronald cool out I don't want to fight you". I could see it in his eyes he couldn't believe I was on top.

Ronald shouts, "get off of me nigga, get off me". He struggles, but I held him down, with my forearm on his neck. I didn't hit him anymore I just tried to calm him down and let him know I had control.

Ronald grimed and said, "get the fuck off me".

I said, "cool out then," he stopped struggling and I let him up.

I let him up thinking it was over now. He gets up.

He gets his composure and said, "lets go".

Dude was determined to get me. I said to myself, "this time I am going to fuck him up. He just won't quit. I was never a person at the time to just clean you out. I would give you a few shots or a slam and it was over, but Ronald kept coming.

Usually a person knows when he doesn't have a win. All right we square up again. Again, I give him a couple of shots and he rushes me again. This time he got me backing up. He forced me off balance and he tackles me. I landed on my shoulder. When I fell I landed on it awkwardly. He didn't slam me; it was like a tackle.

Do you think dude gave me a chance? He just started trying to beat me in my face. He hit me a couple of times, but it was my shoulder.

His big ass landed on my shoulder and I was in tremendous pain. I couldn't raise my arm or really protect myself.

That's when Emus said, "that's enough get up Ronald". Emus started to pulling him off me. Ronald got up talking mad shit. "What's up now?"

I said, "you ain't did shit". I would've went back at him, but my shoulder was dislocated or something.

I didn't want to let on that I was hurt.

Emus was like, "it over Ronald," after he saw I didn't get busy. This is the first time I was TKO. I couldn't finish the fight so Ronald wins. If, we went to the scorecards though, I would have won. This is the first fight I had lost, because I couldn't continue. Up until that time I never quit or couldn't continue a fight.

Ronald went one way and Emus and I went the other way. Nobody saw Ronald do it though! It was just us three so that was good.

Emus say, "you had him beat why you let him up?"

I replied, "I don't know why. I thought he had more love for me than that. I thought we were homimes". Ronald got a couple of shots in while I was on the ground. He swung like seven or eight times, but he connected only twice.

I was moving my face while I was on the ground. He didn't even get any good shots. Emus saw I wasn't aggressive anymore and knew something was wrong. I was holding Ronald off with only one arm.

This is the first fight that I was even in a position to lose. I get home and go in the bathroom and looked at my shoulder. I looked in the mirror knowing I had dude and had mercy for him. I asked myself, "Why I let him up?" I told myself, "I shouldn't have done that I should have clean him out".

Ronald didn't show me any mercy when he had me. If Emus weren't there he probably would have fucked me up bad. He didn't know my shoulder was fucked up because I played it. I wasn't favoring it at all. He probably thought it was a draw. I hit him more while we were on our feet. Ronald didn't know he won the fight. Emus just broke it up.

I get up and he was talking big shit. I didn't quit. Emus threw in the towel.

That day I made a pact with myself, "never to show any mercy". When he's down don't let him get up. Finish what you were doing. That buddy shit is out the window, if he's trying to hurt you".

I barely could move my shoulder for two, three weeks. I didn't go to the doctor or tell my mother. I believed it healed wrong in fact, I know it did. After that altercation happened a little love had left out of my body. I won't show you any mercy once in a fight.

Ronald and I were cool after that! Every now and then we would have words. That day took a little out of me, being cool almost got me banged. Ronald one up me so it just not resting easy with me. That day Ronald took something from me, my compassion for people. You can't be nice in a fight you can't be fair. You can't have mercy on a motherfucka who wants to kick your ass, for no reason.

For now on the only mercy I'm going to show is right before the fight begins. I damn sure don't want to get on you and you are my friend. A friend will not fight you for any reason other than stealing. Anybody else fuck them!

The School Plays

One thing about Rock Manor I liked was the plays we put on every year. One year I was Louie Armstrong. I had to fake like I was playing the trumpet. Victoria Johnson had to sit on my knee was the final move. I like that part when she got to sit on the knee. I wanted to keep practicing that part. It was like a musical. I had to lip sync of course.

The one play I saw when I was a shortie that had a lasting effect on me. I learned something from Michael Evans. 'Mike' Evans played football in the back at lunchtime with us. The upper graders did the Christmas play Scrooge.

Michael Evans played the main character Scrooge. Now to me Mike was reserved. He was well balanced. He played sports and was a smart guy that talked proper. He wore glasses and he could play quarterback. He threw the sweetest spirals.

Anyway he had the lead role-playing Scrooge. We were all in settled in the auditorium and the lights went off. They pulled the curtains and when they opened scene 'Mike' was sitting behind a desk. This is the first time I understood what acting was, and the process.

The telephone rang and when Mike I mean Scrooge, picked up the phone. He had transformed from Mike and was talking like a different person.

He voice was old with a crackle. He was aggressive and loud. He was telling his workers they had to work on Christmas and he meant it.

When he talked it wasn't Mike anymore. Mike rarely raised his voice. He had me totally mesmerize of how he could change his persona. Baa humbug you could here a pin drop when he started talking in that scene. The kindergartners all the way up to the teachers were quiet. I picked that up from Mike later when I needed to act in the streets.

Mr. Norris

Now this happened at the end of my sixth grade. Well I was really in the sixth but when the test came back of course I had to switch classrooms to the seventh graders. The seventh and eight graders were located on the third floor. The men teachers, Mr. Alexander and Mr. Norris taught the upper grades up on the third floor.

Back then the teachers were brutal and would discipline you. They could yard stick you across your butt. Teachers would tell you to hold your hand out and ruler your hand. The paddle was supposed to keep you in line. These two teachers maximized the use of physicalness they could apply to you.

I spent 1 ¾ of a year up there on the third floor my sixth and seventh grade. Mr. Norris was the assistant principal in training at the time.

Mr. Norris ran through me a couple times with the yardstick on the hands. You can't do that anymore nowadays. A student will raise up, on your ass. Later that year Mrs. Rodgers took over the eighth grade.

Mr. Norris was the assistant principal now. You did not mess with Mr. Norris. He was a father figure to those with and without fathers. He wore a fro and reminded me of a Black Panther. He was stern, but compassionate. All of the thugs in the school didn't mess with Mr. Norris.

When he had you, you respected what he had to say. When you didn't he used physicalness. He wanted you to succeed and he wasn't going to let you clown everybody out of an education. I respected this man.

This is the worst move I could've made. Now I am up stairs with my hommies, brothers and sisters. Marcus, Mitchell and Rodell brother Chris were on the third floor. I was upstairs with my friend's big brothers now. These guys were fourteen or fifteen. They didn't take too likely to our smart asses up there, showing off how smart we were.

They probably were saying, "here goes this nigga always raising his hand. Here this little nigga always got the answer".

The year before I get up their, Brandon Reggie and few others were in the assembly with a gun. A real gun! Somehow word got to one of the teachers that it was a gun at school. They bring it up at the assembly. Once they heard that they were looking for a gun. They started passing the gun down.

I look over and see the gun and was like, "these niggas got a real gun".

Anyway Mr. Norris told everybody in those rows to come out. I don't know what happened after that. Anyway I'm going up stair with these types of guys.

I take my smartness upstairs with the big kids. I thought it was a challenge for me to keep up. The teacher was playing us off at first when asking questions.

I'd wonder when we'd raised our hand she or he would look over us. Our hand would be up for about five minutes. She'd be calling on people who don't have their hand raised. Why'd the teacher played like she didn't see Fester, John or I?

After a few people got it wrong I eventually blurted out the answer. I never thought of it like that, way back then. All I know is John Strong, Stacy, Fester and I had the answers to the questions so we raised our hand. You know the girls are smart. It was the guys who had a problem. That's all I had was to be was smart against the older guys. Especially, since they were trying to strong-arm us.

They had this game called neck respect. You have to say neck respect or if your neck was out in the open. They could come by and slap the back of your neck. You didn't want to come to school with a shirt with no collar. That was a perfect opportunity to slap your neck.

They didn't give a fuck, if you wore a collar or not! They still slap the shit out of your neck, if they seen meat out. Manuel and Victor Page and Todd Smith used to play this game. To avoid that I cocked my head so it would be touching my back.

I never thought about slapping their neck I was just protecting mine. Todd and Manuel used to be elbowing us in the top of the head. Aton was the head butter. He would grab your head and head butt you. I did not play games with these guys. I couldn't be aggressive back to them. I just didn't walk up to them and slap the shit out of their neck. This was some bullshit.

When the questions came to them, they just cracked jokes. Chris, Rodell's older brother used to be cracking jokes. We talked in class just like everybody else, but usually us four got our work done first. After that we'd started clowning, drawing and trading comic books. What we did mostly on our free time was to signify on each other.

The "Good Times" sit-com had a bad effect on us in the school. You know how JJ cracked on Thelma and Michael and vice-versa. We took cracking to a totally new level. We were good and mean, mean good, with the capping shit. My meaning, we were mean and good. We had no mercy on you. You could cry and we wouldn't stop cracking.

Stacy was fat, but so intelligent that you couldn't fuck with him. 'Stace' came about in the sixth grade. He wore scruffy looking clothes and never no new shoes. He would bust you out so scandalous. Don't fuck with him! He was an artist too so he could draw a comic book about you.

He was a much better artist than I. 'Stace' drew so well that I started drawing all the time in school. I was trying to catch up with his ability.

One of his names he had for me was Night Roach. He made up a picture with my face on a roach with big lips and a cape with a roach body.

Andrea starts to laugh and repeats, "Night Roach". Yeah this guy had an imagination. All he had to do was show this picture and he didn't have to say a word. The whole class would be cracking up non-stop.

He didn't even have to put my name on it. The face on the roach looked just like me. It wasn't like the picture was on the wall and everybody seen it at the same time.

The picture would have to make it around the room one person at a time. Low-key so the teacher wouldn't take the picture. Each person who saw the picture fell out. Their laughter is drawing on the last person laughter. Until it builds up and the whole class is cracking up on you.

The teacher doesn't know why everybody is laughing.

The picture has only made it half way around the room. When somebody is cracking on you good, you got this blank look on your face. You get this warm feeling racing through your body.

You are trying to conjure up something to say, but it's got, to be good. You can't come out with a dude. You need something to break up his momentum. I could get Stacy some days, but it was just best for you to leave Stacy alone. Just like Emus is to a lot of motherfuckas, leave him alone.

There was Lenard who was the only one who could get Stacy constantly. He told a joke on Stacy that I still laugh when I think about it. It went backwards and forward with those two.

Fester was good and then I. Everybody targeted me on certain days, but it worked around to everybody. It was an equal opportunity with the cracking. I was good, but fucking with them would lead me to greatness, as a signifier!

The older students didn't crack jokes like we did. You could crack a joke, if you wanted to and we were some little niggas.

It was okay as long as we kept it to just us little niggas. The whole class would laugh at us, cracking on each other. Don't give the older guys a reason to smash your little ass.

These guys were teenagers and I am a little peep squeak. It's a difference when you're eleven and they were fourteen and fifteen. Wayne Willis was going on sixteen. Physically there's no match.

Here they were in the room, with these little smart eleven-year olders. We know the material. We probably were making them feel dumb as fuck. I've felt like that before. In a room with people and you don't have a clue. It had to be soul searching for them. So they acted out with physicalness.

I'm bigger and tougher and the girls and boys showed out on us. You little geeks are showing out in class. They would push us around a little bit. That's the reason why we didn't have girl friends. We were too little and the girls paid us no attention.

Brenda Phillips, Teresa Miller, Linetta Smith, Melody Mincy, Lynette Newsome, Latonya Downs, Brenda Phillips and Pamela McNair I couldn't even look their way. I named these because they're the one's I liked. They paid me no attention.

I got a lot of attention from one girl. This girl named Zora used to fuck with me so much. I never fought a girl in school. That was a no no! She was a girl bully. She would pinch me and push me around.

She could not stand my ass. Now that I think about it, maybe she liked me. I hated to see her coming. She wasn't fat, but she was over thick. She was brown skin and kept her hair in a little bitty ponytail. I hated to see her coming, because she fucked with me.

Transformation of a Nerd

Dealing with Thugs

Mitchell Thomas and Todd Smith used to run together. Manuel, Victor, Anthony, Chris Ward, Omar Hazziaz and Aton Daniels, Wayne Willis were in my class too. Aton used to draw in between head butting us little niggas. He would be in the classroom drawing NFL helmets. All these niggas are supposed to be in high school.

After drawing them he'll let me have the sheet he drew them on! Aton drew the helmets exactly like they looked in the league.

These niggas were the goons back in the eighth grade. Some of them had made the transitions to Folks too.

They tried to sic Earnest on me, somebody my age. Earnest was straight, but he couldn't fuck with me. One day in class I might have flipped off to Mitchell or Todd I can't remember whom. You get tired of motherfucka fucking with you so you have to make a stand. Sometimes and others times, be diplomatic. They give me the 3:15.

They sic Earnest on me, head up, because he was more my age. Earnest was Folks and strong though I do remember that. We started to fight and I had him under control. I hit him a couple of times and he went down. I had him on the ground and I didn't blaze him. I was in fear of someone jumping in the fight. I was checking my perimeter making sure that didn't happen.

I had him where as, he had to turn around and get up. He was trying to shield his self with his arm so I wouldn't hit him anymore. While trying to get up his elbow hit me in the nose. He didn't even try to do it. He was really shielding me from hitting him, but I was distracted trying to look around.

They broke it up and next thing you know my nose get to trickling blood.

Mitchell and Todd said, "Earnest won his nose is bleeding".

I said, "whatever he got a lucky unintentional elbow and it busted my nose". Rodell was watching and said, "you could've killed him".

I was throwing dude around like a ragdoll. I didn't hit him because I knew Todd and Mitch were making him do it.

He had made the transition to Folks so he had no choice in the matter. He really didn't want to fight. I still felt funny on the way home, because he did bust my nose. On purpose or an accident my nose was still busted.

Chapter V

Link Pin

I was the link pin to everybody in the hood. I knew the niggas off 171st, because I went to school with them.

Everybody else from the 169th went to Brownell or Meneen. The niggas off 169th didn't really fuck with the niggas on 171st and vice versa. Nobody really would go up to the park with me from the nine. I had to go up there by myself all the time. I used to beg people to go to the park and play. I'd just kick it with those niggas at the park. It was a lot to do up at the field house on 171st.

It was a dangerous adventure, because the BD's controlled the park at the time. Shit used to jump off at the park. It was also a place where us kids from the Manor had a lot of fun. The field house had all the balls. We played ping-pong and plenty of inside games, in the field house. On the outside we played strikeout, basketball, tackle football, swimming and a host of other things.

The first time we went to the pool on 171st to swim. I thought I could swim because I was swimming in the tub at home. I had the gargles and everything when I took a bath. I thought cause I was swimming in the tub I could swim.

My sister takes us to the pool and the pool is jumping with kids. We barely got in because after a certain amount of people fills the deck up. They weren't going to let you in when it was crowded. I know why now. I get on the platform, take off my clothes and dove in the water I was so frantic.

I thought I was going to be swimming like in the tub. No bet! I was drowning trying to swim. I was getting water in my mouth. I was flailing my arms with my eyes closed. I couldn't see anything and was taking in water. I knew I was in trouble.

All of a sudden I feel my toes scrapping something at the bottom while I'm still flailing. I realized all I got to do is stand up. I stand up coughing like a motherfucka eyes red. I made a B line to the side of the pool. My nose is running and I'm coughing and sucking in air at the same time.

To my amazement not one person noticed me drowning. My sister didn't notice the lifeguard didn't know it. That's why they don't let it get too crowded in the pool.

It had been a couple of deaths up there already. Everybody was just having fun. Andrea, I could have died in three feet of water.

I stood on the side and collected my thoughts. Before the day was done I learned how to swim that day. I taught myself how to swim. I watched everybody else and mimic what they were doing. I'd close my eyes and swim. I stand up to see if I was moving and I was. I soon became a pro.

You couldn't have money in your pocket at the pool. While your swimming and having fun in the pool. Niggas are sifting through your pockets from outside the gate. You go to put your clothes back on and your money is missing. You start to remember all those people who were standing around the gate. I slept that one time the next times I put my money in the secret compartment in my trunks.

After swimming at the pool, my Mom accused me of smoking weed. I was old enough to go by myself at this time. Every time I left swimming at the park. The chlorine made my eyes red and she just knew I was high.

It used to feel weird every time I was accused of something I didn't do. I didn't know anything about smoking at the time, but now I am inquisitive. She was fishing and if that was all she was going to say.

"Boy you bet not be smoking no weed".

Ding ding ding a light bulb went off.

It was fun at the park. One year at the park they even had an ice rink up there so you could ice skate. Ronald, Jeffrey Pettway, Deonte, Fester, Ty hill, Chip, Corey and Ronald Bronson, Ronald Goodwin, Tallie Weaver, Earnest Griffin stayed at the park. Most of these guys knew me from kindergarten all the way up, so it was love.

We had a pool on 169th by the fire station, but it closed down. Before it closed we'd used to sneak in the pool at night and go night swimming.

It would be planned; by the older teenagers in the hood. The word would be circulating all day. We are hitting the fire station tonight. We meet up at a certain time at night and all go went to the pool. Back then we wore a lot of cut off pants when the pants got to short around your ankles. We cut them into shorts.

We only had a certain amount of time to swim before somebody called the police. We would hop the gate and dive in the pool. We would be about twenty deep. When the police came we had to get out and run while dripping wet.

I don't believe they were trying to catch us. They let us know they were coming with the siren on all the way. Once we heard the sirens we hit the alleys and the gangways all the way home. We went swimming in whatever you had on that night. That was some fun shit.

Mob Action

I was just as good as the older guys in sports. Sports transcended my adaption to the upper class. They didn't care how old you were. When you could play, you could play. When we chose up I always got drafted high. I learned how to fight and survive at Rock Manor. I had to use my smarts, to not get into with these older guys.

I could have been a bully, but it wasn't in my nature. Plus everybody had older brothers or was Folks. You fuck with the wrong niggas, if you want too. Their back up is coming. I had no back up and definitely wasn't going to call my sister.

This is when you got to use your scruples to get out of a tough situation. Some people even, if you can, fuck them up, don't do it. They could've started the problem, but they got back up.

This is the reason why I never started anything. That was the only way the older brothers wouldn't come down on you. Everybody has to say he started and they might not move on you. Right or wrong you can still get fucked up just for defending yourself.

You remember Trick who used to be at the park. He was older than us, by a couple of years. This is the first year that I was able to go in the back of the schoolyard. The younger kids had the front play ground. The 7th & 8th were in the back playground. I was back there a year earlier.

Anyway Trick was fucking with somebody and stole on him at lunch break. I can't remember who it was, but he was a made man in grammar school.

He told Trick, "do not be here when he got back to the school.

Trick was like, "yeah right I'll be here" and he kept on playing football".

Dude left and said, "I'll be back".

Before lunch was over my man was back with his Folks. They came in the yard and dude pointed out Trick. Trick was trying to talk and explain. The Folks wasn't trying to hear shit and began to fucking Trick up. Bang ##@@*&boom.

This was the first smashing where I had seen four or five niggas jump on you.

Folks, blew Trick eyes and lips out, fucked him up. After they did it they walked out the schoolyard looking real hard and menacing.

Before leaving Folks told Trick, "you bet not say shit or they would kill him next time".

Right after that Trick transferred and went to Catholic School. He attended the same school my older brother Samson had gone. It was dangerous up at Rock Manor even then you had to learn how to mesh with volatile motherfuckas. You can't get into it with everybody, but you have to stand your ground. Learning these survival skills was most instrumental life. Later they'd come in handy!

Street Family

Around the crib it was different. It was like we were all family even before we were plugged. It was like the whole block was cousins.

Your big brother was my big brother. The guys who were over us: Lace, Todd, Big, Freddie, Emus's brother Coole and Lando all interacted with us. They were a little more exposed to what was going. They kept nothing hidden from us and taught us the game. We were the first crumb snatchers in the hood.

Everybody other than my family had six, seven or eight more brothers & sisters at home. Therefore, the brothers and sisters taught them how to dance, step, fight and play sports. The youngest sibling had a leg up, because they had bigger brothers and sisters, to give them the game.

They also had girlfriends at a young age. The guys in the hood were wearing tailor made suits. The shoes they wore were Frank Foti's and Stacy Adams in grammar school.

We dressed on the Met. The younger siblings started drinking, smoking weed, banging and stealing at a younger age. We controlled the neighborhood at a young age. We were being groomed to be young mobsters. We had no idea what was happening. Right was wrong and wrong was right. "It like that and that's the way it is". That's a little Run DMC!

The first person I knew to smoke weed was John Strong. He was only ten years old. His birthday came late and was still in seventh grade. He had brought some weed to school.

John came up to me at lunchtime and said. "Look what I got?" I am so brand new I didn't know what it was.

The only other time I saw weed is when I spent the night out at my brothers. Floyd Foster he had six kids. This is my older brother from my mother's previous marriage.

Floyd oldest son, Junior came in while we were upstairs getting ready for bed. He opened up something in tin foil. The weed was rolled up. I was about six or seven at the time. They look like cigarette hand-made. I didn't think any more of it. I remember it being a big deal, but it looked like cigarettes to me so what the big deal?

John was like, "we about to smoke some, come on Columbus ".

His uncles probably were doing it in front of him and he got his hands on some. After we ate lunch they went out and got high. He asked me again if I wanted to come.

I said, "I was straight I'm playing ball". They went off in the alley and smoked. I think they got caught too.

John Strong and Rodell Ward were the first to try everything. My first beer was with Rodell. The first time I cut school it was with Rodell.

Next it was John and their favorite phrases; let get some beers, let's cut, lets get some beers, let's cut. Those two things went hand and hand. I wouldn't smoke weed at first. I would drink beer though!

Rodell would know everybody who would cop liquor for us. Jerry with pipe on King Drive copped for us. His cousin big Johnny on Vernon would cop for us.

When hanging with Johnny he always called me Buckwheat from the little rascals.

As soon as he saw me he'd say, "there go Buckwheat, come here Buckwheat".

Other than him calling me Buckwheat all the time, Johnny was cool. I didn't like the name Buck Wheat. We would be chilling in the cut like in Cooley High. We'd drink a brick of Red Rose wine or a couple of forties. Pass it around like in the movies drinking out the neck.

Later on some of those cut days Rodell and I would catch the train downtown to the movies. They had this back way into the McVictis Theater we used to sneak in through the door by the alley.

We weren't old enough to be in the theater early and that was our way in without paying. Sometimes the door was locked and we couldn't get in that way. When that happened. We had to get someone old enough to buy us the tickets. Sometime they would and sometimes it was a while before we could get someone to do it. We were supposed to be at school.

The McVictis or State Lake Theater is where they played all the karate movies. We went to the Chicago to see trading places with Eddie Murphy. The next time it was Doctor Detroit with Dan Akroyd. After the movies we would go to the Treasure Chest game room down town.

This one time we went downtown. I spent all my money and was ready to go home. It's an empty feeling when your out somewhere far from home with no money.

You spent bus fare and don't have money to get back and you are down town. You feel like a fool for putting everything into that game. The games were an addiction to me. I'd put all my money in the games, miles from the crib.

Rodell did the same thing he came up to me and said, "I spent all my money".

I look at him and said "me too we'll just hop the train or ask for transfers 'Dell'".

We heads to the L train and started asking for transfers. We were out there a while trying to ask for a transfer. First we worked the bus stops trying to ask somebody getting off the bus. The train came, but nobody was getting off.

The other way is to hop over and steal a ride. People who weren't going to use their transfer would give it to you when getting off the bus. You could go to the back window of the bus and ask somebody already on to give you one. He'd pass it through the crack in the bus window. Chicago stuck together. Especially, if they see you are about to pay. This time the bus and the train kept coming and I couldn't get a transfer. Nobody was really getting off the L at that time of evening.

Rodell got him one, but he couldn't pass it to me. I was right behind him, but Rodell didn't pass it right. Once he got it back he was suppose to ask a question and slip me the transfer.

The attendant peeped our game she was looking at us. She told Rodell not to pass the transfer, because I couldn't use it no way. I should've just ran down to the next stop with the transfer, a block away. I didn't do that.

I looked at the attendant like, "bitch I'm trying to get home". I finally got fed up and said. "Fuck it I'm getting on the next train no matter what". Rodell is already on the platform. Here comes the next train. I hopped over the turnstile while looking at the attendant.

I gave her a look like, "fuck you bitch". No soon as I do that! The police were sitting there watching the whole thing. It's either she called them or they were watching. They sprang out the cubbyhole from behind the scene and grabbed me, before I got on the train.

Rodell got on the train and watched them take me away. I didn't see this police and I thought I was looking for all that. The lady could've warned me, but she didn't. She was in on it!

I said, "officer I'm just trying to get home".

The policeman responded, "you can't steal a ride" and took me the police station. They put me in the back of the paddy wagon. This was my first time I'm riding in a paddy wagon. I see the blood splashed and dried up in the back of the wagon. The arresting white police officer wasn't really tripping.

I give him some bullshit about I wanted to be a police officer.

The officer was telling me, "you can't do things like that".

I told him the truth, "I spent my money down town and was just trying to get home".

The officer ordered out to McDonalds and gave me half of his food to eat. Now that was cool.

He asked me, "you want some?"

I said, "naw" at first.

He then broke it in half and said, "here you can have some".

I saw he was genuinely concerned and then said. "Thank you officer"!

He called my mother while I busted it down. I was waiting for her to come get me. My first police contact was eleven years old down town Chicago.

They had to have the police on those train stations. Mass groups of people used to hop the L. Usually, you got to go up or down to get on the train platform. The attendant was posted on this platform.

We would wait right before the train was going to take off. You had to time it. I'd run then jump over the turnstile like Jessie Owens, doing the hurdles. Hopping the bus was different. Usually, if caught, the bus driver would just tell you to get off.

The Harris's and the Larry's went to day camp on 161st and Prairie. We had to catch the King Drive bus to 161st and walk the rest of the two blocks. Everyday we worked the bus driver to keep that bus fair. I'd hustle a transfer and then we'd get on the bus.

Once on a crowded bus we had to space ourselves. I'd get on then let a few people get on go to the window and pass it out. Another way was while he was handling passengers. Double back like you going to get off and smoothly pass it to my brother. He'd use the transfer. We would use one transfer on a crowded bus, four times.

Once we got 161st and Prairie to the camp. We'd go to this two-floor house and play games, ball, softball, cards and read. I had a fight with a guy named William. Dude thought he was the shit. He was trying to shine on me, but he couldn't.

I can play sports and I was good at the board games. I am a winner and I strutted like a peacock. We got into it about something and he came at me. We were out the hood so I didn't mash him. My mother already told me I was responsible so make the right decision. My decision affects everyone, because I am the oldest

I just restrained him without putting the mash on him. The older guys from the block said he won. I had a responsibility to get us all out and back home.

If I would've smashed him in his hood, it wouldn't have panned out. We would've had to fight all the way home. We couldn't come back to the day camp. I had Alberta with me and she was young about six. I was only eleven. I knew the play and just restrained him. I had Larry, Walley, John and Alberta with me. You have to use your smarts. I've seen several times guys get banged not knowing the deal. This is not your hood.

Toast to Friends Free Ride

Emus pour him a shot of 1738 out the fifth bottle. Next he fills up four more cups.

Emus raises his cup, "We toast to friendship and new friends, clink clink clink, here here". Yeah we come a long way Tadpole just trying to make it.

"Remember Colo when it was cold than a motherfucka and we were coming home from 79Th. I think we went to the movies that day on Rhodes.

It was brutally cold, cut your face, cold. You could hear the wind from the inside of the store. We were coming from the movies and spent our money. The time ran out on our transfers".

Sometimes the driver would take your transfer and just throw it in the basket.

Sometimes they would look and say, "it's expired. You have to pay another fare".

The last thing I wanted to do was pay for the ride. Only lames pay when you can get it free. I did everything I could not to pay. I had transfers from last month, crispy. It had the right date though, but wrong month. I'd get on the bus by myself and give him a bold transfer. Play it off and keep walking.

Colo answers Emus, "Yeah I remember. Emus was acting like a mark. The bus had a front and a back door of course," Andrea. When the bus was crowded or if someone was getting off the back of the bus. Whether we had money or not, can't give it to CTA. Our transfers expired. I wasn't going to risk the transfer pass off. It's too cold to get told to get off the bus.

Why would you pay if you could sneak on the bus? The way we did it we'd sneak on the back and crouch down. After the bus took off get up and go sit down. Most of the time, I'd just walk on the back and just sit down.

Sometimes it work sometimes it didn't. I'd get up and he'd wait until I sat down thinking I was straight. He then would single you out and tell you to come to the front to pay or get off. That was the bust you out and make you feel dumb move, from the bus driver.

Emus and I are freezing and instead of walking to the crib. We're trying to hop the bus it was too cold to walk. We didn't have any money, because we would have paid that day. That's how cold it was, that day. Emus and I were just probably getting off the block. It was too cold to kick it outside.

We got scarves on our necks. My nose is running and the wind is cutting our face. This is the blowing wind like where you had to walk, backwards. The wind is blowing so hard it's pushing you the other way. You would think I was walking in that direction the wind pushed so hard.

We were shorties most of the time the bus driver didn't care. We're in the store on 179^Th we had already walked from Rhodes to King Drive. The bus driver can't see us waiting on the bus from inside the store. We had it set up sweet. It was three people waiting to get on and nobody getting off. Sometimes though, the bus driver out of habit would open up the backdoor.

You can hear the noise it made when the bus driver, activated the door to open. You could hear it on the outside of the bus. Once the bus rides by the store up to the bus stop to pick the people up. I time it and run out the store just as it's passing.

I ran to the back of the bus to check and pulled it open. I was happy than a motherfucka. It is cold and the snow is like ice on the ground. It squeaked when you walked. My ears can't stand the squeaky snow sounds when you walked on it.

I told Emus to come on the bus driver not paying attention. I get on the bus and Emus just looks at me. I gesture waving, come on without saying anything.

I felt the heat of the bus and was home free. The only thing though is, Emus wouldn't get on the bus. We hopped the bus all the time. Now this is the coldest day of the year and he wouldn't get on the bus.

The bus rode off headed toward the crib. I look at Emus starting to walk toward the house. I knew he was about to walk home. It took everything in my body to get off at the next stop. Emus was happy than a motherfucka when I got off that bus.

He said, "Damn Colo you got off. You're my hommie for real".

I just looked at him and didn't say shit to him all the way home. We were freezing like a motherfucka. If I would've said something, he would have been all types of pussy motherfuckas. You scared ass nigga! All the bus driver could tell us was to get off the bus. Emus was my boy, I couldn't leave him. What happened to him, happens to me.

Emus and I were together cutting school on another cold ass day. We were hitting game rooms up. We didn't plan it.

Tadpole start laughing says, "when did y'all go to school?"

Cadillac was the only game room who would let us play the games after school started.

Mr. Reef's open up at 7 am he'd kick us out around eight o'clock so we could get to school. We usually we get there and play a few games then jump on the bus to school. What it was, we played the Pac Man game until the bus came.

We didn't have it planned, but when it was time to go to school.

Emmett asked, you going?

I ask him, "you going?"

He said "naw"

I said "naw".

We were walking up the 169th West toward Wentworth. Emus had on some hard bottom shoes, some penny loafers I think. I had on my boots. The day before it was warm and the snow melted.

The next day everything was freezing. Everything that was water turned to ice while we were walking. I could see the water turning to ice. I see this ice patch and tell Emus.

Dude watch out for that ice patch. I hit the street to get around it.

Emus says, "It ain't that bad Colo" and continued to walk.

He had no chance with those shoes on his feet. When he got in the middle of that ice patch he began to lose it. His hands were in his pockets. Emus next step, he began to slide, he tried to keep his balance. He took his hands out his pockets. His hands were sticking out horizontal, trying to stabilize him self.

His legs were bent at the knees and spread too far apart. He took another step and he was off his feet, bam and hit the ground. I begin to crack up laughing, but this ain't it.

He tries to gets up and he slips again. This time his feet were in the air, bam hits the ground. Now I am falling out on the ground laughing, but not on the ground.

He gets up trying to make it so he starts taking big steps quickly. He loses bad and slips again. This time he went higher in the air off his feet. Each time he fell it got worse and worse.

All I could get out was, "I I ah ha told you Emus. I I I to haa haa hai I I told you". This was funnier than any cartoon I've seen. The three stooges didn't have anything on it. You know when someone slipping and falling on ice or a banana peel? This was real life!

Do you know Emus fell three more times? The people in the cars and on the buses were looking at him fall on his ass. They were pointing at him laughing on the way by, because I was in the street laughing.

The bus past me while I was cracking up so it made them look and laugh. You had to see it Tadpole. He's glasses had fogged up and he face showed, desperateness. This made me laugh more.

He finally made it out the ice patch and said, "fuck you Colo".

My head was hurting bad from laughing.

"I told you, Emus not to walk in the ice patch". I know he had to be sore cause he was hitting the ground hard. I tell my kids about that day. Anytime I wanted to laugh! I just think back to that day. Instantly, I could change my mood. I'd laugh like it just happened.

Great America

We always were doing something, to keep us busy. We went to great lengths to have fun. We had a block trip to Great America. Once they shut down Fun Town on 95th and Chicago and Old Chicago amusement park. We had to go to Great America to ride the rollercoaster's. I even went on this trip. My mother trusted me to behave myself. Before the date of the trip arrived, I had to walk a tight rope for two weeks.

Everything had to be in order or I was not going. I saved my paper route money and was riding out. I never rode out with the hood on hood events. Any events I went on were church oriented.

I'm going this time by myself with the hood. I did it I made sure I stayed in line and got to go with Emus. The bus got there late. The people who were going, were on the corner of 169th & Calumet, waiting.

Everybody was restless at first talking about, "where's the bus?"

We started playing baseball on the lines, then the gambling broke out.

A lot of people jumped on the lines, pitching hard. Six people were pitching on both sides of the lines. Everybody had their money for the trip.

I didn't pitch, because I didn't want to lose any money. I had to use my smarts. I can win and have some extras or I could lose and fuck the whole trip up. It was too risky pitching thorough breds on the lines.

I had about thirty dollars to spend. I worked two weeks for those chips. Lace, Todd, Coole, Big, Big Darrin and a few others were thick on the lines. The more people the bigger the pot. You can win some chips quickly on those lines. It was three pitching on each side of the lines. Emus and I didn't play we just watched.

It was so thick two games were going on at the same time. It was big money dropping on the lines. It was also a game for people with a little scratch.

Big Darrin lost all his money on the lines. After losing his money he started walking back to the crib.

While walking off he said, "I'll be back before the bus come. I got to get some more money".

When the bus came Big D wasn't on it. It was a couple other guys who didn't make the trip, because of the lines.

Lace and Todd was out cold on those lines. These boys would bust sister all the time. Sister is when both of your pennies landed in the line. It seemed like, anytime they needed it, bam then yell, "liner nigga".

Sister paid double so, if its four guys pitching. When the other guys pitched before you and already landed in the line. Now, if you pitched a liner; you can win a nice pot.

It was fifty cents to start the game and liner double. The 1st guy pitch lands in the line that's a dollar to everybody. When he gets busted that two dollars, somebody bust him that's four dollars.

The last man who pitches bust him and that's eight dollars. You get two pitches, so on and so on. You always wanted to pitch last. That means you got the best chance to win. If not last, you got to call, on the man. This means you pitch next to last.

It really didn't matter anything after that. It went like this I'm the man, I'm on the man, I am on him and so on. You got to be fast.

My strategy was, if I wasn't the man. I had to get as close to the line as possible, without going in the line. When you're the closest to the line after the first pitch, you pitch last. You're the man.

That day the pot was too rich for my blood. They were playing fifty cent, liner double. Someone could hit you for two three dollars a pitch depending on how many of us were pitching.

It depended on how many jumped in the line. Jumping in the line could bust you quick. It wasn't good to jump in the line with guys who were for certain was going to bust you 75% of the time.

That's how Big D fell off. Big D could pitch, but his strategy was off. He kept jumping in the line and getting busted. He could pop the line, but it's when you popped the line. Why jump in the line if you're the first one to pitch? Oh yeah! We used to gamble our ass off, on those lines. Andrea. Anyway to get a couple of bucks, out of your pocket. We did it.

You can hit for two, three hundred out there, on a given night while drinking beers. You always want the best lines to pitch. The lines by the 169th St. bus stop were good. We also used the lines in front of my sister's house.

The most I ever won on the Met was about eighty dollars. That was good to be a teenager. While gambling we still had respect for grownups walking by.

We would stop pitching until they walked by while speaking politely. "Hi you're doing mame or sir. This was to let them know they didn't have to worry. We had people watching to see, if the police came or if our parents were in the vicinity.

The bus finally came. We load up and are on the way to the amusement park. We get on the back of the bus and start getting in our bubbled. We were cracking jokes on each other tripping out and having fun. We finally get to Great America and pulled into the parking lot.

No soon as we get in the park. I see Lil rich running the other way. They were laughing and saying we just tore them off. Everybody we came with was stealing their ass off.

They'd lose their money playing the game for a stuffed animal. They waited until the attendant turned his back. They'd grab the biggest prize and run through the park with it.

I was with Emus and wasn't doing anything big. I had a few dollars so I didn't have to steal. I didn't play those rip off games. I didn't want a big ass stuff animal anyway.

All you saw was niggas flying through Great America on something scandalous. Security would be chasing them. Boya, Lil Rich and a few others were wide open at the park.

The most the park would do, if they caught you stealing, was throw you out park. I was laughing my ass off. I didn't want to get caught stealing out there, because they did call your mother.

I would never be able to go nowhere else in my life. If I got caught stealing at the amusement park, I was done. You know we hit the game room, but the trick was to make the money last. Emus and I kicked it the whole day. You want to eat, you want to drink and you want to ride the rides. You want to play the games to have a full day of fun.

When you spend your money up in the first few hour you're in the park. The rest of your stay is bold. I did that before and that's when you start looking to steal. When you run out of money you run out of fun.

I had to pace myself with the little scratch I had. I couldn't come back home broke either.

My mother always told me, "never spend all your money. Put at least a quarter of your money away for an emergency. No man or women should be out, without any money in their pocket".

It was time to go and we were exhausted from the day. I was ready to go I went back to the bus. Todd and I still had some drank left. We get back to the bus and a few of the guys were waiting to go.

Some of them were kicked out for stealing and just waiting to sneak back in the park. They wanted to hit them one more time before they left. They started going over the layout of the park.

People were coming back to the bus with their stories on what they stole. It was a ring of niggas in that bitch, tearing Great America up. I don't remember any more trips to Great America after that! Nobody wanted to be responsible for thieving ass niggas at Great America. Block trips to Great America got shelved.

Concentration Games

Tadpole, even the concentrations games were physical too? Emus explain.
"When you heard somebody curse. They had to say the magic word". When they didn't say the word you got to hit them in the chest or arms. You could fire on them hard as and as many times as you could, before they said, the word 'strawberry', Andrea".

Sometimes you could unleash because when you come at em just blazing away. The person that's getting blazed first, got to comprehend what's going on! Why is this stud or these studs laying into me?

You're saying this while you're trying to cover up. The blows being delivered are shocking you. I know, because that's how I felt when I first was attacked.

Don't get me wrong it was a game, but the game was physical! We were inflicting damage on a motherfuckas ass.

We weren't bullshitting when we got physical. We were trying to toughed up everybody around us. We weren't playing, but we were playing, the blows felt like it was real. As a matter of fact it wasn't no different.

When you swinging as hard as you can there's no difference in the pain you feel. A couple guys could get off about ten or twelve blows. Before the person squeezes out or remembers the magic word, 'strawberry'.

The only thing different is everybody is laughing at you. That's the fun part, because of the look on your face. You got to suck it up and absorb the blows. Whoever the victim has got bruises all over him. The main rule is you can't swing back. That was the only rule. The only thing you could do was say, strawberry.

Believe it or not you could get a real smashing. We were coming hard before the onslaught prevailed.

You could move and get out the way and say, "oh yeah, strawberry". I would cuss and play like I was sleep. I'd see them coming and before they get at me I'd say it fast, strawberry.

We made that game up because one of the kids was cussing out of control. He said it when a lady of respect was walking by. We were taught to respected older men and women.

Cussing was a no no in our circle in front of adults. One of us could be cussing. Whoever see a grownup warns the other, "Mrs. woo woo is coming, cool out cussing". When you on the porch with six guys and one of them cussing. We all are cussing.

When there's a grown up around and you're still cussing. That is no respect and I wasn't brought up that way. They knew we cursed but cussing in front of a grownup. This made us all look bad. It's funny how we made up games that built character, unknowingly.

Emus and I was playing the phone game at my house. We get on the phone and call a number in the phone book.

Emus starts laughing huh aha has. Emus gets him a vic. He say's hello I was wondering if your frigerator was running. They would say yes it running. Emus then would say go out and catch that motherfucka. We'd both start laughing and hang up.

Emus was snapping on the phone you stupid motherfucka go out catch the motherfucka and my mother, picked up the phone and heard everything.

She came down the steps and asked. "Who is the little boy with the dirty mouth?" Emus starts to sweat and I say it wasn't me mother. She says I know it not you, Emus your mother knows you got a dirty mouth. Don't you ever use my phone, if you got to say those cussing words Emus.

Emus said, "Okay Mrs. George".

Then she said, "have a nice day", meaning get up and out of here.

Yeah your mother caught me bold Colo. Emus says and continue to laugh.

Time for Bending

The mental and physical game we played had two positive effects. One is to toughen you up. The other was character building. Time for Bending is a game you couldn't bend over without saying, "time for bending". You could get kicked in the ass for doing it.

Andrea asked, "You get kicked in the butt for not say time for bending".

John assures Andrea, "the kick didn't hurt baby!

Now think how many times you bend over in a day? Everybody who was playing the game would be on alert. When caught bending over! You had a chance to with the instep of your foot, kick the vic's butt. I used to love, "Time for Bending," because I was on my toes".

"I got Colo ooh I got Colo so good though". Emus say while trying to hold back a laugh then starts telling the story. "Aaahhh haa some chicks ahaa rolled up and were hollering at Colo. We were all chilling it was about six of us, on John's porch.

Colo jumps up and runs over to car, real smooth. He bends over on the driver's window and started hollering at the girls. First, I waited so I could line it up. You had to line up the kick.

I didn't want him to peep me out. I tiptoed like a cat with my big ass. Hee Haaa Emus laughs, while doing the reenactment. I was just hoping he didn't say, "time for bending", before I could get to him.

I already had pictured in my head the wind up of my leg and the follow through. I had to keep from laughing. He starts to laughing again and then continues".

"Just as I thought the girls had his total, attention. You were bent over with your elbow on the car propped up, looking cool. I got a running start. I had to get in an angle so the girls wouldn't see me and alert him.

I grabbed my pockets so you wouldn't hear the change in my pockets. I ran tiptoeing all the way from John's porch to the street, wound up and "BAM". I kicked Colo dead in the ass.

Everybody in the room starts laughing while watching the reenactment.

"Hold on, hold on Hee hee I kicked him so hard. He hit his head on the rain guard of the car. That was a haa haa haa, a double wammy, bam bam, I got him good". Everybody laughs.

I looked at Colo face and his face was fucked up. Raymond and Smiley were sitting on the porch laughing their ass off. I was running around laughing with my big ass. I'm looking at the girls, look at Colo and then me. The girls started giggling too which made me laugh more.

After everybody calmed down, from the laughing I had to agree with Emus. "Dude I was so embarrassed, because the girls in the car was giggling too. I bent over again and I lost concentration. That's why I say it's mental. I was trying to save face.

I was about to explain the game we were playing to the girls. I bent over again trying to escape the situation and talk to the girls. Now Smiley, Fat Cat and Emus lines me up.

All three of these motherfuckas came and kick me in the ass. They got me all at the same time, bamm, bamm bamm. I felt like a goofymark this time. Everybody on the porch was falling out laughing at me. My face told the story. I got played like a goofy mark.

I didn't even feel like talking to the girls after that.

They asked, "Why they keep doing that to you? They're kicking you all in the ass and shit".

The girls probably were saying, he must be a real mark. You know you don't get any play, if you're a mark. You can't protect the girl. Now my own guys are kicking me in the ass. I must be a mark. First here's this big motherfucka with bifocals coming, kicking me in the ass. Now everybody on the porch is kicking him in the ass.

They kept looking at him then looked at me. What was going through their mind is you must really be a mark. That's exactly how they were looking at me at me like, nigga please.

I'm downplaying it by saying, "Aw it's a game we play, you know what? Then I said, "I'll get with y'all later". I couldn't pull it off! I had to escape the situation. All you heard was continuous laughter while I'm trying to talk to the girls. The laughter behind me was too much. Now I didn't have girls riding up on me and when they did, I get kicked in the ass. Ain't that a bitch!

Everybody on the whole porch was laughing. The girls, even the people driving by looking were laughing. You got to suck it up and you can't get mad. I look at Emus like you kicked this shit off. I looked closely at him and saw he had tears coming down from up under his bifocals. He was laughing so hard. You do go through some emotions.

"Yeah I got you that day Colo," Emus says while laughing.

I agree, "yeah frustration, embarrassment, goofy like and markishness set into your emotions. You didn't want to look like a mark in front of people at all. That's the last thing you want on earth. Markishness will cause repercussions from the goons.

Yep Andrea, just cause you didn't say time for bending. You get kicked in the ass?

Andrea asks, "everybody was mean seems like in y'all neighborhood. I thought it was just you".

Emus let's her know, "Andrea you slipping you slipping. It was no room for a person falling off".

I goes to the side and tells Tadpole, "how I fell off on the second kick". The first kick fucks you up, mentally. You start addressing emotions immediately that's when you bend over again and you still, forget to say it. That's how they got me the second time.

Your discombobulated and stunned it's almost an out of body experience. You ask yourself, "did this motherfucka just kick me in the ass?"

You laugh it off, but it's a phony laugh, you got me. Next thing you know, you bend over again without saying time for bending. I was trying to play it off the first assault. Here they come again, bang boom boom.

I'm not the first person that happened too so I know. They get you the second time and now you say, "time for bending, damn". Now you are getting mad, Tadpole. When you say it, your say it pissed off, "time for bending motherfucker, damn".

Everybody else is just laughing his or her ass off. Right now, right now, you are, looking like a goofy mark. A mark is a target or a description of someone soft. A goofy mark is someone who's a target all the time. He keeps falling into the same trap. I was a goofy mark that day in front of the girls. She didn't give me any play after that either.

One time an older person was walking by watching us. He sees somebody get kicked in the ass.

The older gentleman stopped, looked and said, "damn did he just kicked that boy in the ass?" Why are y'all kicking that boy in the ass?"

Now you know this is funny to us. Someone you don't know stops and ask you that shit.

The kickee got to say, "it's just a game we play".

Dude looked crazy while going through his thoughts for a couple of moments. The older gentleman started walking again. He was walking while looking back watching us laughing and said.

"Y'all shouldn't be playing any games like that! You all kicking each other in the ass and shit".

Everybody starts laughing at what the old man said.

He gets a quarter of a block away and say, "what type of game is that, that you kick each other in the ass?"

The gentleman then slowly walks away, shaking his head. I know he was probably saying to himself. You young motherfuckas are out of y'all mind.

It's the getting laughed at, that gets you, not the kick in the ass. The kick in the ass with the side of the foot doesn't hurt. It's the laughing that throws you all off balance mentally.

The laughing draws the embarrassment. Playing Time for Bending you always wanted to wait until it was a crowd around. You needed other people to see you get kicked. That's when you catch somebody slipping. You get a lot of points for the level of embarrassment. I think Emus kick was the best on the block that year. He get's the "Time for Bending" award.

When you were slipping badly, you get got, like they got me. Before he kicked me the 2nd time. Emus wired everybody else up before he kicked you. Tell them to join in on it. Now you got three people kicking you in the ass.

The only people who could kick you are the ones playing the game. From a distant what does that look like? It looks like you are a goofy mark. If you got, got, you had to play it off by saying, "it ain't shit, it ain't shit, I'll get you back". This is while not showing any emotion and hiding your true feelings of being humiliated.

Y'all remember Pepee? Pepee was playing time for bending from off Prairie. Guess what he did? He was playing time for bending just like Emus did me. Dude kicked him in front of some girls.

He got so embarrassed he went in the house got the missile. Came back and blew dude and his boy away. The one who was laughing and the one who kicked him, was killed. He came back out and said, "time for dying motherfuckers".

"He's got premeditated murder and doing 25 to life for playing that game. Dude was young and couldn't handle being humiliated. It was humiliating, to get kicked in the ass and you can't do anything, but you developed focus. You have to say time for bending.

The people that watched you getting kicked in the ass think it's real. They don't know were playing a game. They're wondering why are they playing you like a pussy? After that happened with Pepee I think that game got shelved. I don't remember anybody playing after that!"

Coming Up Athletes on the Block

Yeah from about twelve to fifteen we were goons in training in the hood. What held our attention the most was playing sports. We had to start making our mark. Back in the hood though! We still had to get out there earlier to play on the basketball rim. We were getting better and getting close to not getting eliminated.

It was a strike out box on the Henderson's garage. We played strikeout on his garage too. Sometimes he couldn't stand the noise of the ball constantly getting threw against his garage

He used to come out and say, "not today boys". Then we would go down to the skyway. I think that's why we able to be so versatile. When the bigger kids came they would gradually kick us off the court.

We started staying on the court back then, not getting eliminated. You played elimination, if it was too many people were playing 21. Elimination was at seven and thirteen. You needed at least two points to stay in when somebody scored seven points.

You needed seven to stay in at thirteen. When you didn't score the minimum you had to sit on the sidelines. This means this game is competitive, until someone won, from start to finish. When you get close to eliminating the pack you got to play.

It was no way you wasn't going to get, tripled teamed. Everybody playing was blocking you off the boards. Nobody wanted to watch you play. The game was so competitive you could be watching for an hour after being eliminated. You get to twenty and miss your free throw you went back down to thirteen.

We would play 21 with Jason, Macado, Bird, Lagon, Rock and even Bruce the storyteller. We weren't ready yet for their game. These were alley ball legends. These guys took it personal back in the alley. The games were physical and intense and borderline dirty when you played against certain people. They weren't letting any shorties get down.

The older guys wanted us out the way. They would play hard as they could, until they eliminated you. You come to play with the big boys. They didn't give you mercy. You can't dribble they'll take the ball. You trying to shoot they will blast your shit down the alley and say.

"Little fella get off the court, if you can't play". They were another level, but that would soon change

The Game 21 was another way of getting the shorties off the court. This was a better way than them just telling us to move. You made your bones back there on the court.

This is how the hood all knew you, if you were cold in sports. Now, we shorties, were around all the time. We started to play the older teenagers in basketball tough.

We started being competitive with Big D, Todd, Big, Freddie, Lando, Darkness, Lace and your brother Coole, Emus.

To me all these guys were my big brothers. They got the game from their older brothers. I am getting the game straight from them. I kicked it with everybody family for a while I'll get to that later.

I stole a little bit of everybody basketball moves and incorporated them in my game. I would get out there and practice soon as I woke up. After Jeffrey Hudson beat me at basketball and baseball I was sick.

I go back there in the alley and practiced all my moves. Shoot all my shots over and over so I was getting sweet. I worked on that left-handed lay-up from all different angles and release points. I practice the English that Big used to put on the ball. I practice my outside J from 25 feet like Lace used to shoot. I also stole his left-hand hook shot from eight to ten feet.

When I missed I had to chase the ball down fast. I never let the ball stop I'd catch up to ball while it's still rolling. I'd shoot it from where ever I picked the ball up. I'd turn and shoot while I was tired and exhausted, building stamina. I learned to shoot from all over the court. It wasn't a shot I didn't like to take. I knew I could hit it. I shoot the fade from the corner like Lando shoots.

I practice the fade away I stole from Todd. I'd practice my handles spinning, back dribble, cross dribble through the legs, wrap around dribble with both hands. The only person who handles were better than mines was Big. Big and Pookie from the park had the sweetest handles on the South side.

I stole a lot of shit from him on how he could control that ball. I sped up my release for my shot cause big fellas were blocking my shot. After I practice their shots I practice my new shots.

Shots that fucked them up Tadpole, John and Emus know.

"Yeah, Colo came up ugly in the dungeon," they both shake their head in agreement.

Well the mid group thought they could come to court. They'd come bubbled & high and still try to put us off the court. That was over I'd practice long and hard and I was whipping Arron and Emus into shape.

I would come get them after I had practice a couple hours early that morning. Kenny who stayed up under Emus met me out there early a lot of days. He was high energy so that helped my stamina. He would never quit. I hated to lose to those guys. They talked so much shit especially, Todd, Lace and Big.

I never wanted to stop playing and I hated losing. Emus and I would go head up for hours. Emus had that jumper. He used to try and use his size to back me down. I would try to go around him quick and get the ball.

I beat Emus so much, because he would get tired. Emus had a jumper and a slow spin move to the hole. He would've beat me a few of those games. He had to play me when he was mad all the way through. He couldn't get me playing one on one, but he did win a few 21's.

Emus cuts in, "If it wasn't for Colo I wouldn't have been as cold as I was. He used to coax me into playing when I didn't want to play or when I was tired. The person who used to be my nemesis was Todd and Big Darrin".

I hated to lose to those two guys. I hated losing to Todd the most, because he was antagonizing. He brought out the best in me, because I didn't want him to beat me. I had to win and have bragging rights. He was short, but he knew how to win. I remember losing a lot of close ones to Todd. Todd would get in your head with the bullshit.

I agree by shaking my head and say, "one time Emus and I had a block party on Todd shit. We blocked his shit about 11 or 12 times in a row. It didn't matter what Todd did. He drove and it got block. He tried his fade away; it got blocked. He tried to back us down; it got drove to the earth. Emus and I had so much fun that game of 21.

You got to realize these guys had us for a minute. These guys were good they all played for their school team. Big and Lace played for CVS. Lace played all three, baseball, football and basketball. Slick Freddie and Big D played football for the Robe. It was nothing, but athletes on the court in the alley. They were doing something at the time. Todd played football for Communication Metro his first year.

That game right there, was the beginning of the end of Todd. Killed him in that 21. That was one game we had Todd frustrated he couldn't get shit off. What it was with Todd.

He had a drive game, because he was quick so he could get past you. His jumper was suspect though! He would hit it when he needed it, so that was good enough. That's another thing I stole from him, his strategy.

Todd would not shoot his jumper until the end of the game. He'd shoot it, but that wasn't his game. The last couple of points after he did all that driving he'd shoot.

That's how he beat me a couple of times. He'd have me on my heals waiting for the blow by. He'd hit the last two shots from deep. I would give him the jumper from 20 feet and out and just guard against his drive game. His little fade game I added to my arsenal. Back then there was no three point shot.

Yeah Todd was tough, but he cheated. He'd just call travel on you and walk back to the out line.

I would plead my case, "Todd I didn't travel" then I would reenact the move.

His response, "you traveled nigga, ball out. Oh oh if he shot and missed, after he missed, he would call a foul. The ball would hit the ground and then he called foul.

I'd yell, "hell naw Todd that's some bullshit".

He yelled back, "you fouled me nigga, you hacking ass nigga".

I'd say, "that's okay, you still ain't going to win. I don't care how much you cheat".

He'd then say, "ball out and stop crying, you a hack".

He wouldn't' wear it out, but he had at least two of those calls a game when he needed it. The person I loved to play against was Lacey. He had a jumper and could shoot with his left. He had a sweet left-hand hook shot from eight to ten feet out. That's was something I added to my game too. In order to beat Lacey you had to guard him tight or he would get his jumper off and it was deadly.

I had to force Lace to go to the hole. Which he could do also, but his game was his jump shot. In order to beat him I had to take it away. Lace and I used to go, I started to get him as I got older.

We had legendary one on ones, back there in the dungeon. Sometimes it would be just two people in the back shooting.

Mike Stables Todd's little nephew used to come back there and watch, laugh and say, "ooohh! He fucked you up!" He used to be the ooh he fuck you up guy on the sidelines.

The Physical and Mental Games Smash em'

Emus changed the subject and said. "Tadpole, as we got older the games we played got physical. We played catch and smash with the older guys in the hood. They'd chase us or we'd chase them. Who ever had the ups would get chased.

This game would aid us, if we were being attacked. It could be four or five guys trying to catch you. Later on when we started the banging and strong-arming, it was good training". Before you can strong-arm you have to practice hood maneuvers.

The fun came when they chased you. As long as you didn't get caught and smashed, it was fun. It was two groups back when you used to play.

The mid groups like my brother Coole, Lace & Todd. We teamed together against the older teenagers in the hood such as Steve, Dave, Lando and Darkness.

We'd chase each other and giving the business when we caught you alone. Can't get caught slipping. You got to be on your toes at all times. Someone could pop up from anywhere: a gangway, jump off the roof, in the alley or out from behind a bush.

Anywhere we could lay a trap for your ass. This was low-key training on hunting a motherfucka down. We'd figure out his movements and catch him in a spot where he can't get any help.

The only place you were safe was inside the crib. When you were caught: on the sidewalk, in front of your house, at the store, on the porch or one foot in the crib. It was all-good to smash, if caught in the streets. As long as you could be snatched, before you got that other foot in the house. You could get banged.

When you got caught you got the business, bango bango. You'd have to take a couple or a few. Gives some back then find an opening and break out again and start running.

This did develop some survival skill just in case you were about to get moved out on for real. It was getting smashed training or smashing someone training. This was the prerequisite for when the real thing goes down. Everybody has and knows their expertise.

Colo jumps in and say, "Yeah, I used to do John and Teddy bad. Even though John is only one year younger, he was very small. He couldn't even play with us. They wanted to play so Emus, Lamont and I chased them.

I did it for a reason though! Y'all were coming up under our wing. I wanted y'all to be able to handle the block. A couple of times I caught John and did him bad. I was hitting him with my knuckles on his bone. I was really targeting the bone area. I was training them like I was getting trained, no mercy.

You know John is light skin than a motherfucka. Those bruises would turn, yellow, green and black. I stopped because John was looking and yelling at me like he wanted to kill me. You supposed to punch back get up and keep moving.

John interrupts. "Colo you caught me and did me bad".

I laugh and say, "everybody, John just laid on the ground. He was like a wounded rabbit and I was the lurking wolf. I did what you would do, if somebody were laying on the ground. Whale on his ass, but it was just on his legs.

John frowned and yelled at me, "pick on someone your own size," he kept yelling, "pick on someone your own size".

Andrea begins to laugh and ask John. "He was picking on you baby?"

John answers, "I was much smaller at the time baby he can't do that now.

Colo just looks at John and continues, "Now were playing the smash em game, but for anybody walking by. I am straight beasting him and he looked white.

I just walked away and said, "get tough little nigga. You playing the game and got caught you get smashed".

John replied, "fuck you, go get somebody your own size". Those words kind of hurt too, when he kept saying those words. I had to think though! Everybody is way bigger than me and I'm handling it.

I stop gangstering him and said, "just get tough little nigga. You got to hold down the block".

I said to myself, "I am only a year older than John anyway".

It wasn't that many people to chase up under us. Who was going to run from John and Teddy? They were too little to run from and too small to beat down. We had to join in with the mid team and chase the older teenagers. How would that look looking from the outside? I am running from these guys.

This one particular night everybody was just chilling and hanging out. You knew the time when you were playing 'Smash em'. You also knew the time when you weren't. You couldn't play all day. When everybody was mingling on the Met, then it's peacetime. It's a truce.

How you got caught was in the morning going to the store for Moms by yourself. You got chased at night when you coming home from school functions. You'll see the double team coming. You heard the words smash em when we were coming at you.

This day all three groups are just standing on the Met just chilling. We may have just got through playing some basketball. Darkness opened his door to his house and sees my back turn. Runs up behind me and swung with all his might and hits me dead in the back. Boommm, is how the blow sounded off!

Everybody out there was like, "aaghh oooh Darkness why you do that?"

This nigga knocked fire from my ass. I grimace in pain as I tried to recover. My back had a concave bow in it, until the pain went away. All three different levels of niggas were pissed at him.

Everybody spoke up for me and asked him. "Why you do that Darkness even his guys?

Darkness said, "he's playing and I got him. Keep your head up".

Todd said, "everybody is chilling and then you bang him in the back. That's some hoe shit, Darkness. Bust his ass back Colo. Todd told me to go straight at him.

"I bet you can't get him head up Darkness, with your weak ass".

Todd and Dave kept shouting, "go at him head up. He don't want to do that!"

I was John and Darkness was I, in reverse situations.

I thought about that and agreed and said, "I bet you can't get me head up". I said to myself, "you can't be a dog, if you only fuck with people you know you can smash. You can't be a dog, if you stay on the porch. Time to jump off the porch, if you are a big dog".

You still got puppy nuts, if you stay on the porch. You want to be challenged and meet the challenge. Especially, when the outcome is unknown. You have to test yourself to see where you at, anyway. I wiped the little tear that trickled out of my eye away. Squared up toe-to-toe and we started to bang. His front toe was touching mines and mines touching his. Let's go! I give him some and he gives me some.

Everybody was rooting me on, "whoop his ass Colo". The energy does help when people are rooting you on! I got him, my shit was more combination and his was more power. I wouldn't let him get those big shots off though.

The last time we played I was about fourteen and he was about nineteen. The guys on the block saw me rise to the occasion and didn't back down.

I was used to getting hit by big niggas anyway. Darkness shit didn't phase me. My nephew in law Derek was about six years older than I. He was cocky than a motherfucka, you remember Derek, Emus.

I used to body punch him coming up. He prepared me for this moment. Derek wasn't giving me no room. He let them go, boom boom boom.

I stood toe to toe with Darkness and threw back, bing bam boom boom. My combinations were tighter and I was thudding his ass. The hood gave me P's for having heart. I had enough heart to stand in front of this big motherfucka and throw back.

That day I said to myself, "it doesn't matter how big or how old. You got to have heart and know how to throw. You will fuck a motherfucka up with your skills.

My nephew showed me what I could take, without breaking down. It felt good for the whole hood to feel me. I had to get up and handle him.

I didn't lose because I was crisp. He was trying to load up, but I am too fast for that! Darkness moved out the hood shortly after we boxed. This was the first sign of me being a beast on the block. After that day, that game got shelved.

Chapter VI

Bootie

"**H**ow about Colo when we used to play bootie in the dungeon?" John asked.

Andrea interrupts, what, what back up, you played what John?

Tadpole starts laughing and says, "sound like some kinky shit to me, Andrea".

It was a game we played y'all check it out.

They want let him talk because of the laughter.

I answers John, "hell yeah! I think that game took me to the next level of handling pressure.

Playing booty helped your game? Emus asked.

I answered, "Let me explain. It's the pressure of not only losing the game. It's standing on that gate bent over at the waist. While everybody who was played gets three throws as hard as they could throw at your butt.

Bootie was a game that the big fella's used to play. It's something just to past the time when they weren't playing real games. It was that or horse, but horse, was no pressure. Booty depending on the people you were playing, added tremendous pressure.

The way the game went is there were valued locations, all over the dungeon. They had about eight different spots on the court with different values.

You had to hit from each one of those spots in any order to get to 100. Now the shots were 10' to 35' out. The last one left to booty out, had three shots to get to 100.

When you didn't get to 100, the booty is out. Now you could run and try to get away from getting bootied. What detour you from doing that move?

Everybody picked up sticks, bricks and rocks for ammunition. You could run but we could stone you for doing it. We'd be locked and loaded with ammunition ready to throw them, if you try to run.

When you lost you had to turn around on the gate bend over and you can't flinch. You flinch they get another throw. Some people would just toss it at you soft. Most people were trying to kill you back in the dungeon. We'd rare back and sling it like a baseball at your butt. If they hit you in the back then their turn was over.

That's why you got to bend all the way over looking like you ready to get banged in the butt. Believe it or not getting hit with that basketball and just standing there bent over feels like hoe shit.

It just doesn't feel right bending over on the pole waiting on the throw to the butt. I felt though I would never get bootied, because my shot is accurate. It was only a couple of times I could ever remember being, bootied. Everybody I played booty with at the time. I shot better than them anyway and rarely lost.

Well, this one day everybody was out playing bootie with the big fellas. Jason, Bird, Mackado, Rock all the way down to us. It was about eleven of us. I figured I would play since it was so many playing. I wouldn't be the last one out.

All the big fella's asked, "you sure you want to play? You know if you try to run we can pick up anything and throw it at you Colo?"

I looked unconcerned and answered. "Dude I'm not going to be the last one so bootie ain't out".

I said to myself, "I can shoot better than half of them anyway," even though younger.

I'm in the game I am a big fella. The game was going and I couldn't get on for some reason. My shot wasn't falling it was either long or short. The thing about bootie is that while everyone else's taking their shot.

You're still pondering about your next and last shot. Over compensating or under compensating for the shot you missed. It's going through your head I got to hit this next shot for sure. If you hit your shot you keep going until you miss.

When you miss your first shot, that's just one shot. Only thing is you have to wait till everybody else finished a round of shooting. When it's eleven people playing you could be on ice a while.

Some of the guys were hitting shots going out in the first round. You keep shooting until you miss or go out. Four of the eleven went out in the first round. While their going out, you're still waiting and you don't have a rhythm. This is when anxiety creeps in and now your next shot is clango, you shoot it's short.

That ain't shit, that was just my second shot. While I'm waiting, I see more people gradually making their way out the game. You start to hope they miss, but they are hitting.

Now the big fellas start looking at me like, "oooh Colo your ass is out". Everybody smiling and grinning and looking at me like I'm the vic. Now this is when you start to get desperate. My next shot I shoot and missed again. Now I'm cursing. Fuck, shit, damn motherfucka.

This is who was out there. Big, Todd, Lace, Pauly, Pauly, Big D, Lando, Freddie and then it was Bird, Jason and a few others… My thinking was I got to cross over and get my respect on the court. I can't stay little all my life.

Emus didn't play, he was sitting on Mr. Henderson car. They asked Emus before we started was he playing?

He answered, "Nope" very quickly.

Emus wasn't ready to play with the big guys. I on the other hand had something to prove. I wanted to be a big fella on the court. Everybody has gone out and it was down to Pauly and I.

I had a shot from that line crossing the Stables gate, connecting to Miss Lane's gate. It was probably equivalent to the first NBA 3 point line. I had a shot from the corner right next to Santos garage. Pauly had about four shot, but went out on his next turn.

That's one thing Pauly could do, was shoot that ball. He could dribble, but he couldn't dribble sweet. You just couldn't steal the ball from him though! I was the king of the rip.

When it's down to about two of you, the pressure mounts. People start to harass you adding pressure.

"Don't run, don't run, I'll hate to brick you".

That's some of the shit they'll say, when it's time for you to shoot. They were trying to shake your nerves.

People who lost sometimes might try to run so we implemented, "the if you run rule". You can be stoned, sticked or bottled if you ran More pressure to help mess up your shot.

When Pauly went out everybody started picking up rocks, sticks and everything else. The fear of missing the shot was excruciating. Even more was the consequences afterward.

I said to myself, "it is eleven people with three throws apiece. That's 33 throws in all getting thrown at my ass".

These niggas I am playing with now. They won't have nooooo mercy on you. They'll throw the basketball as hard as they can. I had three shots to go out. I chose the shot at the top first. I missed the first one. Two shots left so if I miss the next one. I was getting bootied anyway. It's a hundred shot, but it's way down the alley.

Everyone who was playing and went out already was around me hooping and hollering.

They were hollering, "yeah! yeah! yeah, your ass today Colo".

I composed myself. I needed a fifty so that was back by Lando's backyard approximately 40'. I blocked out everyone else and shot. If I missed that shot I was going to make a break for it.

I wasn't about to stand up there like a slave, while getting beamed that many times. I took my time and shot and it went swish, all net. I knew I could hit that shot I just dribbled three or four times and got in rhythm. Instead of just aiming and shooting.

I shot it like someone was sticking me. All I needed was a 25. I walked over to Santos house. Which is about a 22 footer from the side. This is Lando's shot I'd been practicing it.

Everybody got kill objects in their hand just in case I ran. Encircling me like vultures. Their swinging the sticks and throwing the brick against the ground so it breaks in half. Now he's got two throws, if I run. I am watching all this while I get ready to shoot. I looked at Emus sitting on Mr. Henderson car. He barely could look at me.

He shakes his head like, "I told you to chill over here with me".

Emus starts to laugh and says, "hell yeah".

I got one foot in the wind and one foot in my shot. I poised myself, got my mechanics together, as if I was just practicing back their by myself. I blocked those niggas out who were hollering, waving the sticks and shot it high.

Shooting it high increased your odds for it to go in the basket. I let it go with the perfect rotation.

While the ball is in the air they're making noise and shouting, "he missed, he missed".

I felt it was money when it was leaving my hand. I watched while the ball was in the air high then swish, I sanked that shot all net.

I immediately started talking shit. "Fuck all you'll niggas. I don't miss shit like that; my ass was on the line. I had it all planned just to see y'all face. I was just fucking with y'all.

I could've been went out. It wouldn't have been no fun, seeing how stupid y'all look right now. Even if I would've missed, y'all wouldn't have caught me".

That pissed them off even more. That was extreme pressure on me. Right then I knew I could play with the big boys.

That shot wasn't even in a game, but it made my game better. I knew I could hit the pressure shot. This increased my confidence two fold. Not only did I hit that one shot. I had to hit two shots, to save my ass. After I missed all those other shot before and that took focus.

I shouted out big shit, but I didn't play after that. I looked back and saw they were pissed off that I hit that shot. They were going to try and kill my ass, literally. They really hate when a little nigga is talking shit, but when you back it up. You have to respect it. All I heard was, "that nigga hit that motherfucka".

The game against Big D and Todd was when everything changed. Todd grabbed Big D. He won the 21. It was Arron and I against them. Now you know Big D is the beast. He plays basketball pretty good.

Rod and 'D' jump out to a big lead. Rod was going to work on Arron. Big D was going to work too. He was hitting shots from deep calling out Larry Bird name and hitting it.

Here go 'D' after he ran to the corner to shoot, "BiiiiirrrrrDDD!"

They had gone up like 24 to12 and game was 32! The ball went out of bounds and I looked at Arron in the eyes and said pick and roll and give me the ball.

I commenced to, going to work, with every move I practiced. Cross over left hand roll. Cross over right hand roll. Hit him with the fade away. 'D' was draped over me, but I was getting my shot off.

Rod was looking and saying, "This nigga looking like an all star on your ass 'D' switch".

My handles were awesome and 'D' is trying to stay in front of me. He couldn't do it. I rocked him one-way and went the other with the Ice Man George Gervin finger roll layup.

Rod was like, "switch 'D' this nigga is eating you up".

D didn't say anything he just looked at Todd and pushed him over to Arron.

It's 24-20 I hit him with eight straight. I missed the next one and 'D' did the same thing he did at first. If 'D' would've used his strength, to back me down he would've made it easy. He still tried to shoot that same jumper from deep.

Todd was like, "no D stay in the post" 'D' wasn't listening to Todd strategy

He was on target, but it was short. I get the ball and go on a roll. Arron started picking and rolling and when the switch came I was raising. Bango we hit five straight plays in a row.

I dropped dimes to Arron and he hit a couple of buckets. The score was 30-24. Todd and 'D' were arguing at this point and Arron and I are laughing. Todd wanted to stick me and 'D' had too much pride to let him do it.

We take the ball out and I had style points on this shot. I showed him every dribble I had and dumped it to Arron for the game winner. 34-24 game over! They never scored another basket.

After that game I didn't have to talk. They started letting people know I was the new king of the alley.

Super Rat

The reason why we called the alley where we shot ball, the dungeon? All types of criminal activity went down back in the alley. Not only that, it was all the obstacles we had to play through.

Massive cracks in the ground. You'd be dribbling the ball and it hit a crack and the ball would go the other way. It seemed like it would happen during crunch time.

It was a rock patch next to Mrs. Lane house. It was two piles of wood and garbage about eight feet long and six feet high. One pile was next to House's house. The other obstacle was in the rock patch.

It seemed for a while that it was going to get took over from us. It was hectic playing back there one year. One day Lace and I had just finished a game back there and was walking back to 169th St. We we're talking shit about the moves that we just hit each other with in the game.

We bent the corner of the alley at Santo's house. Just then a super rat came scampering down the alley. No, the rat was walking in the middle of the alley along the side of my house. Lace and I look at each other.

This is while we were squinting our eyes trying to get a bead on it.

Lace taps me with his elbow pointed and said, "is that a rat walking down the alley?"

At first we were trying to shoo it away by making noise and stumping our feet. The rat kept coming walking without a care in the world. As it got closer it seemed to get bigger and bigger. Like the rat was it growing as it walked.

Now we like shouting and stomping our feet harder. The rat looked at us and kept coming. We couldn't make it to the gangway to escape. The rat got close to us thinking the rat was going to turn and run.

The rat kept coming so Lace and I hit Santos eight-foot gate where the dog were. We couldn't jump the gate, because of the dogs. We just clung to the gate and watched the rat walk by while clinging to the gate. As the rat walked by us it looked at us unafraid then scampered to a cubbyhole.

The rat took his sweet time as if to say, "it's a new day motherfucka".

It was big and around the neck, was built up, like a pit bull. While hanging from the gate we were the one's looking like we were out of place. The rat supposed to be hopping on the gate, trying to get away.

The rat had the alley that day. Once the rat walked away Lace and I hopped off the gate. We just looked at each other and laughed.

Lace said, "we are some real pussies right now!"

The only difference I saw between a pit bull and the rat. The rat had a long rope like pink tail. Y'all remember those Super Rats?

"Hell Yeah" Emus replied. "I remember that time that all that garbage was out by our yards and in the alley. Living next to them Houses you just had everything back there piled up. The King Drive block club had to come clean it up.

They had to come from King Drive to do the job. Nobody from Calumet was out there, but us cleaning up. My grandfather orchestrated that one. When we got out there we were moving shit around and picking up shit.

Rats were everywhere. People had pitchforks, shovels and boards trying to kill the rats. That's where we used to play. The block clubs used to come around with poison. They'd look over at us playing basketball and tells us not to mess with the poison.

They put up rat posters with an X overlaying the rat. It was like the pied piper story in the city. The only thing different was these rats were big as hell. It used to be the main topic in the news "Super Rats" and the growing problem.

The mayor had no solutions. It was all on the news. The news was showing these super rats getting pitch forked by groups of citizens. Dozens and dozens of rats stuck on pitchforks.

The alley cats couldn't fuck with them. Just like in the pied piper. Let a regular size cat walk up on one of those rats. That cat is coming out of there scared, like in the cartoons.

The cat had to get bandage up after the war with the super rats. For real though, when the cat got to the crib. It had to get bandage up like in the cartoons.

Whose cat used to fuck them up though? I asked.

John replied, "Lacey's cat I forget his name though I agree,

"Hell yeah, Lace's cat used to fuck those rats up. Everyday Lace had to go out and clean up rat guts. I'd see him with the shovel scooping the rat up and throwing it in the garbage can. His cat used to leave them lying in the backyard ripped up.

I guess he was letting the other rats know don't fuck with us. The rat was soufflé like Swiss cheese. We walked past Lace crib just to look and see, if his cat had torn up a rat that day. His cat used to leave them in Raymond yard. He stayed only two yards away. I guess he left them where he found them or chased it to the yard.

The rats just didn't stay outside they came in the crib too. You could here the scampering of a big rat from time to time, in the crib.

This would scare the shit out of me. You could here the rats scratching at something inside the wall. I think the girl rats just came into to lay babies. There weren't too many big rats inside my house. We had a problem with mice everywhere.

My mother would go to the store. She'd buy about 10 mice traps and grab up a couple of rattraps. My brothers and I used to have fun catching the mice. We'd just lay and wait to here that sound. Ssssnap and a low-key whimper from the mice, sss..queeek, sssqueek.

We would laugh and go around and find out what trap popped. Every morning we used to check the traps.

I would ask, "how many this morning Samson?"

After checking my brothers would reply, "three or four".

The only thing I didn't like was to dispose of the mice. I didn't like to pick them up. Blood would be spewed around the trap, with a mice laying limp. If it was still alive, the mice would be trying to wiggle his head, out of the trap.

You right though Emus. The block club helped keep it straight and safe for us. We were back there all the time. No telling what would've happened, if we fell in the garbage or stepped in a hole.

After that summer it wasn't as bad for us to play. The neighborhood came together on that issue. The super rats were literally taking over the hood. I guess the poison worked. We didn't care really where we were playing ball, at the time. It was a come up from Mom's lampshade.

Mary Jane I Love You

I had to break the weed pact. It was a saying that weed stunted your growth. Now look at Todd, Lace, Freddie and your brother Coole. All of them are two to three inches shorter than all the rest of the males in their family. Prime example Emus you are 6'5" and Coole is about 5'10" and he's your older brother.

Coole started smoking way earlier around ten or eleven years old. Emus didn't really start smoking until he was about sixteen. Emus wasn't trying to follow Coole back in the day. He didn't hang with Coole at all. It was height in Emus family.

Coole was the coolest he'd give you the shirt off his back. I was Emus hommie so Coole looked out for me too. Coole was scandalous or a slick dude from the block I should say both slick and scandalous. They came from the white building. It was a low-key project down about a mile away from the Met. Mike got a little more project life than Emus.

Didn't he have Slick Coole tatted on his arm? Emus was the exception to the rule. He started smoking late keeping to the pact we made. He drank on some occasions.

You know the little brother always wants to do what big brothers do. That means you're on your way, to being a big fella. Why?

You're doing what big brother was doing young. You're doing it too, so you're a little big fella. This makes you cool with the big guys. Other than Coole the older brothers started smoking at sixteen or seventeen.

The younger brother usually is going to do whatever the big brother do. The age difference means nothing. You have access to what you want. Your big brother would get it for you or show you how to get it.

That's how Rodell was exposed to everything earlier. His older brothers Carlos and Chris were plugging him to big brother shit. Carlos rest in peace was ten years older than Rodell. It trickled down to me what Rodell did, cause I hung with Rodell. We started everything years earlier.

You were around your brother's height. My research and evidence that I presented, shows weed stunts your growth. Your brother group, were much more advance than we were.

The older group of brothers and sisters taught Todd, Lace and Freddie at an early age. This was our link to older guys on the block. They mid group even had girlfriends in grammar school. Not just, chase a girl freak a girl. That's what, we were playing, catch a girl freak a girl. The girls they had, they used to bang and get the poonany!

I remember us three setting a pact that we would not smoke weed. We weren't going to gangbang or drink like the rest of the hood. We were ten or eleven. We also were going to graduate out of high school.

We made the pact while we were walking down the alley. We were going to the dungeon when we said it. We made those goals because of all the negative influences around. One out of four isn't bad coming from where we came from. We kept the most important goal. We all graduated.

We all tried to keep the pact, but that peer pressure was awesome. One thing we can say is we started a little later than everybody else our age. At least I waited until I got to high school to smoke on a regular basis.

I was about thirteen when I started on a regular. Up until that point I didn't know how to smoke. I did the Bill Clinton at first. I didn't inhale. You see Clinton did what I did or just said he did. He couldn't get around the smoking part. Tell them what they already know. Clinton might not have inhaled, cause check this out.

You know people seen him smoking before. All he could say is, he didn't inhale it. No harm done. I kicked it with y'all only when playing sports and hanging. That's because y'all wasn't smoking yet.

I had my get high hommies on the Met, which was the next group. We would get bubbled with our drank, in the cut. I was first to break the other three provisions in the pact.

Todd will call me off to the side and say, "Colo lets smoke one". Todd kept weed and money for drank.

This is how they caught me doing a Bill Clinton, I will never forget. Lace and I was getting high with Todd in his basement room. Lil Todd pulled out the pad and they start shooting dice.

I wasn't gambling just chilling as always. Todd and Lace was going head up while smoking weed. They were choking on the weed talking about it was fire.

I said, "man why y'all keep choking on the weed it ain't all that fire?" Lace is coughing; Todd is still coughing minutes later after he passed it.

When it came to my turn I'm blowing it all through my nose and everything. I was doing tricks with the smoke. After taking a close look at what I was doing.

Lace looked and said, "no wonder you ain't choking, you're not inhaling the weed. Nigga hit the weed".

I said, "I am hitting the weed what the fuck you talking about?"

You see all that smoke going through me and I ain't coughing.

Lace busted me out, "nigga you ain't hitting the weed. You fucking the weed up, hit the weed. Todd this nigga is wasting the weed.

Lace then says, "give me the weed nigga".

I passed it to Lace and he showed me what I was doing wrong. He inhaled and sucked in a cloud of smoke into his chest.

He started coughing and passed it back to me and said, "now," then started "coughing, cough cough hit cough, hit the weed like that!"

After showing me I said, "It ain't going to make a difference. I still ain't going to cough. Y'all got some weak ass lungs that's all".

Lace said it again, "just hit the weed and take it in your chest nigga".

This time, that's what I do. I inhaled a lot of smoke thinking I could handle it ssswwwwwhhhhh. I inhale swwwwwaaaa and my chest expands like it's on fire. I couldn't hold it. I couldn't wait to blow the smoke out of my lungs.

The smoke stayed in my lungs no more than two second. I started coughing uncontrollably and couldn't stop. By the time I let all the smoke out of my lunges. I was high than a motherfucka. My eyes were blood shot red.

I'm still coughing and coughing and by the time I calmed down. I was totally blew out. The veins in my head, neck and eyes were stressed while slobbing saliva.

Lace and Todd was laughing like a motherfucka. I looked back at them and this different feeling came over me. The properties of the THC had raced into my blood stream in a matter of seconds. I looked at Todd and Lace in another state of being. I was glazed over in the face.

I said to myself, "he's right I wasn't hitting the weed". This euphoric smooth ass cool chill out sensation whisked through my body.

While still laughing Todd said, "all this time we've been smoking cuz and you ain't even inhaling the weed?"

Todd has been calling me to the side to smoke and I never got high. That kind of tripped me out too. Things didn't matter as much and stress was off me immediately. I was hooked.

I was like, "oh this is what you talking about". It was like my whole world changed after that. I got a problem smoke some weed. My momma on my back, smoke some weed. The sun came up smoke some weed. I was just a weekend smoker.

We'd break out the session that day. I hit the block high for the first time. I just thought I was high those other times I was blowing. It was just the drink. All the other times I smoked I was just catching a contact.

The first people I saw on the block were Emus and John on John's porch. I felt kind of funny. Here are the guys I made the pact looking me dead in my face. Drinking and smoking out the window for me.

I just broke that part of the pact, but I thought I broke it a long time ago anyway. I knew at that moment it was broken and I didn't give a fuck. I was laughing like a motherfucka at anything. Lace and Todd was snapping on me in the basement and all I did was laugh.

I'm sitting on the stoop with this breeze from the wind blowing. The sky was the bluest of the blues. I felt good. I didn't tell Emus and John anything, because I was the first to get high. I just laughed at anything that happened. I did that anyway so they couldn't tell. I could, cause this was one of the best laugh.

Of course Todd and Lace told everybody. How I'd had been fucking up everybody's weed.

"Colo is doing tricks and playing with the weed wasting our money".

I didn't buy weed at first. They'd always bust some out when we were drinking. I'd hit it a couple of times, just like I did that day. They were telling the whole hood I ain't even been inhaling. That's one thing! There weren't any secrets on 169th & Calumet.

Everybody knew the business about you. Everybody knew the business, but nobody else knew the business.

All that time I thought I was smoking and I was just blowing smoke. That was the first time I got high, high off of weed. The rest of the time I was just getting a contact, ain't that a bitch.

On the Road

We tested how good we were in sports and went to other neighborhoods to play. We went on the road to play games. The first time we left our comfort zone to play I recall playing Michigan in football or the guys across the track.

We'd play against the guys at the park. 171st street nigga's used to come down and play against us or we'd go up to 171st. First we used to play in the sandlot by Big Mike's crib.

Everybody in the hood would play football in the sandlot at night. I could catch so I always got in the game. The last play of the game in the last game we played in the sandlot. I caught a pass for a touchdown.

Playoffs we would go up to Midway, to play tackle football. Midway was behind King John College on 169th & Wentworth. It was about three hundred yards of grass. It was perfect for football games. Sometimes it would be two games going on at once. I wonder did they name both of those civil rights leaders for the name of the college?

It was a badge of honor to get pickup by the, mid group. That means they think I can help them win. Lace and Big D told me to come play with them, on Sunday up at Midway. I got the call up from the kid league.

They knew I could play so they came and got me to play at Midway. The guys off the Met going were Lace, Big D, Lil Todd and I. We swooped Dirty Red along the way off of Indiana. We all went up there together. We met the rest of the guys on the team, up at Midway.

Snow was up to the middle of my leg on the field. Before we left Lace told me to put on two pair of socks and wrap my feet with plastic bags. I taped around my ankles so the bag won't come off or slide down.

This will keep my feet warm and they didn't get wet, because of the plastic bags. This is before I went to high school. They let me play defense, strong safety.

First play of the game after the kickoff we were on defense. The runner back gets a handoff up the middle. He busted past the lineman and the linebackers. He got up on me so fast.

I come up and plant my feet, but wait for him. He gave me a move that broke my ankles. Left me stuck standing in the snow looking at him scoring.

All I hear was Lace saying, "damn Colo come up and make the tackle. Damn nigga, if you scared get off the field".

Lace was playing linebacker.

He shouts at me, come up and make the tackle or get off the field. I look and see that they got by the linebackers too. I felt like an ant, because I didn't even get my hands on dude. After that it was a wrap. The game gets going and Big D is clowning on defense.

If they got past the line, D was cleaning them up. D was in the backfield sacking the quarterback. Big D is all over the runner back. Big D is going crazy and our defense started shutting them down.

I made up for my debacle earlier. Their quarterback was cold. He would break out and run around the end with the quickness. He was shaking niggas up trying to tackle him. This particular time he shook past everybody and was heading down the sideline.

I had to come over and the corner was coming back up. The linebacker was Dirty Red and he was running paralleled trying to cut him off.

Their quarterback was trying to get past Red and cut in between the corner. I was the safety entering the alley. I come in the alley full blast and hit him low, bam then picked him up in the air.

By that time Red and the corner met me a fraction of a second later. Bamm bamm then we slammed him to the ground. I looked up dude had fumbled the ball and we retrieved it. Red got the fumble. I got up and looked at dude.

He just laid there for about three or four minutes. I was glad cause my face had taken a beating on the tackle, cause I went low. He was straight, but we popped his ass good. They were going to respect the safety position.

I made somebody else fumble entering that alley. I made sure I came up and filled those gaps they were trying to run through. We won the game like 35 to 14. On the way home I didn't hear anything about that missed tackle.

All I heard was the hit of the game went to me. They expected me to play high school caused they knew I could get down. I had heart. I was going to play for the Darobe when I got to high school. I had made it up in my mind.

This was my school of choice. It was brand new and they had sweet school colors. The colors were reddish orange and gold. The Robe was rank high in the state and was winning city regularly.

Coach Murry played for the Steelers at wide receiver, was the coach. He's got the college and pro hookups.

Freddie was already on the team and was getting mad ink in the papers. He was playing cornerback.

Mike Jones was from our hood and was going to Wisconsin that year. He was playing safety and receiver. Mike was so fast, he was a blur on the field. One time we were at the park playing the guys on 171st. He ran a kick off back that had me mesmerized. He had true speed. That's where I am going to go when I get to high school, Paul Darobe.

Hood Rivals

The Taylor's used to come to the dungeon to challenge us in basketball in the summer. The Taylor's had about seven brothers and all of them could play not just basketball, but baseball and football.

They had a certain swagger about themselves. Like they knew they could play and they were going to win. Mills, Red and Legion were the ones we always ran into.

They played as a team. Their team threw blind passes, because they knew where each other would be on the court.

You couldn't double you had to lock down your man. They knew each other moves and how to cut to the hole. The used to cut, pick, box out and used screens. When we beat them it gave me great satisfaction. In order to beat them you had to hustle. It a must you play airtight defense and your shot had to be money.

We also talked mad trash on the court. We'd try to psyche each other out of each other game. The shit we talk to each other was legendary. At the end of the game it was no trophies or money. It was just bragging rights. We play two out of three games.

When we won we'd say, "y'all niggas better take your ass back on Michigan with that weak ass game. Nigga, y'all are playing on the Met in the dungeon nigga. This is like, the Boston Garden back here, we won't be defeated".

When they won the series they would retreat back to Michigan saying, "the competition is weak back here. Let's go somewhere else and play where we can get some competition".

You always walked away after the series talking shit. The words would eat into our souls, if we lost. Therefore, both teams played like it was the game seven of the NBA Championship.

We had competition that would come on the block. Let me see Arron Fonville and Diago Mckenzie both stayed on Prairie. Both of those guys could play baseball pretty good.

Arron was about 5'6" and could throw heat. Diago had Popeye muscles and used to throw heat too. He was also known for his bat. He was always big and when he swung he looked like a big lumberjack or something crushing the ball.

Both of those guys were competitive at the other sports too. They fit right in on the block. Diago played for Darobe football team as a linebacker. Gang banging kicked his football career to the curb.

In fact that's what happened to a lot of people from the hood. They couldn't play because the coach was scared. He was scared that they'd get shot at on the field. Thus, cheating them out of a quality environment, because he wouldn't let you play, if you got caught banging!

Same thing happened to Slick Freddie. Freddie had a chance he was ranked as a junior. Coach Murry wouldn't let them play, because of his gangbanging activities.

Freddie retaliated from a confrontation that happened to him earlier at that week. I'm going to jump ahead for a second. I was there it was my freshmen year. I was still a shortie.

Freddie stole on dude and Dicky and somebody else jumped in the fight. Freddie was going to go head up with the guy. When they jumped in to aid and assist the fight, it changed things.

Now it was gang activity, not just a fight. Coach Murry came down hard on him. Coach Murry wasn't from Chicago. He had no idea about the atmosphere in Chicago. The gangbanging and street life was unavoidable for some teenagers.

Instead of Murray cuffing and shielding Freddie he should've gave him an outlet out of the life. He made an example out of him. He could have taken Freddie out of the life. Freddie grades were straight and he still wouldn't let him back on the team.

Bonner the assistant principle gave him the go ahead to play. He told Curry he was straight. Murray told Freddie, if his grades were straight and he stayed out of trouble. He would reinstate him back on the team.

Once grades came out he went and showed the coach. Coach Murry went back on his word and still wouldn't let him on the team. Had Freddie knew he would have transferred to another powerhouse school. It was too late and this crushed Freddie chance to go to division one.

Murry was thinking about himself, because if he went to another school. He could have come back to bite him back. He fucked Freddie. It something about power it goes to people head.

The Robe was going to city and state championship game during these times. I wished I would've played sports, coming out of grammar school. The possibility of me gang banging would've been a much lesser Emus. I made it out grammar school and didn't plug in with the nation. I was going to play ball.

Did you all know what I was getting into back in the day? I kept a lot of things to myself. My mother was a private person and I was picking it up from her. Around this time is when playing ball transcended, into gang banging.

I was a pretty good kid. I wasn't scandalous until life started making its mark on me. It all changed after I graduated out of grammar school. I had a couple of dilemmas that I needed help handling, which I dealt with by myself. Things that were instrumental in the path I would take, as a young teenager. Right now I'm just enjoying my last year in grammar school.

The Jokes

Up until then life was ball, fun, a lot fights and jokes. Todd had his jokes planned or something. He just walked up one day out the blue. It' was D who only had one leg and wore his hair buttered. He had a sweet car and had a hardy laugh.

Even with the one leg he was pulling some fine women. I peeped that and would take that from him later. While we were sitting on Darrin's porch Todd came walking up

He said, "Emus big momma looking for you, big momma looking for you Emus".

Emus was like, "big momma looking for me" with a bewilder look on his face.

I had the same look cause big momma don't get out. She's eighty years old with gray hair and barely moves.

Emus asked, "where you see her?"

Todd said, "big momma was riding in a helicopter Emus looking for you. She just flew threw the dungeon and repelled down on a rope, like a paratrooper in her bath robe. Everybody on the front porch started laughing uncontrollably.

Todd was looking in the air and pointing like that's where he saw her. He said it happened while they were playing ball on the court.

I was looking up at her Emus like, "damnnnnn big momma up in a helicopter".

After repelling to the ground she asked me, "Todd you seen Emus?" and he's saying it in big momma feeble voice.

"I told her you were on Prairie so she hung on the rope. She pointed toward Prairie to the pilot in the helicopter.

She then said, "that way and she hung on to the rope as they flew away". You better hide she kept asking where's Emus? "What you do?

Now Emus grandmother is eighty years old and repelling out of helicopters.

This was the funniest joke to me. I would immediately visualize what he was talking about and crack up. Big momma is in her robe and glasses repelling out of a helicopter. You know that was funny Emus. Emus never laughed at that joke. He got mad when I laughed at it. He just looked at Todd with the fuck you look.

The mid group had a person who they talked about every time they saw them. For me it was Big. I loved Big's game on the court, the way he handled the rock. He had trickery involved with his handles. He learned it from his brother Jason who was cold.

Every time Jason came out in the dungeon he'd put on a show.

Anytime Big saw me or I was coming to the dungeon. He'd be sitting on his father's Mr. Henderson car.

Soon as he saw me he'd yell out, "it's a Gorilllllllllaaaa. Could you please tell me how much the Gorilla cost in the alley.

Another one was Cornelius, Cornelius, Cornelius and he would say it loud. He was calling me the name of the smart gorilla in the movie, Planet of the Apes. He'd laugh and laugh and laugh.

After laughing so long he would then say, "I am just bullshitting Colo".

My reply, "fuck you Big" while warming up shooting ball.

I hated to see Big coming. I still loved him, because when they came to Rock Manor to play. I was bragging on my guys from the hood. At the time I was in the sixth grade and wasn't on the team. Lace and Big dropped 60 points on us.

Rock Manor had 23 when Meneen came to play Rock Manor. We had Wayne Willis who was tall and could play. We had a girl on the team her name was Irene Singleton. She has a twin sister named, Inez. She was quite good.

Wayne and Landress got down, but it wasn't enough. They had bragging rights in the hood. I wasn't on the team that year anyway.

All Big and Lace used to say, "Rock Manor ain't shit. We blew yall asses out".

I couldn't wait until it was my turn, but it never came. Big I say, in the hood, used to get under my skin. I loved him, but I hated to see him coming. He used to crack on me and it didn't matter who was around.

His big brother Jason was the same way, but evil with it. I was sitting on the porch with Emus and Pia. Pia is Emus fine ass cousin. Jason came walking down the Met from Stag house. Jason cracked on me about me being a black ass. I crack back on him and don't even remember what I was saying. Pia started laughing at my joke, a little too hard.

All I know is Jason walked up talking smooth like it wasn't shit. As I relaxed, he grabbed my legs and pulled me off the porch fast as hell. I couldn't even put my hands down in time. Bam, my head hit the concrete steps. My head made the thudd sound and I was dazed.

Pia was like, "oohh damn Jason you didn't have to do that to him". I am about twelve and this nigga is about twenty-one.

I wasn't big enough to fuck with him. I just held my head to contain the pain.

He just walked away and said, "watch your mouth little nigga". That was one thing if you weren't old enough to talk shit to the older niggas. If you couldn't back it up with the physical. It was best you kept your mouth shut. I had to learn that the hard way, but I would have my time.

Same thing happened with Dirty Red who stayed on Indiana. He was a little older than Freddie. They did used to hang. DeJuan Black used to be up at the park playing baseball with the semi pro baseball team when I was on the Cardinals. He also used to play softball with us when we played Piggie.

DeJuan used to hit the softball so far. He hit the ball from the baseball diamond, over the outfield gate, over the swings, over the merry go round and into the sandbox. The sandbox was located where you first walk in the park.

I was sitting in the swings and when he was leaving the field. He said something to me. It always had something to do with my color. When you crack on my color it was an instantaneous comeback.

He asked, "what your black ass still doing up here?"

I said something back smart. I had a smart mouth even back then with anybody.

Red said, "you better shut up.

I told him, "you shut up, you ain't going to do shit to me". Red walks over to the swings and grabs my legs. He pulls me out the swing, to the ground and I hit my head.

I didn't cry, but the shit hurt. I just looked at him and couldn't do anything.

He said the same thing Jason said, "little nigga you better watch your mouth. This taught me a lesson with fucking with older nigga's. Don't talk shit unless you could back it up. Even if the older dude is talking shit to you. These niggas didn't know I was mad ass fuck! I couldn't wait to get bigger.

I reminded myself every time I saw them. "When I get bigger I was going to fuck these niggas up". That 's why I practice so much boxing and karate.

Other than, the older guys who were fucking with me. Emus and I would tear the neighborhood up as far a sigging. We would go into Mr. Reef's game room and it was open season. Emus and I would have motherfuckas on the verge of tears. You try to leave the game room. We'd follow you home talking shit about you.

We'd follow you home from school cracking about you all the way until you got home. They way we did Woody was scandalous. Woody had a haircut like Woody Wood Pecker. His hair stuck up in the middle of his head. He was also poor like me, but you could see it. Woody was cool, but it just, what we did. He'd leave out the game room crying sometimes. This would be even funnier, because that was our objective. We wanted to make you cry. That means that you are good signifyer.

We were some mean kids and we did not give you any air. To be honest this built mental toughness. Emus and I was the tag team champions together we would crucify you. I fed off him and he fed off me. We'd be in the game room playing Pac Man or Ms. Pac Man laughing our ass off at a motherfucka.

I was the king of those games. I had my own patterns different from the patterns everyone else had. I loved when Emus was around because we had so much fun.

Emus also would calm me down, because I was disturbed a bit.

He be like, "Come on Colo that ain't right". I would be ready to snap. I needed Emus around, because he was a voice of reason.

Now it's one person who had the jokes I couldn't fuck with him.. Fat Cat used to go hard on niggas with the nonstop sigging.

Meaning he wouldn't let you get in a word. He would just go on and on! When you tried to get on something, he would get louder and louder.

"Youuuu ugly gorilla looking, cookie monster chewing, big lip slurping Oragatang haaa haaa haaa".

I'll try to cut in while he's laughing. "That's okay you fat ass…" no bet!

He'd start again, "look who just come from the jungle, bone in the nose, where's is your grass skirt, out in public like a monkey man". I'd have to laugh myself, because he was sweet and I learned.

He'd just go on and on, on your ass. You couldn't get more than three or four words out. His real name was Raymond and he was about three years older than we were. He was from Parkway. Raymond and his family moved in the hood when we were in the sixth grade.

The only thing about Raymond he used to have those seizures. When he didn't take his medication, which was a lot. He would pass out on us right before our eyes.

I saw him blinking out while we were getting high. It would happen all of a sudden. He would be cool one minute and the next second he'd fall down pass out. Raymond didn't like taking his medicine.

He played sports with us. He used to shoot the ball funny. His fingers would be wide apart when he shot. He had a little game. We mostly played night games with Raymond in the dungeon after a bubble.

Revenge

This type of activity was going to stop! I don't care how old you were. This is what was going through my head when Darkness and I boxed. I was ready for the moment. I had to get off the porch I still had puppy nuts. Me getting my head bashed in those couple of times is what preceded that moment.

I told my mother I wanted to take karate classes. She paid for my brother and I to go to class. I'd go up to the park, where there was a man teaching the lesson. He had the practice in the glass house on 171st. A brown skin man with a baldhead and wore a white gee.

Marcus Thomas from school was going too. He was in there doing high-flying kicks. He already jumped in the air, high as hell, from all that tumbling. Doing karate helped me with my speed and my blocking and head movements.

I was already cold at fighting, but now I am ruthless. I didn't have to worry about Walley. Everybody had to worry about him. It was only so much you were going to say to Walley.

It was only a couple of times I had to come to his defense. I was intense with my training. I couldn't wait to go to my lessons. Once I finished with the classes I was fast. I told myself, "I ain't letting no body get away with fucking with me. I don't care how big they are to me".

Leaving Grammar School

That was life in the hood. In school during the same time I had to make a transition. I had to make my first big decision. I had a chance to graduate a year early out of grammar school. At the time I was twelve going on thirteen. My birthday was in March and we graduated in June. The reason why? I scored high enough on the Iowa test for my age to move on to high school.

I wouldn't even say that it was just year advancement. I was already picked to excel in another level. I couldn't graduate, if I didn't make at least an 8.0. I was ready to leave grammar school. Especially, since I went there ever since kindergarten. My math was straight I scored at a eight grade level

What was cool Emus transferred from Brownell after the sixth grade. He did 7th & 8th grade at Rock Manor. It felt good having somebody from the hood now going to school with me. Everyone on Calumet mostly went to Meneen except Lamont and Kenny. Lamont went to a Catholic school.

Kenny lived up under Emus, but he wasn't a hood guy. He was from our hood, but he really didn't hang. He played ball in the alley though!

He never hung on the front block with us. He was good competition, but he couldn't mess with me. It was either Kenny or I who got back in the alley first.

I plugged Emus to what was going on at the Manor when he transferred in the school. It was no joke at Rock Manor, if you were a mark. They'll be on your head.

Emus had those gargles for glasses back then and was chubbed out. Everybody starts to laugh. Shit I worried so I sent word around, that's my guy. I couldn't let them fuck with him. A lot of niggas knew his brother Coole so they knew he had backup. Coole played for the Cardinals and knew a lot of 171st niggas.

I told everybody he was my guy and he had a relatively easy stay at Rock Manor. We played football at lunchtime, like clockwork. They knew I could play, but they didn't know Emus could play. The older guys in the class usually picked. Jeffrey Hudson or one of the older guys usually picked. He wasn't get chose at first so he had to just sit the bench.

One day Kevin Stroles picked him up. Kevin is a smooth guy. He got along with everybody. He didn't have to pick Emmett up that's how smooth he was.

"Naw they wasn't choosing me at first, Emus comments. When they saw I could catch and was sweet with it. I was the talk that week. They didn't expect it".

I knew Emus was sweet. Stroles threw him a pass over the middle. Emus caught it ran and did a little move before he got tackled.

That had motherfuckas looking around at each other like, "damn dude can play".

Emus got up and came to the huddle. I had a smile on my face, cause I knew he was in the game now. He used to just stand there and watch us play for about two months. I would say get Emus and they would pick all over his head.

The only reason I would've stayed is, because Emus was at the school. I made the basketball team in my seventh grade. It was my last year at the Rock. I was going to be a beast for the Rock. This was the only reason I was staying. It was my time to shine as a Stallion. I waited six whole years.

Rodell made the team. Rodell didn't play like we did, but at tryouts Rodell did not miss a shot. I couldn't believe it. Rodell had very little skills on the court. That day, dude was unconscious.

I saw how Mrs. Bulkolz, the gym teacher was looking at him. I knew he had made the team. She was like, "wow he can shoot".

Rodell never hit two shots in a row anywhere. At tryouts he couldn't miss.

The test results came back and I made an 8.1 or something in reading and 7.7 in math. Back then that was excellent.

A lot of people didn't get that high of a score and was in the eighth grade year. Most often you were probably behind in both areas. I only went up a few points from the year before.

This meant I didn't learn much my 7Th grade year. I started transforming my self from being considered a nerd. Once I knew the material my interest waned. I got more into sports.

I attribute the high score due to reading so many comic books, newspapers and encyclopedias. I read the newspaper from front to back. I read every section from: Jobs to finance, movies, politics, horoscope and sports.

I would start with sports and work my way back to the front. Comprehension of words opens your whole world up. The more words you know the more powerful your intellect become! I would gobble up things to read.

My love was the comic books though! The comic books took me to other places other galaxies. Something that was different than the life I was experiencing. Comic book indirectly helped make me smarter without knowing it.

When reading the comic books you could get educated. A lot of comic books would talk about current events. It would be a picture and a passage underneath. Some words you didn't understand until you match the picture to what you didn't know. This is how I began to figure out what words meant. This expanded my comprehension.

Everybody who traded comic books scored high. John Strong, Fester Delldow and Stacy Smith all graduated a year earlier. Stacy I think had a 10 or 11point reading score. I would have scored higher, but I was working at that age. Now that I look back working knock down my will to study like I used too.

Another thing I was getting plugged in the hood. I knew everybody. Especially, since I was out there working my paper route in the alley and playing for the Cardinals.

I knew my classmates and hood mate's mothers, fathers, brothers and sister. A lot of people got the paper so I was known. I used to study and everything at first. Now studying took a back seat to playing and getting the money.

It still showed how smart I was at the time. I was working my route getting money, playing sports and pulling my grades.

Stacy was the best artist. He used to actually make up his own super heroes. 'Stace' could draw them better than they were in the comic book. A guess it's true that smart people becomes comedians, cause boy could he sig on your ass. He was fat chubby and his clothes looked worst than mine. He didn't play ball or anything.

Try and fuck with em if you want too. He'll have the whole classroom laughing at your ass. Even the teacher Mrs. Rodgers couldn't hold back her laughs while trying to do so.

Mrs. Rodgers took over for Mr. Norris eight-grade class. When Stacy cut into you it's not just for that moment. He's on you for weeks. Stacy will go home and come back with more jokes. I went home and thought up my jokes, but Stace was another story.

Yeah all of us were comic book feins. I wasn't just collecting the books and just looking at the pictures. Like Emus and my brother Walley did. I was reading them. That's how I got over on trading comics in the hood. I knew which one's to trade. Emus just liked the pictures.

I started reading them later, Emus replied with the look of embarrassment.

I used to be like, "Emus you got to read them or you don't know what you getting".

Oh I loved to read and I would read anything.

My mother left the decision to skip a grade up to me. She often would tell me when I was coming up.

"You can be the President of the United States if you want". I would then look in the encyclopedia and see thirty-eight in a row. No black presidents, but she did inspired me. You got to set your goals high and go for it'.

She said "if you think you are ready for high school and can make those grades then go ahead".

I was so eager, because I had been at the Manor eight straight years including kindergarten.

This is what made my decision much easier. Rock Manor disbanded the basketball team that year. I was going to start and I couldn't believe it. It was my time to shine as a Stallion. Now there's not going to be any team, this was devastating. That was it my decision was made up to go to high school.

It was no basketball team anymore. I waited all these years and made the team. Now it's will be no more teams. It seemed like I was always out of tune somehow with team sports. I never was in the right position. The Cardinals and now the Stallions are disbanding.

The only thing I regretted was leaving Emus behind. I wanted to go to high school with Emus. I should've played one year of organized basketball before I got to high school. It was nothing else Rock Manor could teach me.

I would've just sat around learning the same material. What good would that do? I already didn't learn much my last year at the Manor. Ever since kindergarten I've been waiting on my turn to walk across that stage. Be careful what you ask for in life!

I think we were all on the right path. Something's can change the course of your path, if implemented into the equation. We were good kids, a little mischievous, but basically good kids.

Now I know back in the day it was discussions on me. Even though I did my dirt away from the crib, it got back to the Met. I think life came at me all at once. I had to grow up and face reality and the stresses of life as a kid. This is where we differ a little, as far as struggle. I had to grow up faster.

Chapter VII

Finding out who is who?

It wasn't too many people who looked out for me as far as money. I didn't have blood relatives that I knew in the city. I had one cousin named Otis Bankhead. Every once in a while we'd visit him or he'd come by.

We did a holiday with my cousin over his house. I don't even remember where he lived. He always visited us. He had a 1979 Lincoln Continental with the oval for a window in the back. He was my mother's age though! He would drop me a couple of bucks.

I had Mrs. Carmelita Frank who was my godmother. I loved her. She bought me my first watch when I was four. It was a digital watch. When I was in church I'd see her and she'd give me some change. I'll get the change to go get me some snacks at church. Mrs. Hellen also gave me money. She was my mother church friend they'd talk all the time on the phone.

Other than that Mom gave us money for lunch at church. We'd be at church all day though! We bet not ask nobody for any money at the church. I f she heard that it was immediate discipline.

I used to love when it was Palm Sunday or Ladies day. These are the days when they give the young people the yellow coin bags or a box to collect money. They had different days they celebrated, for the congregation. I was good at collecting the money. I'd hit up and ask everybody.

Excuse me, and I would know their name. I got to call them by their name that gets me in the door. Excuse me, Mr. or Mrs. Woo woo woo! Would you help me help the ladies out on ladies day? I am collecting on behalf of the ladies today. I usually would get a quarter all the way up to a dollar.

Now you already know I didn't turn that money in to the church. Not all of it anyway. I got my cut. If it was twenty dollars I collected, I kept fifteen. I had to turn something in everybody saw me collecting. If you don't get away with it, why do it?

I usually left the dollars and kept most of the quarters. I'd leave a few quarters in the slot, for quarters. I kept all of the dimes left the pennies and nickels. You received more quarters than anything.

I had a thieving demon that was self-activated anytime around money. Now you know that shit ain't right. I didn't even have a second thought. It was no question once the money hit my hand. It was mines.

One of the reverends used to look out for me. His named was Rev. Cody. Now dude was cool. Every time he came to church he dropped me a couple of dollars. When he saw my face his face would light up a bit.

He'd see me and say, "what's up doc?"

He automatically started reaching in his pocket.

I be like, "nothing,"

He then ask, "you're doing good in school?"

I answer, "Yep I am ahead of schedule. I could be graduating this year if I want too".

This is when I was on the usher board. I would be one of the people in the back of the church anyway. He seemed to always get there a little after the service started. He'd hit me up with the bucks, real smooth.

I used to sing in the young adult choir. He would be in the pulpit and when we came down to sing he would hit me. Nobody really saw when he gave me money. He was smooth with it.

Now this went on long as I could remember. The ice cream man was Reverend Cody son. He came to the church after morning and evening service, with the ice-cream truck.

Every time he came, I got free ice cream. All I had to do was just stand there and look at him.

He would see me and say, "what do you want?"

I'd tell him and he'd hook me up. His name was Butch. He was big and had a super fat butt.

The only thing about hooking me up, it was a secret. I never saw them looking out like that for the rest of my brothers and my sister. I never told my Mom he was giving me money.

I still wanted the money she had for me. It was a candy and food truck that sold hot food in the parking lot, foot long polishes, hotdogs, cookies and candies. I had to hit the truck up constantly while at church. When he didn't come to church it was like a big disappointment. I was looking to see him.

Periodically, he used to take us home from church. He drove a sweet black 79 Cadillac. He was taking us home and I started to wondering about him. Other than the folks I named earlier. I didn't have a lot of money coming my way. Mrs. Carmelita is my Godmother and you are my Mom. I'm young, but old enough to know! People just don't give you money.

My momma told me, "nobody gives you anything for free. Anybody giving you something for free it's a trick to it".

I'm in the car sitting in between my brothers and sister looking around in the Caddy.

I asked her because dude was too cool, "Mom is Rev. Cody some kind of kin to us?" They look at each other, but didn't say anything. I asked her again, "Mom is Rev. Cody some kind of kin to us?" I said it much louder thinking she didn't hear the question the first time.

She just replied, "boy be quiet I'll talk to you when I get home".

I just thought that was the funniest answer. It's a yes or no answer to me. Forget about it, I didn't think anything else of it.

Later that evening, my Mom called me in the room.

She reminded me, "you ask me earlier is Rev Cody some kin to us?"

I responded, "yeah I did," and she answers the question while sewing on one of her patterns and watching TV.

"Well he's your father".

Just like that, he's my father. I turn my head looked bewildered and asked, "how can I have two daddies momma? Why don't I know he's my daddy?"

She tells me how, "Daddy Samson adopted you and Cody helped brought you into this world".

My next question was, "Rev. Cody is just my daddy? What about the rest of my brothers and my sister?"

Mom answered, "No he's just your daddy".

It didn't really register, because I was young. Why the big secret? Reason being, I didn't understand what the full concept of conception. You know back then shit like sex was a secret to the kids.

I just said to myself, "okay I got two daddies to look out for me". I was kind of happy I had something nobody else had in the house. I got three daddies so I am blessed. I'm thinking I got two people giving me stuff on my day.

My birthdays and Christmases I should be getting it, two times.

Before I left the room she said, "one more thing don't be around the church talking about he's your daddy".

I asked, "Why not that's my daddy?"

She replies, "Don't nobody need to be in our business. Just keep it to yourself". That right there bothered me, but I would have to figure it out later. For about a year I had three daddies that cared about me. Don't forget about daddy Curtis.

Dealing with Death

My dog Tiger died or was put to sleep. Tiger would leave for a couple of weeks and come back. He was a hood dog. He'd hang out with my friends. I took him everywhere as a paperboy. Tiger knew how to get around.

The times Tiger would take off for two three days. I'd come outside in the morning and he'd be sitting on the porch. This time Tiger had been gone. He was gone the last time for two weeks and came back.

This time he left, but didn't come back for a while. He had a dog tag on and we were notified. Tiger was in the pound. I was like bet cause I was missing him for about month.

My Mom went down there to check on Tiger. When she came back we all were waiting for him, because we all missed him. She gets out the car and no Tiger.

I look all in the car and asked. "Where is Tiger mom?"

Her reply, "Tiger was vicious and he didn't know me. He was growling and foaming at the mouth. I told them to put him to sleep. Someone got a hold to him and abused him, turned him vicious.

I was stunned, "this fuucccCCcKed me up!!! My face went blank. I said to myself, "Tiger is dead. You got to be bullshitting. I couldn't even see him before you gave him the needle".

That's why she didn't take me with her. They told her he was vicious on the phone. I know if Tiger would've seen me, he would've snapped back. My dog hung out with me.

When I was on punishment it's him and I. He's with me kicking it through the hood it was it was him and I. I cried like a baby in the house. My mother got tired of me sulking and gave me something to cry for.

She said, "it was just a dog".

It was more than a dog to me Tiger was my best friend. This was preparation for something much more tragic. The summer before I went into high school my adopted father died from a heart attack. When my father died that summer I was crushed.

When my dad called the house to talk to us. I'd be the first one he wanted to speak to when he was on the phone.

He'd tell my mom, "let me speak to Hollering Jack first". It was one Sunday morning my Mom got the call.

At first she said, "your father was in the hospital, but he was dead already".

She was just probably trying to find the words of how to tell us. He had a heart attack and was found dead in the house.

I remember feeling very somber, but hoping he would be O.K. Later on that morning she gives us the real news.

She said, "your father is dead from a heart attack".

I should've known the deal. She didn't run out the house the first time when she told us. She was looking for words and probably searching herself.

That's one thing about my momma she gave it to us cut and dry. No sugar this is what it is! Same for Tiger it seems as, if she put it behind her. She had to show us strength. It seemed as, if I cried the whole week before the funeral! I really loved my father, even though he didn't live with us. I still knew he loved us and cared deeply for us.

This is a feeling that I didn't have at the time with my biological father. Yes, he says he loves me and probably did. My adopted father showed us he loved us, because he came around. He'd always call to see how we are doing. Often drop by to kick it with us. He made me feel like I was his favorite son. He had a big red dog he kept with him.

Hollering Jack was his nickname for me. He used to tell me the reason why he called me that!

He'd say, "you know how you got your name".

I'd say "no daddy!".

He then tells me how, "boy you would not shut up when you were a baby!" You hollered all day and all night.

He used to say to my Mom, "that boy is hollering jack".

The word back then was jack. Cool out jack was the saying! It stuck with him and that's what he called me, Hollering Jack.

He'd call and say, "Let me talk to Hollering Jack".

The day he died or night he died is the night my world crumbled. I had memories of a real father. Here's a man who loved me just as much as his own kids. You wouldn't be able to tell me that wasn't my old dude. I didn't know the reason why my Mom and him were separated. It seems as, if they had a good cordial relationship when they talked. I never heard her say one bad word about him.

His funeral was at the Without a Spot or Wrinkle Church. During the proceedings I looked over at my Mom. She didn't shed a tear during the proceedings. I remember her telling me she had to be strong for us.

I never saw my mother cry in all my life. She didn't that day, either. My father had a lot of friends, because the church was packed to the hilt. I didn't know one person, but everybody was coming giving condolences.

My brother Samson and I carried my father casket out the church. I was hoping and praying I would not drop it. After he had his funeral in Chicago. His family shipped his body back down South to Mississippi. This was for the second funeral in his place of birth. This is where my father would be buried.

My mother couldn't go, because she had to take care of things at home. I was the only representation for our family in Mississippi. I was thirteen years old when he died. I don't have recollection of my family members from his side of the family in Mississippi.

I don't remember any of my cousin's aunts or uncle's. I went down there with my father's people who I never met or knew. I really don't remember who took me down there I was so fuck up. My mind was shutting down the whole thing. This was a very traumatic event.

The one person I wanted to see was my cousin, Franco Harris. He didn't show up at the funeral, if he did, I didn't see him. The only thing I could remember from going to Mississippi was the people lowering his body in the ground.

To this day I can't forget that moment or shake that feeling every time I think about it. They slowly lowered him down on these ropes. The minister was saying some words, ashes to ashes dust to dust.

Up until that point I pretty much composed myself through the funeral. They started to lower him in the ground. That's when a chill shot from my head to the tip of my toes. It instantly paralyzed me. I couldn't move and began crying uncontrollably. The tears were shooting out like rapid gunfire. Once he retreated back to the earth I lost it.

My family had to literally drag me back to the car. You could see my trail marks for real! These are the emotions that were exploding in me: sad, sorrow, and mad. This was my man who was in my corner. At this point, realization had sunk in to my soul. He wasn't coming back and I will never see him again! At thirteen, that's very hard to handle, for any kid.

For a long time after that! I did not want to go to any funerals. All it did was made me think of my daddy. People would think I was crying for the person in the casket.

It was my dad I was crying about and he looked much different dead. I can't go to funerals. My logic was I rather remember them alive and not dead. He did not look like himself dead.

I blocked my father's death out for a long time unknowingly. The feeling of loss was incredibly unbearable for me. To think about him was to bring those feelings back like it happened today.

My mother brought his name up sometimes. I'd blocked out what she was saying, unconsciously or quickly tried to change the subject.

All I remember is when I got back to Chicago, The next day I came out on the porch.

Emus and John walked by and said, "we heard about the old dude. You okay?"

I answered, "yeah".

Emus said, "Let's go to the game room and play some games".

I replied, "bet" and after that day. I rarely thought about after that day.

My middle twenties is when I started to think about him. It still was unbearable, but it was time to grieve. Each time I thought about him I ended up sobbing and a man ain't supposed to cry.

The tears are streaming down as Colo tells them that part of the story. At least that is what I thought, while wiping away tears. That's why I blocked him out all those years.

Later on my mother said she notice that my father's death, hit me the hardest. She says she saw a change in me. My dog and now my daddy are gone. At the time they were my two best friends. I missed them both. I really missed my daddy. RIP

Stanley Darobe High School

I didn't know how to handle certain situations that confronted me in high school. I wasn't very smooth at adapting. I was out of place totally. The school I was going to was Stanley Darobe High School. At the time Darobe had a good football and basketball team.

I tried out for both and was cut from both of them my freshmen year. My boy Freddie was a senior that year and was on the football team. He was one of their best players. The scouts from Michigan State, was looking at him, his junior year.

I was hoping he would speak up for me, if he could. Everybody wanted to play for the Robe. I didn't know junior varsity tryouts weren't held with varsity tryouts. He could have given Coach Murry the heads up on me.

They always picked me No# 1 draft choice for the shorties. Like I said earlier he had his own problems. I figured I go there get on the football and basketball team and become a star. I had the hands, I could hit and I was fearless and relentless even at thirteen years old.

I was ready. All summers I had been practicing blocking out everything else. I was trying to catch up with the rest of the hood. I developed sweet handles and could finger roll with both hands.

I could hit the 15 to 20' footer consistently with D in my face. I had much hustle. My defense was good as hell. At football I was a receiver, I could catch anything and had evasive moves. The moves I learned playing hill dill. I also could hit.

Well Coach Murry was the head coach of the football team at the Darobe. He used to play wide receiver for the Pittsburgh Steelers. My cousin was still playing for the Steelers. He was one of the all time greats. Franco Harris was my adopted father nephew. My pops was his uncle. His brother is my Uncle, Cedilla Harris is Franco's father.

After I found out Franco Harris was my cousin. My passion for football was even greater. I often bragged about him to my friends. They didn't believe me until we got some photos from my father house after the funeral.

The Steelers had just won the Super Bowl against the Rams the year before I went into high school. I was leaning toward football.

Franco had scored a touchdown in the Super Bowl. That intensified my dreams of becoming a pro football player. I wanted to score a touchdown in the Super Bowl like he did. Now, Franco didn't know me from a hole in the ground, but I knew him. He was my temporary role model.

I was going to follow in his footsteps. I tried out for the Darobe Raiders. I came to practice every day giving my heart and sweat and loved it.

Back then though speed was the name of the game with Coach Murry. Don't get me wrong I was fast. The position I was trying out for was receiver or corner like Freddie. First of all it was about 150 people trying out for junior varsity.

It was people there who could run faster than I could. I thought, I was fast I was right there, but they got me by a couple of steps. They were a couple years older than me, but I never used that as an excuse. One thing about me I was crafty. If there were any way to catch the ball I would catch it. I'd make over the shoulder, diving, stretching or leaping catches and come down with it.

Check this out one time in the schoolyard. We were playing tackle football after school about twelve of us. I was in about the 6th grade. The game was tied and it was getting late. Whoever got the next touchdown wins the game. It was our ball. I'm in the huddle I tell my partner Fester to throw me the bomb and the game is over. Hike the ball on three. I go out and line up in the receiver's spot and he hikes the ball on three.

I shot off the line of scrimmage. They were double covering me, because they knew I was the threat. I still beat the corner off the line. Fester saw me open. He threw a spiral high in the air and over my head just like I like them.

Now, it is a steel post gate encircling the whole schoolyard. I'm running and looking up at the ball. All I was thinking was to catch the ball and game over. I was concentrating so hard I forgot about the gate.

Most kids would stop running five to ten yards before the steel gate. I leaped up and dove for the ball caught it and ran into the iron fence with my head. I came down with a hellva over the shoulder catch and held on to the ball.

I had a hickey big as the rocky mountain, but I didn't cry. I got up with my football and went home. I didn't drop the ball, game over we win. That's when I knew my passion for sports were rank supreme. If you needed somebody to get open, I could put a move on you and bam I was open. I was quick with the ball and I'll trick you.

I wasn't scared to hit especially playing with older boys all my life. I could read the quarterback eyes and anticipate where he was going and often intercepted my opponent's passes. I should have being trying out for safety.

I was also small, because I left grammar school that year early. I needed that extra year to grow and put more weight. I was short with little above average speed, but I could play and had heart.

You can't measure that doing drills. I did all the drills and was crispy. I knew I had made at least that cut. Once we start on the football field. That's when I can show off my skills.

Cut day came, Coach Murry addressed us on the bleachers. Everybody who name I call, step out here. If I don't call your name come out next year. It was about a hundred people trying out for thirty-five spots.

I felt, in my heart I was going to make the team. Everybody else in the hood makes the team off 169th. I got to make the team, I'm from 169th & Calumet, we ball. Everybody coming out our hood was making his or her school team. I was better than most of them already.

Big D didn't even have to try out. He was practicing with varsity while he was in grammar school. Everybody knew I was trying out and had high expectation of me.

Coach Murry said, "and last but not least Johnson".

I just knew he was going to call my name. He didn't call my name and this was the second cut.

I didn't make it to the part where I showed him my skills. I was running with the runner backs and receivers I was coming across 6th in a race with 12. I was there in the running, but it was five people faster.

I was devastated. I knew, if we just started running plays I could show them what I knew. I didn't even get to that part.

I can't blame the coach. He didn't know me from a hole in the ground. I had too much pride to try and hang off my cousin's name. Hey coach you know Franco is my cousin.

I should've did that though! Receiver is what I played in the hood. Yeah I was one of the fastest in the neighborhood for the position, but in high school it was another story.

Coach Murry did not know my love for competition. My will to win in any sport I played. I hated to lose. I wasn't a sore loser, but I hated to lose. I did what it took not to lose.

I'd tell a guy if he beat me, good game. It was so rare that I didn't know how to handle it. Jeffrey Hudson made me realize loss on a low level. On the inside I would be feeling funny and all fucked up about the loss.

I would go to the house and be thinking about the lost all night. Get up the next day and go practice. I practice whatever it was I needed to practice. One thing I knew is when I play, I play to win. If I was missing jumpers I practice jumpers.

When I missed the layup, because of the ball rolling off the rim. I'd practice putting it in a spot on the board so it would drop right in the bucket. I knew losing was a feeling I didn't like and didn't want to lose again. I didn't have a father around to coach me on going out for what position that I could make. I had to figure football out myself by watching it on TV.

I didn't know what shit was called, linebacker, safety, corner or the rules for lineman. All I knew was check him or stay in and block. What I do know how to do, was catch the ball and run patterns. That's the position I wanted to play. I watched it on TV all the time. I didn't comprehend football not all the way.

I never figured out why when the quarterback got in trouble. Why he just wouldn't throw it to the guys standing in front of him. Those guy are ineligible I later found out. I played the game, but didn't know the game. I would've tried out for a punter or field goal kicker anything. I could later change my position if I wanted once on the team.

I was dejected and didn't know how to handle being cut. I walked home from Hamiltion Park by myself. I had to face my friends and tell them I didn't make the team. Worst of all I embarrassed myself.

I always bragged about how good I am. No one could beat me in the hood my age. In grammar school I was always the top pick. I'd go up to the park no later than the second round. Grab Columbus up cause they knew I was the difference maker. That's even with the niggas off of 171st.

I went to school with a lot of people who tried out. They knew I was good. The older kids who played before I did, knew I was good. Coach Murry didn't though. Yes, I was embarrassed.

I know I cried walking home at least once or twice. It wasn't a boohoo cry. It was a disappointment cry. The tears trickled out. I thought about my Mom and how my dream to get her out the hood was done. It was a long mile and half walk from Hamilton park to my crib. I came up with something for the hood. I lied and told them I hurt my ankle and couldn't finish tryouts.

Inside I handled it like maybe they are better than me, so fuck it. I liked basketball anyway. I tried out for basketball during basketball season. I got the same result. I got cut after the first cut. I think that put the finality on me trying out for sports for a while. I was too small again and was real nervous for fear of being cut.

I didn't relax and didn't play like I knew how to play. I am running guard and I kicked the ball off my feet and it went out of bounds. Alley ball is one thing-organized ball is another thing.

I knew the fundamentals, but wasn't used to the atmosphere. This never happened to me kicking the ball off my feet. I played like I never picked up a ball before. I wouldn't go that far, but I was much sweeter than I performed in tryouts. That football cut hurt my confidence. I didn't know nobody either is what killed me.

The players that were trying out I knew I had more skills. I needed more court time. Other than the park I didn't have much court time. I didn't perform so I was cut. I knew I was going to get cut from basketball team, because of my weak performance in scrimmages.

This anxiety and fear of getting cut wouldn't let me perform up to my ability. I was playing guard and couldn't get the ball up the court. Here I am kicking the ball out of bounds. The outcome of my dreams shattered before I could start. This would ultimately later on push me to join another team. The Black Disciples!

I didn't have anybody to share my dejection. I had no one to push me, to be persistent and not give up on my dreams. Come back next year. Work on trying to get faster. Coach just said I was cut. No one to me tell me what position you should try out for. This is how I got cut.

I just signed up and tried out for the position I like to play. Truth is I would have played any position and could've later work on the position I really wanted to play. I did not have any guidance and no knowledge about organized sports. I was embarrassed for being cut from football no doubt, then later I was bewildered.

I couldn't figure out what happen. Now, I know I didn't have any exposure. No one knew me outside the neighborhood for ball. It's just like trying to get a good job. You got to know somebody. The coach didn't know me. Nobody on junior varsity knew me. Here I am this skinny short kid trying to walk on.

Most people grammar school, park district or father would wire the coach up. I needed someone to give Murray what he needed. Tell the coach to keep an eye on me I'm good.

I wished I had someone in my corner to tell him about my talents. He has above average speed, he's quick, he's a playmaker and he hates to lose. Those few words to a coach would get him to look at you harder. I didn't have anybody to do that and my heart wasn't seen on cut day doing drills.

I learned most of what I knew about sports watching television. Put in mad work playing in the hood, hours after hours. I never played organized ball except for little league baseball. It seemed that I kept missing the boat.

It wasn't going to happen, now what? My dream is cut short. I couldn't get on the field. My conclusion on the situation was, "fuck it".

I never tried out for Darobe again. I would've tried out, but it just wasn't in the cards for me. Something always happened. I still played endlessly in the hood.

People in the hood always asked. "Nigga why you ain't on the squad at school?"

I would answer pissed like, "fuck trying out for school".

In my mind though I was saying, "They don't know a good player when they see one". Well with nothing to occupy my time and I'm always in the hood. I began to really chilling out more with the older guys in the hood.

I am in high school now. I can't go up to the grammar school. I couldn't go hang out with my old buddies after I graduated. Even though I wanted too I went up there one time to see Mrs. Rodgers.

King of the Dungeon 21

The game that made transformed to being a legend back in the dungeon is the time we played a 21. You have to beat the best. The game of 21 is big in Chicago. It's you against the world. It was Big Lacey and Lil Todd. This was the best the dungeon had to offer.

21 is a game of endurance. You can't get any help to win, it's all on you. You got to rebound. You got to play defense. You got to dribble and shoot to win. To win a 21, it was a badge of honor. When you won the 21's it was like you were King of the Dungeon.

Everybody believes their skills are better than yours. This game you do all the shooting. You do all the dribbling. This is when you have a chance, to show your shit. You don't have to pass to nobody.

When you won you had first pick, for the team game or you call your game of 21. You can play no tips or tips from the line. You can call no fouls. You can call elimination.

When they were ten people playing, it was ten against one, when you got the ball. You had to have real skills to come to the hole. Elimination made it so every possession was challenged. You call seven eleven elevation. They weren't going to let a young nigga win. I had to start winning the 21's. I had to start taking over those games.

You know when you get close to 21 and close is like 12 or 13. You are about to start getting triple team, from out of bounds. Not only that, everybody is blocking you out for the rebound.

I had every patent move working this day, the J, the hesitation, the cross over and the drive. I am doing this with intense defense on me. You just don't win against the big fellas unless you earned it. Too many reputations were on the line.

They couldn't stop me I get to nineteen. I try to go out from the line and missed, but it came off awkward and went toward the gate.

"Yeah right you missed on purpose," John commented.

I answered, "No I didn't, I never tried to miss at nineteen. I wanted to go out at the line, like the big fellas. That means you got confidence in your shot".

It was off and I was off and running soon as it left my hand. Just like I practiced. I knew it was off. It comes off the gate. I blocked them from getting to it. I pivot back toward the middle. Back crossover and bounced off Big's chest, he reaches, I cross through my legs, I up head fake Lace, he jumps. I spent back the other way and faded. Big jumps and tries to block it, as I fade, no bet.

I let it go high from 17 feet, all draws. I used all the stuff I stole from them on them. The handle and the up fake was Big. The fade was Todd, but the shot was Lace's.

While the ball was in the air I said, "game over" then I walked away.
You got to leave after dramatically shit like that! You got to savor the flavor! Those niggas were mad. You could hear them snapping on each other as I walked away.

Lace would say, "Damn Big you let him do that to you".

Big then said, "Todd, you had him, he spent on you".

I tell them all before I bent the corner of the alley. "I got mad game now and y'all can't stop me".

I started being the number one draft choice even when the older niggas was shooting. Now that's respect. I went right after Big. You got to beat the best to be the best. cal

I heard the older fellas calling me. They called me "Earl the Pearl Monroe", a hall of fame basketball player. Another name I had gotten, because I'd let my shot go from all angles. World Be Free!

They give you names Tadpole, when they see pro shit. I got the older guys so bad one day. Lagon, Rock and a few of the older guys got it bad.

I remembered when they wouldn't let me play. I remembered when they were smacking my shit to New Orleans. They kept eliminating us at seven points. It was three eliminations seven, eleven and fifteen and the shorties were gone at seven.

Once they got to seven they'd be like, "now get out of here shortie you can't play with the big boys".

We have to leave or watch the rest of the game on the sidelines. The sidelines were for the busters and you couldn't help, feeling like a buster.

I got them back all back one day. After my father died I stayed in the alley, shooting ball. I got up early in the morning and left the dungeon late. My stamina was like the energizer bunny.

I was on every loose ball. I rip them every time they put the ball on the ground. I could see it in their face I had frustrated them with the quick stop and pops. I won like three in a row and they were out.

I think I retired them. I was all over the court. They couldn't dribble the ball, if they did I was ripping it. I was shooting their lights out and it felt good.

Joining the Black Disciples

That fall King Shorty Freeman got out of Jail. He was one of the Black Disciple leader's King. Now the BD's got a King on the street. King Larry Hoover was still was locked up. Prince Derky was locked up and David Barksdale was dead.

I wanted to meet King Shorty Freeman. I saw him from a distance in 1982. The king was Floyd and Lil Jerry's family off of 171st. We all knew these guys from the Manor. We all played ball at the park for years.

If, you were going to join an organization, you might as well, get blessed in by the king. It was a meeting up at the park so I could plug. All BD's from 169th, 171st & 175Th had to be at the park at three o'clock Sunday. I was contemplating going, but I was in fear of the OG.

That's one of the things my Mom says she wasn't raising any gangbangers. I still was in fear of her. I don't care what anybody said I couldn't get peeped. She had people everywhere watching me. I couldn't be seen at the Disciple meeting.

I didn't want to be on no list either. I did not want anybody to know other than my guys. I was joining the Black Disciple.

I said, "fuck it I am there, I am about to plug". Big D, Lace, and Freddie were going. They were already BD's. I wasn't a BD yet, but I was ready. I go up there and we were all standing around on the basketball court waiting on the king. Here comes the king and his bodyguards.

He sent one of the guards over and he said, "everybody who's plugging to get in a 360, on the field".

I am at the court, but I stay on the court. Everybody on the court went to the meeting. It started to drizzle rain. I was just watching the meeting and was shooting the ball. I probably was so small I look like I was just a kid, shooting ball.

What am I talking about? I was a kid just shooting ball! Tadpole laughs! All while they had the meeting. I was on the court by myself. I was the only one on the court and I stayed until the meeting was over. I didn't want to be seen out in opening attending the meeting. I wished they had it inside somewhere.

I was still too scared of my mother for fear of her finding out I had joined. I figured I get everything I need to know from Freddie, Lace or Big D. I walked up there with Big D.

After the meeting they asked, "why didn't I come over?"

I told them, "y'all just don't know my mother. She knew somebody around the park that was probably telling her my every move. She had somebody observing me while I was playing on the Cardinals. I never knew who it was that was peeping me. I used to be looking up in the buildings to see who was watching. She had me paranoid, she had a good look out system for me.

That's all I need is for someone to tell her I was at the Disciple meeting. I would never see light again. She was constantly telling me she was going to send me to the auty home. This is one of here favorite lines to my siblings and I. I brought you in this world and I will take you out. I believed all the shit out of that.

I thought she was going to take me out one time. I had to be about nine or ten. We went down South to Jackson Mississippi to see my uncle. We load up and go down there on the greyhound. It was just my mother and I on this trip. We went a couple of years earlier and everybody went.

This was a long ride for a shortie. I was cramped up with all this energy for twelve hours. It was different in Mississippi once we arrived. I looked around town and took notice.

There weren't any skyscrapers, not even a colt way building. The houses looked like small barns with windows. My uncle came to pick us up down town at the bus station, when we arrived. He was driving a pickup truck.

He told me to jump in the back with the luggage. There weren't any seat belt laws at the time. I jumped back there thinking we only had to go a couple of blocks. We were riding a while going down all sorts of trails.

I'm in the back gripping and clutching the side so I don't get thrown out the truck. I wasn't used to riding like that and was scared as hell. I didn't let on though! We get to the house safely and get settled. I was happy ass hell to jump out the back of the truck.

I had a bunch of older guy cousins. My uncle had about eleven kids. They got up every morning and went to the field to gather cotton. They were sharecroppers. This is like one foot in slavery and one foot out of slavery.

The people sharecropping didn't own the land they worked. It seemed that time had stopped when I went down South. I was only eight or nine and could figure that out.

In the morning the rooster would crow at five or six in the morning. Just like in the cartoons and that had me amazed. They were raising pigs so they had a pigpen. It was a chicken coop off to the side.

My older male cousins got up and fed the pigs slop. My aunt would get up about four in the morning and start breakfast.

I never seen people get up and eat breakfast like they did. The practically cook a whole pig, literally. Those biscuit with butter and jelly she made, were famous. After breakfast was done.

My uncle and cousins jumped in the truck and went to pick the cotton early before the sun came out. One morning I told them I wanted to go to the field with them. They took me to show me what they do. I couldn't understand why they were picking lint. The shit they were picking, looked like lint.

We all took a big jug of frozen ice, in an empty plastic milk gallon to the field. By twelve o'clock the water was steaming hot. The guys had to drink one of those jugs everyday or you would get dehydrated working in the field.

We drove the truck to the field on this orange red dirt. The mosquitoes were big as birds, with long ass skinny legs. I was really scared of those motherfuckas. I would take a bath and they'd have this sheer see through material that went from the ceiling to the floor. That was so the mosquitoes couldn't get through the small holes. The mosquitoes would come in and just land by the tub seeking water.

This was much different than city life. During the day the women stayed at the house. The girls shucked peas and broke down the corn and cooked.

Sometimes after work we played softball. That's where I got my P's. I could hit run and catch very good. My cousins were surprised of my skill level. They complimented me on how good I was at baseball. I would be the talk when we got back to the house.

While down in Mississippi you know me I am the adventurer. I wanted to sneak off down the path, where I seen this candy spot. Momma wasn't letting me go anywhere by myself. I had a couple of dollars and it was a pack of fifteen Now & Laters that had my name on it. I never saw a fifteen pack before in Chicago. We only had packs of seven.

I slid out when my mother was distracted and went to the truck without permission. I get the pack of Now and Laters and I cool out for a while. I was just checking out the sites like in the hood. I was sitting on the curb watching country life in Mississippi.

I busted up the whole pack while cooling out by the stand. I asked the lady for a pop.

She said, "a pop what's a pop?"

I looked at the lady like she was crazy. I just pointed at the orange Nehi.

She said, "oh you want a soda".

I said, "oh yeah a soda pop". I've been gone a while so I say to myself, "I better get back".

I knew the way home I hit the back trail. I was hoping she was talking to my auntie and wasn't worried. Mom knew how I was and she told me on the bus going down south. She also told me when we got to the house.

Do not go anywhere without my permission. I need to know your every move this ain't Chicago. This is what's going through my head on the way walking back home. Before I left I didn't think about it much.

I started to shake in my boots, because I had, to get back before she knew I was gone. I had done it before and everything went smooth, but I didn't stay long. It something about disobeying, it's cool while you're doing it.

Once it's time to see, if you got away with it. All of a sudden you get a nervous feeling in the pit of your stomach. I knew, if caught I would have hell to pay. I had a couple of Now & Laters left, but I couldn't even eat them, my stomach was so jittery.

I knew it was over soon as I was coming down the trail. It was a gathering in front of the house. They sent people off looking for me. I saw them before they seen me. Once I saw them looking for me my heart drops to my knees. I instantly got weak. It's time to pay the piper.

I get back and she's not only waiting for me, but had been looking for me hysterically.

I pops out and say, "hey y'all," as if nothings wrong trying to play it.

"Where have you been?" She asked.

I told her, "I went and got a pack a Now & Laters down at the candy stand". Wrong answer! After telling her what I was doing she snapped. She just grabbed me threw me in one of the rooms and closed the door.

She had to find whipping material, because she didn't bring any. I think this is always the worst part for me, watching her hunt for whipping material.

Once she found something she doubles the cord up and she whipped me so bad. The screams that my cousin's and uncle heard coming out of me. They came from the core of my stomach.

I was trying to escape her scraping and clawing to get under the bed. My Mom would pull me out and turn me upside down between her legs so I couldn't run. She commenced with an extension cord to whale on my ass. After ten or twelve lashes, I'd wiggle away. We'd then start the process all over again.

My uncle couldn't take it. He kept hearing me, hollering after every lash. They had to bust in there and save me after about twelve minutes. They literally had to pull her off me while she was whipping me. She was breathing hard and trying to bust through their grip. This was the most painful and horrifying moment of my young life.

My uncle said to her, "you're trying to kill this boy".

I looked at him like my savior. The look he had on his face was of concern and of surprise. He stood between my mother and me until she calmed down. He couldn't believe how strong she was and how persistent she was at trying to keep beating my ass.

My mother thought the worst when I drifted off. She thought the white people had got me like they did Emmett Till. A few years earlier they found Emmett Till in the water with a cotton gin around his neck beaten, dead. Emmett till was from Chicago too. This was all because he whistled at a white lady.

I didn't know anything about racism at the time or the incident. In Chicago my whole neighborhood & area for miles were black. Now I could see her now praying. Yaweh please don't let these white people be done gotten my child.

She knows I get into shit. She was really happy to see I was all right, but I had to pay with my ass. She also made sure I never and I mean never, walked off down there, ever again.

I wasn't going to test her. That beating was still fresh in my mind years later. I had to be real crafty or the consequences were devastating. Everything had to be planned, even down to the escape.

She would brush up on my teachings whenever I disobeyed. This was three years later. I still was petrified of her wrath. Now what I figured, if she didn't know I was at the court, when the meeting went down. I would be at the next one. I would plug at that next meeting. That didn't work out either.

I'm at home watching the news with my mother. They had just locked King Shorty Jerome Freeman back up. When I found out what they locked him up for I was flabbergasted. They caught him in a house and found over a hundred guns and weapons.

That's what they showed on the news. You know how they can spin you. The FBI had surveillance on an apartment where he was located. I'm glad I wasn't in the 360 now, because he was being watched at the meeting.

I said to myself, "what in the world was he doing in a place like that?" He's a boss and shouldn't never been around shit like that! He was just getting out. Even I knew that and I wasn't old as shit.

Well, so much for getting blessed in by the king. They gave him 25 more years. Taught me a lesso,. if they on you, they on you, don't make it easy. Don't think there not watching, if your are high profile regardless of what you do. Those alphabet boys are watching.

You can't do shit because they are watching. Now you know they got surveillance on somebody of his stature. He is the living King of the BD's. How did they know to come in there at that time and find those guns? They were watching his every move. Not just the police the FBI and maybe the CIA.

Lil Todd

Around the crib I started to hang with Todd a little more. We started saying we were cousins on the block. Now I had true back up at the time. I had someone to go get for the first time. I never used him in that way though. It felt good to have some back up just for other people to know.

We were linked up through my niece, April. Todd brother Will and my sister Regina on my father side conceived my niece, April. Todd started put me up on game once he knew Regina was my sister. He took me under his wing and I'd say. He was like an older brother to me now that I think about it. Todd never left me hanging.

He taught me about a lot of things that I needed to know. In order to get through high school such as: girls, gangbanging, clothes, stepping and cologne. He helped brought my courage out as far as being tough. I was tough to people who knew me. People who didn't know me and I didn't know them. I was always quite hesitant in getting into squabbles with people I didn't know.

I didn't have any back up until now. The Met backed me up from the outsiders. You still needed in hood backup. I wasn't worried about guys my age I was fearless. My worries were that someone big brother was going to come back and bash.

Like Folks did Trick at Rock Manor. Almost everybody had older brothers. I have seen retaliation for messing with little brothers of big brothers and its nothing nice. Who could I go to my mother? No I could never do that!

Lil Todd was short stocky and stood his ground with anybody who confronted him. I never saw him concede on a squirmish or anything. He usually was the first to say something about a situation. Todd had three bigger brothers and three older sisters that schooled him.

Todd was already riding the Black Disciple Nation Organization. This was the organization that a lot of the teenagers in the hood were representing. I was sweet with drawing the symbols in grammar school.

I used to occasionally turn my hat to the right and wear a fake earring in my right ear when I was a shortie. I wanted to be real though only Folks wore their earring in the right ear. I was wearing a fake one for fear my mother would kill me if I got it pierced.

Other than 169th I wouldn't wear my hat cocked representing Folks. This is for fear of someone knowing I was false flagging. That was representing an organization you were not a part of. Back then you could check niggas on a set, about the literature.

Folks with rank could ask you to spit knowledge and what set you representing. Who are you riding under? When you didn't know the literature or didn't say the right names. You could get smashed on the spot.

Another reason why, because the opposition might catch you slipping and break you off something. Now you getting smashed for something you're not. This happened a lot in the hood.

Either way it was quite crucial, if caught in one of those situations. Everybody in the hood was Folks and that's where I grew up. Most of the Folks from that area I either went to grammar school with or knew them from the hood. I was cool in the hood because I was hood without being Folks.

After a while though! You got to break off your boys that are plugged. It's either plug or break off from them. You got to ride, if squabble broke out.

The opposition is not going to say, "oh he cool," if you with him. You're going to get smashed too. You either ride or fade out from your hommies to stay out of shit like that. You got to fight, if you are with him. They considered you Folks if you were hanging with Folks anyway. It was just a matter of time before I was a full-fledged Black Disciple! I didn't fade I was on the team. I needed to be on somebody teams, if I can't play ball I'll play this!

Todd was sixteen when he took me under his wing. I was about three, four inches taller than Todd. It looked like we could be the same age. One day we were walking up to 169ᵗʰ & Indiana to get a drink or something from Bennies.

Bennies were the store where you waited out in front, until you see an OG. Give the OG a dollars to hook you up so they cop you some liquor or beer. We see Donald Bird and he always cops for us.

You usually would give them a beer or something for their efforts. After we got our drink and came back out. Todd looks across the street and says there go Kenny Bowie and Karate Kevin.

I responded, "who is that?"

He shouts, "They are some motherfucking Hooks from the white building, what are they doing over here?"

Hooks was a disrespectful name for Black Stones, Vicelords, Cobar Stones or anybody riding under the five-point star. The "All is Wells", organization had a cane for one of their symbols so there's your analogy.

He knew them from Meneen grammar school. Folks would call you a Hook in order to start squabble.

Todd shouted out, at them, "Black Disciple" then he started throwing up III's and dropping the five to disrespect them.

I am like, "awe shit" to myself.

They shout back equivalently the same. They used to call Folks glazed donuts or cole pricks. We started walking toward each other. Todd knew the guys, but I didn't. I'm like damn damn damn this shit is about to kick off. Kenny Bowie was standing in Todd face and he's about five inches taller than Todd. He reaches out and tries to mush Todd in the face.

Todd steps back and in one-motion snatches off his belt buckle. The buckle spelled his name Todd and started swinging at the bigger and taller Kenny Bowie. He landed one and kept dude off of him. He did it by swinging in a back and forth motion. 20 to 70 degree angle on both sides up and down.

Now I've heard of these dudes, but never saw them before. I knew they were Stones and there have been a couple of squabbles with these guys. His name sounded dangerous. Karate Kevin and Kenny Bowie so who I got to fight Karate Kevin? My man had karate in front of your first name. Does that mean you know karate?

At first I looked in amazement of how fast we got in to conflict. I just stood there watching at first. This was my first encounter with somebody that was known out the hood from the opposition.

Again, I was quite hesitant in getting in that since I didn't know of the guys. Karate Kevin didn't jump, so I didn't either. One on one, I did step up though and had Todd back. I stayed right next to Todd and I got in my stance.

I was gazing at the other guy to see what he was going to do. Dude didn't move I guess he didn't know me either. I was dark-skin so I had an automatic rough and tough look.

All of a sudden the police rolled up. The crowd dispersed and we headed back to the Met. Kevin and Kenny went back toward the white building. We still got the drink and headed back to the Met.

We went and sat on the back porch steps next to the gangway to get to the Met. We bust the drank open, blessed it with the III's. This was an introduction to holding down your hood. This was quite normal for Todd.

I wondered to myself while we busted open the drank. "Did I have his back or was I too scared to move out?" I didn't know, because it didn't happen. Todd and I made a pack on that drink to have each other's back.

After that I slowly started making the transition to being Folks. I was hanging with them, drinking with them, shooting ball with them, playing games with them, and fighting with them. Now I am a BLACK DISCIPLE.

Who else was I'm going to roll with? These were my boys, my hommies, people who got my back, if squabbles are going down. That's what I need I was known from 169th to 171st & Rhodes to 171st & State. I knew the Folks all through the land anyway.

When I got plugged it was like family all around the hood. The school I went to was predominantly Folks. Eddie Holmes had my back when I was a shortie. Ed Holmes was major so what he said, goes. Ed and my sister Barbara went to Rock Manor together. I used to deliver the paper to his house. He got a couple people off me when I was a shortie.

Therefore, it was easy for me to pick when it came down to my team. I was going to roll with BD's. The Black Gangster Nation organizations united as one under the six-point star. As long as you were Folks you could go on any Folks set and kick it. As long as you were Folks and it was Folk's neighborhood.

GD's and BD's cooled out together without tripping. If there was conflict it was usually handled on a one on one basis. I must say after becoming Folks it did feel like family. It was instant.

First it was, "Colo is Todd cousin, don't fuck with him". To that's Folks with the handles on and off the court. I was carrying my own weight.

Little did Todd know that day, I had a few butterflies. These guys were much older and bigger than I physically. We were about to straight squabble just walking to the store. This is a whole another level than a school-fight.

Your name travels squabble after squabble. People know your name before they see your face. That's how I knew who they were. They couldn't say who I was until later. The opposition didn't know me like that. They were no Stones we were fighting like that for miles. All the Stones in the neighborhood we knew, we knew them and were cool with them.

If, Todd was scared he didn't show it, shit, he kicked it off. His actions on how he moved spoke for themselves. Even though! The guys were bigger than him and he went straight at him.

Todd gave me a clear-cut example right then about banging. Go straight at them no bullshit. Whatever, you do to him he would have done it to you, so if it's on, it's on! Todd didn't know that I was scared or not sure of myself. He didn't let on he knew. After that day I wasn't scared anymore after seeing how it's done. The butterflies didn't come anymore.

Well it got around the hood Todd and I had squabble with Brothers from the white building. We defended the hood. I think Todd told the story that way and he knew I didn't say a word. Todd would always tell the story Colo and I moved out on those niggas. You couldn't tell in my face, I was scared though. If there was a stomach meter, for butterflies, I would've been on full hilt.

That was Karate Kevin. I'm not a rocket scientist, but if you have karate before your name. Does that mean you've been trained in karate or know how to kick very well? What I would learn later nicknames are just names. My nickname should have been Ali, if that's the case.

I don't know why, but Todd sort of looked after me. Even before my niece, April came along. He often bet on me in slap boxing matches or body punching matches. He went against others in the hood for me. He wasn't nothing but sixteen. Rod had a father in the household and it showed in his independence.

The fact that someone else believed I could do it, motivated me. When these confrontations took place I had to win. One thing he was doing, because he knew I was sweet with my hands. I just needed the confidence.

Todd low-key was promoting me. He knew I was cold with my bangers. Everybody around the house didn't know at first. Todd knew cause we always body punched. I fought Robert, but that was a couple years earlier. The next time I was straight for the battle.

Tookie on Prairie lived in one of those colt way buildings. You know where you walk in the corridor and there are about four entrances. There are six apartments with three floors in each entrance. Two entrances were in the front and two in the back of the whole building development.

'Took' had a party in there one night and invited his Black Stone friends from Simeon. You know Tookie was a Stone. That was one thing about us if you lived around there and you were a Stone, you got a pass. If you brought some Stones in the hood then you got a problem. You couldn't let it go by. The reason why the next day more Stones are going to show up. These Stone might not be that friendly. Got to let them know, we ain't no hoes over here.

Anyway Lil Todd, Brandon, and Big D planned for me to go to Tookie's party with my hat banged to the right. I was a shortie and had to go on a mission. We knew it was going to be a bunch of Brothers and Sister at the party.

You can get smashed in some hoods just for wearing your hat a certain way. You can get smashed in the hood for what colors you wear. We weren't on that, just respect the hood and you can be who you be.

First, we got bubbled and put the plan all the way together. The plan was I was going to walk in the party by myself.

Who made that plan? John asked.

Lil Todd was doing the talking. I had my blue leather union hat on banged to the right representing to the fullest. We were walking down 169th street alley in between Calumet and Prairie. We were getting our bubble in and smoking the weed. Now it's time to roll.

Todd was like, "Took is cool so we just ain't going to bust up his shit. We just going to get on there hoes and smoke and drank they're shit up. If they don't fuck with you Colo then fuck it. They try some shit, we got their ass".

I went in first, Took knows me I say, "what up Tookie?"

He responded, "what up?" and let me in the house.

Todd and them came in about three minutes later. Everybody, else who came with me came in the house with their hat, bang to the left. Yeah, it was a straight Stone party.

At first! None of the Stones said anything to me they just looked. They were so surprised, I'm blatantly carrying the nation and I am all by myself. I went over to their bar and poured a drank.

If looks could kill I'd be dead. I just played oblivious to what was going on! They might have thought this nigga can't know, he's doing too much. He might not know about his hat being broke off.

When the music came on I started to dance with this girl. I was bubbled and wasn't worried about shit. While dancing I started throwing up the treys. Oh they know now I am a Disciple. I'm peeping them, but playing like I don't see shit. I'm dancing with a drank in my hand and I'm having fun.

You could see them gathering like they were ready to move. I wasn't disrespecting them. I was just letting them know how I carry it.

They get aggressive and they asked me while piling around me, "what's up nigga, what s up, all is well?"

I replied, "You already know what's up. I kept throwing the treys up. They were sleep. I got my niggas in here figuring out who is who. After they all started rushing me.

Brandon and Todd said, "take it outside".

The Stones start pushing me toward the door. They didn't want to move inside Tookie's house. I'm figuring Took should've told them to cool out, since he knows I'm hood. Instead he was going to let them move on me. We play football all day long with Took in the hood and he didn't speak up.

What he told me is, I had to go. When I was leaving out Todd and them went out before I did. That's what the Stones wanted. They were waiting on me to come outside. As I'm coming out the door two or three of them start throwing up fives.

Next, they tried to mush me in my face with the five. I was keeping them back by pushing them out my face. I was keeping a good distance, my three feet and shouting, "Black Disciple".

Once they tried to mush me. All the Folks turned their hat to the right and started throwing up the treys. Todd stole on one of the Stones then I hit dude in front of me.

Todd stole on him again then shouted out "BD nigga". Shit broke out. Now everybody is running outside. I get down the steps and walk outside. I see Big D just pick this nigga up and slam him to the ground, Dboe style. He then grabbed someone else and did the same thang, bam.

Todd told me to get on security. At that point I ran outside and gets out to the front entrance. I get on security to make sure the law didn't sneak up or any more Stones block or us us in the entrance. Some of the other Folks came and then it was over. All of us who came together, left, because we kicked it off. Can't be around when the police come. Why do it, if you going to go to jail?

Well really they kicked it off, because they started it. Later on that night I heard they fired up Tookie house for bringing those off brand nigga's through. I heard a Flower got shot in the hand. A Flower is a female riding under the five. The equivalent for us were called Queens.

Word is she was throwing up the five and got shot in the hand while doing it. A nigga got shot in the chest, but they got him to the hospital.

Before he got shot heard he was shouting, "he wasn't scared of no gapper", pop pop pop shortly after he said that! He lived though!

We wouldn't have done shit. If they would've, respected our hood. That's one thing about the BD's. You would get a pass as long as you didn't disrespect. I didn't disrespect any of them. I just was throwing up the III.

They fell into the trap, if it was just me there, they would've smashed me with no question. That's why they got smashed. Do unto others as others would do to you, so we smash them.

Todd little ass showed me what heart is about. I was gone off of Muhammad Ali and Bruce lee. I talked shit like Ali for sure and was just as confident. Bruce Lee used to fight multiple opponents and run through them. That's what you had to do in the hood. The move out factor could be the equation of 20 to 1. That's when everybody and they momma is whooping your ass.

I practiced boxing and karate relentlessly. The move out factor causes a pumpkin head, if not prepared, Tadpole. The pumpkin head must be avoided at all cost. The pumpkin head is when your head is beaten swollen.

Your head could swell up to two three times the original size. Your mother wouldn't even recognize you.

I imitate a ladies voice, "That ain't my boy is it? No that ain't my boy, but somebody boy is fucked. She looks again and screams, "oh shit that is my boy". Those are his clothes he had on this morning". Your own momma won't even recognize you.

Slick Freddie

Getting challenged happened at any time. You could be walking the hood and challenged to a match. The time Freddie called me out. I'll jump ahead a bit. I was walking with the GD's Grimes and Sacks. We were high than a motherfucka. Freddie was over there by the Germans sitting on the car. This is after Freddie graduated from the Robe.

He said, "Colo word getting around that you're cold with the hands. Let me see what you got".

I always looked up to Freddie and he's calling me out.

I 'm high so at first I'm like, "naw Freddie you my guy".

He started laughing and said, "just what I thought".

He said it in front of the Germans like I was a hoe. It wasn't like a hoe, but in a sarcastic voice, while laughing. Like I am a little nigga. Now I've looked up to Freddie for years.

My first year at the Robe we had a party at King Martin College. I was with Cassius. A buddy I met from school. He lived across Halsted. On the way out the party I see Freddie get stole on by some guys.

Three or four of the Folks was on his head from off of Halsted. Instead of taking a stomping he got chase a bit, but came back.

Cassius was like, "they moving on your hommie".

Freddie looks at me, but it doesn't resonates to him I can go. He still thinks I am a little nigga. I had his back though!

Big D came out of the party. Freddie told Big D what happened. By that time all the Folks from across the tracks came out. Lace, Big D, Freddie and I were off the Met and it was about ten more of us. Freddie was looking for the nigga who stole on him.

It was about ten of them guys from off Halsted. Freddie found one of the guys who tried to move. He had about ten guys with him. All twenty of us were all in a 360.

Freddie pointed at one dude.

The dude he pointed at said, "what up?"

Things understood don't need to be spoken upon! Freddie blazed him with about five or six blows in an exchange nonstop, real quick. Dude name was Dee Dee he attacked. Dee dee was swinging back, but he wasn't connecting. It was one on one and nobody moved.

Freddie was in football shape and Dee Dee was in banging on the block shape. Dude didn't have a chance. During the may lay the police rolled up. Freddie was still fighting the guy. The police jumped out and grabbed Freddie. He then put the pistol to Freddie head and grabbed his shirt. They were in the middle of the street on 169th & Wentworth.

Once Freddie saw it was the twisters and not someone else with the gun. Freddie snatched away quickly from the twister and jumped in the wind. After the fight Freddie had enough energy to jack rabbit out the policeman grasp and jump in the wind.

To me Freddie had done some sweet shit, after getting stolen on! He settled the business before leaving, saving face. That was some real gangster shit. I had his back though!

We all walked up to McDonalds on 169th & State to make sure Freddie was straight. Four niggas tried to move on Freddie and he get away. He comes back smashes dude ass then gets away from the twisters. Yep, I was impressed.

He called me out though! I had to go. I immediately get in my stance and he gets off the car and get in his. When you go toe to toe with somebody you're about to find something out, ding. Gladiators got to go toe to toe, Tadpole.

I jump out the gate, because I know Freddie is fast as hell. I can't let him get off. I was so fast, off the faint. You couldn't see where the swings were coming. I was releasing from different angles. Smack, smack smack and down goes Freddie, down goes Freddie, down goes Freddie.

Everybody looked in amazement at Freddie on the ground. Shit I looked in amazement.

I was bouncing and said, "I told you I ain't no little nigga no more". When we slap box Adrian, it ain't no pitty patter shit. We're trying to slap the shit out of you, leave that handprint on the face. He couldn't believe how fast I swung probably.

If Freddie was a little high, he wasn't high anymore.

He gets back up and looks at me and says, "come on".

I said, "all right. He comes at me, I swing, Freddie ducks. I swing three more times and he ducks those real sweet. He is bobbing and weaving. I'm trying to time him on the bob. I swing three more times. I miss them all off the bob and weave.

Freddie comes back up, swinging on his last bob, back up with two quick slaps, bow boww. I hit the ground. This is the first time I ever hit the ground. I get back up quickly and jump in my stance.

The Germans and Grimes immediately says, "that's enough Folks". We both had that look in our eyes, some beast type shit. You can see it in the eyes, warrior type shit was going on!

They all said, "leave it alone" while laughing at what just went down.

Freddie looked at me like he couldn't believe it. Yeah I've grown up now and I've watched you for years. I was going to get him, still.

I had a whole bunch of shit people hadn't even seen yet. I learned from that move Freddie did on me. It was a cold move off of an aggressive opponent. I've been slapping people to the ground with that very move ever since.

Earning Stripes

Everybody came after what they heard I did to Slick Freddie. It's getting around the streets that I can't be fucked with, with the hands. I had to go through the whole hood. I went through the Met and Indiana. Lace, Todd and Freddie were the best competion

Your brother Slick Coole and I challenged me. Coole came out the your house and saw me walking by.

He was just looking at me at first and said, Colo I heared what you doing with your hands let me see what you got".

He wanted to body punch. I let him get off to see how he punched. He had looping upper cuts. I was going straight at his chest. After a couple of exchanges he was straight.

He was impressed and said, "Colo you hit hard ass hell", while laughing. White boy Slopes got the same treatment in the game room on Indiana. He had looping upper cuts too. I can get off three shots before you land one. We had a couple of exchanges and then he was straight.

White boy slopes said, "you got guns Colo".

I never quit, so if you are the one who stops first I count that as a victory TKO baby. I body punched wrestled or slapped boxed them all and they were impressed. White boy Slopes has a older brother named Lucien that joined the service. He had a sister too and they all were light like Pete. They both were Folks but they looked white.

John, Lace tried to go up against Emus and I at one time, remember Emus.

Emus answers, "You know I remember".

Emus and I were coming back from the dungeon through the gangway. We pop out on the Met and see Lace on his porch.

He saw us and just jumped off his porch and said, "you and Emus. I'll take both of y'all in slap boxing right now.

I responds, "Lace you ain't ready for me. You can't take both of us. Emus and I cross the street in a hurry once he said that!

We caught him coming out his gate.

He looked confident and said, "you ain't shit I'll take you and Emus".

I squint my eyes in disbelief and looked at him crazily and said, "Lace both of us".

He looked grim, got in his stance and said, "come on". Andrea people couldn't understand how quick I developed. I went from this type of dude to this type of dude with confidence. The transition was maybe six months in all areas. It didn't matter how old you were. When I was thirteen going on fourteen my wings spreads.

I get on the left side and Emus get in on his right side. Lace was more worried about me so one of his eyes was preoccupied. I'd halfway attack and diverts his attention. Emus and I knew how to attack from playing, smash em.

I diverted his attention and Emus reared back and slaps the shit out of Lace. Whaaccckkk, slapped him hard as hell. Hit him so hard he had to shake it off!

I said, "damn Emus, hell yeah". Oh yeah Lace had the five fingerprints on his face. Lace was light skin too.

Lace got off me so quick and made quick work out of Emus. I tried to interfere, but he was too quick. Whaack wackk whaak after he got three or four slaps back.

Emus was straight. Emus was like, "all right I am straight".

I'm bouncing around and said, "don't quit Emus, lets fuck him up".

Emus started straightening his glasses and said, "y'all go head".

Lace had knocked them sideways on his head. After that Lace and I went head up on the Met.

Lace was like, "it's just me and you now".

I said, "you think that's a good thang?" We didn't go toe to toe. Lace and I didn't have too because neither one of us steps back much. We did a lot of footwork in a small space, but had the whole street.

It was like art or a symphony, Barisnicoff. Lace could really slap box. We really didn't get any licks in hard. We were just nipping each other. That means our defense was scandalous.

He'd go on offense until I could counter off a miss and make him go on defense. It was music how we boxed and defensed each other. We utilize every option not to get hit: The ducks, the head movement, the faint and the dancing. Everybody on the block saw us getting down.

You see Lace was on his tiptoes swinging and me the same locked. Swing, swing he counter, I counter, I swing, he counter Lace was the best defensively I've slapped boxed.

When you can't hit a nigga and he's right there in front of you, he's good. I got him across the head on the duck, but no clean blows. I see though I am retiring motherfuckas, because after they slapped boxed me. They don't do it again.

I was always challenging people after that, cause I was working on shit in my basement. I never let people know I was on their heels. I always practiced or was trying to spar.

Emus and Matt were my sparring partners for some of my moves. It used to be funny going with Emus. I used to be smacking his glasses in the bushes. We'd square up and I'd faint and swaack and his glass would go flying.

He'd pick them up and I do it again the same exact way. I'd laugh my ass off because the glasses landed in the same bush and in the same spot, like a replay. Emus was better than most people thought. I really taught Emus to slap box so I knew he was good. That's how he got Lace he was sleeping on Emus. Emus just didn't really have problems. His older brother Coole was a true goon.

I only went against the goons, cause if you couldn't fuck with them. You damn sure couldn't fuck with me. I was polished when I hit Prairie and Indiana up. After a while I was respected all through the land for my hands. If you don't take the challenge I count that as a victory too. You concede that I am superior. Which puts me in a class of, don't fuck with that nigga, class.

Only thing though! That would only last for only so long. Niggas started shooting. If you ain't got no heater the toughest niggas is the one's pulling the trigger. This variable evens the odds dramatically.

A weak skinny niggas, who couldn't fight, but will pop your ass. Now he has the power because he's willing to do it. You can talk all the shit you want, if you willing to pull that trigger. Things have changed.

It used to be like you went and got a gun when niggas rushed you. Going to get a gun when you had squabble, was a sign of weakness. Especially, if the fight was one on one you were a hoe to go get a gun. When it was two on one we still didn't go get a gun. We just came back with more niggas and had a brawl.

Now niggas are getting guns if you in a one on one fight. Step on his shoe if you want too. The nigga with the gun got all the power. No more of the tough guy running shit. The boxing shit was becoming obsolete in the street once the shooting started.

We still kept on our toes in the hood. It was always somebody to walk up and challenge you. When your good everybody wants they're shot at you. Goons want to know if you can or can't beat them. They just got to know, if you worthy of the respect people are giving you. They found out quickly when challenging me, you can't fuck with me.

The only one with the guts, to try me more than once on the Met, was Smiley. Smiley would try his hardest, but he couldn't touch me. He would fuck up a lot of other niggas with the hands, but he couldn't get me.

I'd hit him with the snake style. Striking from all angles like a cobra. I'd laugh, while slapping his face red as a beet. I'd connect with the rake slap. That's slapping your opponent's forehead all the way down to his chin.

This blow touches eyes, nose and lips and it has to be set up. This slap works when your opponent is leaning back or trying to duck. You hit them with that and all those facial areas you struck are on fire. I could see the blood coursing through his face. I heated him up with that slap.

Oh no I didn't run through him, cause Smiley could box. He just would make a mistake and you just couldn't do that with me. When I slapped box Smiley I had to quit, because he was not going to quit. After I heated him up four or five times I'd stop. You win, if you stop on the mercy rule.

I'd be like, "that's enough".

He would be like, "come on".

He'd be squinting and red all over.

I'd be like "Naw you my man Smiley that's enough. Let's go tomorrow or something, but today that's enough". I would be laughing of course. I'm looking at his face when I come to this decision.

He'd be like, "fuck it I'm a going to get your ass one day".

My last test was going against Otis, Bluski brother he was older. What am I talking about? Everybody was older except, Smiley and Emus. Otis knew karate and was a pure thief. He used to snatch bikes. He had the sweetest bikes for miles. I know he had a different Swinn for everyday of the week.

He was fast as the wind and I ain't bullshitting. One day he was smoking a joint and the police rolled up quick. We didn't see them at first and they jump out. Otis looked and jumped in the wind so fast. The police didn't even begin to chase him. He was still smoking the joint while he was running looking at them. They just got back in the car and pulled off.

He was about four or five years older than I. I was taller with the long arms. Everybody started challenging from everywhere once the word spread. Colo is taking out the goons easily.

First they be like, "I don't care who he is he can't fuck with me".

Once they felt or just seen the quickness from my blows. Everybody stop challenging me and jumped on the bandwagon. I was fast and good as fuck.

One day Otis challenged me to some karate and I was hesitant. He just got out of jai and heard that I was a beast. I had some kicking skills, but it wasn't up to his caliber. Otis goes into his stances and poses then starts air kickboxing. He's kicking the air, looking sweet. He's doing round houses, double kicks and shit like that!

I didn't want to seem like no punk so I said, "let's slap box".

I think Lacey and Lil' Todd and Freddie was on the stoop. That's John's porch.

Otis replied, "we can do that, come on".

Wrong answer Otis! This was my area of expertise. I could cut up somebody slap boxing. I had to be careful can't under estimate anybody. I was confident in my skills with a formidable foe now. I had arrived and nobody knew I was coming.

Someone made a bell like sound "ding" and it was on. Since my arms were longer I used the countering method. Anytime he swung either I'd duck and come up with two or three slaps. Or lean back, just out of reach and retaliate. Once I did that he opened up the match. He swings I counter, smack smack smack and you could hear me doing the snake like sound. ssssss everytime I swung. ssssss smack smack sss smack smack ssssss smack smack smack.

I could here Todd in the background "go head cuz, go head cuz. Show them what you know".

After a couple of more slaps Otis conceded the match. Otis was very light complexion with a yellowish like look to his face. When I finished, he looked like an Indian his face was so red.

I left out the circle flawless victory. That bout flew around the hood like wild fire. Soon the coldest guys were coming at me challenging me from out the neighborhood. I would send them on their way. I practiced all the time. I body punched all the time. I did karate and wrestled all the time. Again, I hated to lose so I would practice whatever, relentlessly.

When somebody believes in you, you don't want to let them down. This helped me understand that reputation means nothing or a hard look. See what they've got or where their heart is at? After you bust him one across the mouth let's see what he does? A motherfucka will sell wolf tickets all day long, until you bust em' in his shit.

Something miraculous happens at this point. After getting chin checked he either bows out or now he understands what going on! They understand that I ain't no hoe with my hands.

They've realized that they just fucked up for challenging me. It was just like in the karate movies. You want to challenge me, "come oonnnn!" I say it in Chinese dialect. I love seeing that look on their face. The look when you bust his ass for talking shit.

I'll never forget my sister's boyfriend Wayne. He challenged me in the hallway coming in my house. Let me see what you got little nigga. I tell him Wayne this shit I got is like nothing you ever seen before or let alone boxed against.

I warn him and I'm smiling like I know something he doesn't. A couple of years earlier he used show me some karate kicks. I guess he thought he was taking me under his wing.

Wayne was off of 161st King Drive. We square up in the hallway in my house. He didn't know and I was just smiling all the time. The hallway is narrow I can touch both sides without stretching my arms all the way out.

Anyway I hit him with the snake cobra style. I'd hold my hand by my face while boxing. I would roll my fist in a circle with my elbows cocked sideways. Next, my right arm and fist would be left straight up, ready to strike.

The left hand would be horizontal in front of my face. This gave me a superior blocking, striking and ducking advantage. Both hands are in the striking and blocking position. By doing this it took all the telegraph, off of my swings.

I constantly moved my arms by fainting and striking. You didn't know where they were coming from literally. I used this style, because of the small area. That's releasing backhands, rakes and short right hands due to the small area. I needed to strike and be quick. I couldn't let him use his length. I had to get under him.

I get in on him after a quick duck and release three quick bursts. I did it three times in a row. I get on him, jump off, see where he at and get on him again. After the last attack dude had to shake his head in disbelief or to shake the cobb webs out. He literally shook his head for about three seconds

Either way it looked like in the cartoons. His eyes were bucked out his head and he was wondering what hit him? Todd had my confidence soaring as a boxer. He was making sure everyone knew I was the man with the hands.

Todd taught me more than just how to bang. He fought me like a pit in the neighborhood. Todd would let me wear his gold and silver when he wasn't wearing them.

He just was there for me whatever I needed. He would often put up for me, on the bubbles. Sometimes I didn't have any money.

He'd say "I got cuz on the drank". That meant he had to put up double on the bubble.

He was carrying me and I thought that was real cool. I didn't want to wear it out. Sometimes I would accept and sometimes I wouldn't. I didn't get high all the time. I didn't drink all the time. I cooled out is what I called it.

To get high and drunk was money and time. When I cooled out I didn't do a lot of talking. Everybody was older than me so I just chill. I just sucked up the game. I didn't want to feel like a leach.

A leach is around with no money all the time and a habit that somebody else is paying for it. They talked about leaches bad. They'll let you get high, but you were talked about. I'd just spin them and go shoot basketball or something. You can't be a leach on the strip. At least my pride wouldn't let me be a leach.

My mother says, "a man is supposed to stand on his own feet".

Todd's father Mr. Stables owned his own gas station and mechanic shop. Todd worked there when he wanted too. He always had money stashed always. He always had money in his pocket. He always had his own weed. He had his own drank and own car.

He was a very independent person and did a lot of things on his own. He really didn't hang out with his older brothers. If anything Todd kicked it with niggas in the hood not particular on the block. He always was introducing me to guys out of the neighborhood

This is a characteristic I tried to pattern myself. Todd was good at holding his own down. He didn't care what other people thought.

His favorite phrase, "fuck them suck up niggas Colo".

While cooling out with Todd he'd school me on different things while blowing. We often boxed in the basement. All it took was for one of us to punch each other and it was on!

His younger brother Mark, Abdolla and nephew Mike, would always cheerlead for Todd. We had those battles in the privacy of his basement. They would hear us boxing and run down the stairs and watch.

This would motivate me to go to work. Everybody in the house was cheering against me. Even though Todd was stronger and older I was holding my own. I never let on that those blows were breaking me up. I just kept throwing blows back.

His mother Mrs. Stables would yell down, "stop all that fighting each other down there".

I never quit though! He didn't know I was so glad when someone or anyone intervened. I never showed it. He was throwing blows. He wouldn't slap box me but we would body punch.

He would say, "your lucky".

I'd reply, "naw your lucky" as we stare each other down nose to nose, literally.

Todd was shorter than me so when he swung he was already at my chest, stomach or ribs. I had to bend down to get in position to hit him or I would hit him in the face. This happened a few times. I had to study how to get down on him while body punching a short guy.

After we would finish we would get high. He'll move some clothes around in his stash spot. He'd pull out a half of Martell and roll up a joint. We would get high trip out and listen to some Isley Brothers or some J.B's.

After the high from the weed sets in we'd get up and step.

Mrs. Stables would yell down stairs, "I smell those funny cigarettes".

Todd would ease her concern and say, "okay momma". Todd then would take out some air freshener and spray it in the vents.

Now, stepping is something that Todd showed me how to do. Everybody in the hood knew how to step. Bluski was sweet with the stepping. Some people are smooth and just glides when stepping. He was one of them.

Todd was sweet he had his own style and he was short. Short people really look sweet stepping, if they got their own style. He could get his legs in position quick to do his little moves. He'd throw the JB's on! Pass the Peas would be playing.

He'd say, "come on cuz". We'd practice in the basement for a while. That's one thing about us. We didn't just get high and just buzz out. We got up and did something. We balled or stepped. Todd had a car so we'd go by the skyway to race his Oldsmobile Cutlass. He was always doing something.

He'd be like, "let's shoot down town to Uno's and grab a deep dish pizza". The stepping was the shit though when you got high. I love stepping, because you create your own moves. I had to get used to leading, if I was going step with a girl.

Everybody would have their Frank Foti's or their Stacy Adams over their shoulder in a bag, sporting a tailor made. You never wore the slippery shoes just in case some shit broke out. You put them on only when you hit the floor, to step. Guys would step with each other putting on dazzling moves. Spin moves, splits, slides and a lot of complex turns. Stepping was one dance the Folks could do and it wouldn't be frowned on! Some Folks did the breaking and pop locking, but usually Folks just watched the people who were sweet. Most Folks just does the gangster boogie dance.

Jew Town

When the Folks stepped at high profile functions, you had to have your gear straight. Nothing looks sweeter than a nigga suited up from head to toe sliding across the floor at the party. To get straight we used to go to Jew town and get the suits made. Those Jews down there were cold with sewing the clothes.

Right in the middle of 12Th & Halsted was a team of Jewish tailors stores. These boys were bad. You go in the shop and pick your material and color of your suit. Next, they'd bring out different books for you to look at for styles.

This was the best part you design your own suits. This wasn't a suit off the rack. You tailor made your own suit. Next you would go pick up a Bossalini or a Dobbs for headgear.

Jew town was where all the clothing, shoes, hats, and suits. Whatever you wanted to get for clothing Jew town was a spot. It was the spot where you could haggle and get a good deal. You go to Jew Town it's was people on the streets. The outside market would be selling socks, naked movies, tops, incense and oils. Anything you could possibly want you could get it in Jew Town.

The first time I went Todd and Lace took me down there. It was a deep criminal element down in Jew Town. It was the hood and the hood knew you had money coming down to Jew Town. Niggas would go to Jew Town and get robbed for clothes and money.

Everything was moving fast outside. It was an outside market for hustlers then it was also storefronts. Outside they sold all your accessories. You have your outside restaurants on the corners. The Jews had it banging on those corners. They sold grilled sausages, pork chops, hamburgers and hotdogs.

It was the sweet grilled onions they put on the sandwiches that was boss pimp. They would load them up on whatever you ordered. Lace and Todd used to go every weekend for a while to grab something up to wear. I joined them a couple of times. Lace and I got paid from the paper branch. After we got our clothes we'd eat a Jew Town polish on the way out.

The ride on the bus down to Jew town was fun. The hustlers on bus were hustling three-card molly or pea and cap game. I used to peep they come on in threes. One nigga is going to play and win low-key to get your interest up on a crowded bus. It could be a female too. Dude working the game is going to have a bunch of money in his hand.

He'll cheesed out dude who was betting him and say, "that ain't shit".

He'll say some shit like, "I got plenty of money, you win some, you lose some, you win some, you lose some. You want some get some. You see how easily dude just got forty dollars you can get some too". You got to play to win that's how they get you to play.

Ooops after they get you for a quick hundred you like, "damn". I see them getting the white people on the way downtown all the time. They got me for twenty, one time I got suckered up. I bet dude just knowing I had a come up. I just knew the pea was under that middle cap.

I was watching and just knew the pea was under it. He raised it and it was nothing under the cap. Cracked my head open when I looked and saw nothing. He then slapped my hard-earned twenty dollars on his knot so quick.

Next thing you know, dude who won the money gets off the bus. The dude who was running the pea game and another dude, you didn't know were with him both get off.

One of his guys get off the front of the bus. The others are getting off the back. I'm watching these niggas cause they got my hard earned twenty. They are all getting off the bus together. They are working together.

This was the first and last time I played. Even if I'd a won it was a possibility I would get stuck up by the one I didn't know was with him.

When it was no game on the bus all we did was talk about each other. Mainly they got on me, because I was the youngster. Two or three years older was a whole lot back then growing up. On the way home they would roast me. I bought these Devil jeans one time. They said I overpaid for them.

Here go Todd, "Lace, Colo done paid the rent after they sold him those jeans. Those Jews rolled the red carpet out to bus and Colo dumb ass went for it. He wanted those jeans. I tried to tell him, but he wasn't paying me any attention".

Lace asked, "how much you pay for those jeans Colo?"

I'm like, "fuck y'all I didn't 't over pay, I'm the one who got over. I know how to Jew those Jews, nigga". Lace and Todd got everybody on the bus laughing.

Here's Lace, "soon as Colo walk out the store Todd, they started closing up, pulling the gates down aha aha haaa".

Lace started taking with a Jewish accent, "the Jews in back were laughing at his ass while saying, got another one". We saw him when he got off the bus, hee hee haa. His eyes were too wide open, looking like a tourist. We're straight for the rest of the day. I thought we had to work the whole day. We got us another sucker, early ahha hha".

Lace returns to his own voice, while laughing. "It's only 11 o'clock in the morning and we on our way back home. They're closing up, ain't no refunds nigga". Man they had the whole bus laughing.

They took me down to Jew Town those couple of times and showed me what was up. I went down there all the time to get my gear. I went there or on, 169th Halsted. I made my own money from my paper route. I did my own shopping so momma wasn't dressing me anymore.

I didn't go to parties in grammar school. If it wasn't school sponsored, it was a rap. I was always in church and my mother just didn't fund shit like that. I couldn't dance or step until Todd showed me. This came from no exposure in the kiddy discos.

How you going to get close to the girls if you can't dance?

The girls will be like, "you not on a team, for any sport, not even swimming".

The prospect of you being popular wasn't very high if you are not on the squad. Everybody wants to be popular. Nerds were not in play coming up. The girls weren't ooowwing over the smart guys. They wanted the cool or athletic guys.

If you couldn't dance then the girls wouldn't dance with you. She would leave you on the floor, if you couldn't dance. Therefore, no dance no possible chance to be smooth with the girls. I was very shy and wasn't very popular with the girls. When I did start going with Cassius. Cassius is my high school buddy. He knew I couldn't dance and tried to teach me.

I was afraid that the girl would say no if I asked. I went to those Darobe or King Martin house parties. I'd look crazy trying to interact with the girls. One time I did get a dance. The girl was pretty too.

Cassius would look from a distant and once I started dancing he'd started to laugh at me. The girl would see him laughing and she'd stop dancing and look at me. I tried to keep dancing and play him off.

I was warm inside from Slept Rock laughing and she started looking funny at me. I got off beat and she walked away. I can cut a rug now, but then I was terrified of looking like a fool.

Todd could dance, step and sing. He knew how to talk to girls.
I often said to myself, "his brother's and sisters must have taught him, because he was smooth".

He had this girl friend named Anecia. She was cool and he'd game her. I used to sit back and watch the older teenagers. I don't think they knew, but I peeped my guys on the block game out. They basically helped me through that teenage transition. I watched everybody and took the best part or pick up the best part of their game.

I'm controlling this body, but it's a lot of my niggas that are in me. How else was I going to learn? Mom can't or I was not going to let her teach me these things. She can't teach me how to be a man. She tells me what she thinks a man, supposed to do. It was damn close though! She gave me much game on being a man.

Todd was dumb ass hell. He'd crack on anybody. He used to be mean to these two fat girls who rode by our block all the time. They had this little small car. I must say they did have some of their body parts oozing out the car. That's how big they were.

We'd be sitting on Lacey or John's porch.

Todd would see them riding and yell, "fat hoes, hey fat hoes, hey fat hoes. One was dark-skin with the red lips and real big. The other one was brown skinned and not as big, but big.

They would yell back, "fuck you, we going to catch your little ass one day.

After they said that, Todd would tell them, "go ahead on, fat hoes, faattt hoooes". When they took to long leaving he would make them pay.

He would hold the notes, "Faaaat Hooooooeeees. Biiiggg Faaaatttt Hooooeees". We would join in, "Fattt Hoeess" all in unison.

We would be laughing at them, because this happened every other day.

We'd see the car and let Todd know, "Todd there they go".

As soon as he spotted them he'd yell instantly, "fattt hooess". They must've lived close around the area, because they rode by the block all the time. Todd wouldn't stop he had the girls about to cry.

They caught him one day by himself and stopped the car and threaten Todd. Todd told us he was out they're by himself and he said the girls caught him. They rode up on him and asked Todd, not to say fat hoes anymore.

Todd obliged them and told them he was just having fun. He told them he wouldn't do anymore and we got cool with the girls. The bigger one moved on the block later so she became family.

Chapter VIII

The Stains

Listen Andrea, John, Tadpole and Emus knows. This is something I'm not proud of that I went on stains. I went on my first stain with Todd, well no my second stain. My first stain was with Pauly and Fonz off of King Drive. They were older Pauly was about sixteen and Fonz was fifteen. I had to be about thirteen.

This is what helped turned me into a criminal. We came home from church and somebody had broken in the crib. They stole our stereo and that was all they took. That stereo was really my music. I listened to the stereo more than anybody in the house so it was like my stereo.

I loved music I used to go to Marys Record Shop across the street from the crib. I didn't even know the name of the songs. If it had a sweet cover I bought it. My first record I bought of significance was Prince single 777-9311.

That's all I really did with my money buy comic books and records at first. The comic books were mind stimulating and the music was soothing. Other than clothes, this is all I had to show where my money had gone.

Disco was going out. I remember when everybody brought their disco records to Comiskey Park in 1979. They burnt the records right in the middle of the field. I was wondering why were they doing that, I loved that music?

Rap music was coming in strong. The guys in NY were coming in with the new wave. "Rappers Delight," bust us right in the head. Curtis Blow, "These are the Breaks" was banging.

I'd wait all day by the radio with my tape recorded just to hear those songs. NY had this innovation on how to use turntables and a mic. You know black folks we'll make something out of nothing.

We listened to house music too, but when they came out with the rap. I had very little interest in house music anymore. I was trying to rhythm, but I didn't have a stereo anymore. I was the one who mainly listened to the radio.

We get home and I was the first to notice its not there and asked, "momma where's the stereo?"

She looked and says, "oh my god it was there when we left".

We look around to see how they did they get in the house. They came in through the back basement door. I felt assaulted and then this was my hood. When I look back at it I think Pauly and Fonz broke into my house, I could be wrong.

They were the only one's breaking in houses other than your brother, Emus. Even Coole ain't that scandalous to hit us. They broke in our house, but we didn't have shit. They just took the stereo.

Anyway a couple of weeks later Fonz and Pauly come to me. They were planning to break in Half and Half crib. She used to just come visit in the summers. A couple of summers went by and she didn't come through.

I said, "naw" at first, but then Pauly said.

"They got all sorts of shit in their Colo".

I already knew it. I've been over there before.

Pauly gets to telling me what's inside, "TV's and stereos are in there Colo".

I looked back on it; it had to be them. I just didn't know Pauly was that scandalous at the time. It always somebody you know.

We used to go over Pauly crib to get high. His mother didn't care, if we drink or smoke. He used to talk to his mother like the Mexicans do.

Anyway Pauly said, "stereo" and a light bulb went off. We don't have a stereo. I said, "they got a stereo in there don't they Pauly".

He said the keywords to pull me in on the stain. They wanted me just to look out. I was in, somebody stole my shit so I'm going to steal their shit. Now that shit wasn't right. I didn't give it a second thought after he said stereo.

Pauly and Fonz were manipulator. Pauly lived by the vacant lot at the end of the alley. I knew Fonz from grammar school. He was one of those guys that were fifteen and I was twelve in the same class. They came to the block later. Fonz had to be in the eight grade, when he came to Rock Manor.

Everyday we used to throw the football to each other all the way home. Pauly would put a rim up on that little slab of concrete over there by the skyway. We'd go down there to ball on his rim.

When we got eliminated from the game in the dungeon we would play on Pauly's rim. I got a lot of game time in against them. He had it chained down so nobody would steal it. That's one thing about a thief. He knows what a motherfucka will do.

Fonz was cool until they moved away into the projects. He moved to the projects at about nineteen. He came back to the crib programmed. He was Super Folks with all the gang tattoos all over his body. He was enforcing violations down in the projects. They were using his skills to fight for the nation.

He was just different when he came back. He was robotic like while telling us how it was in the jets. Fonz and I used to laugh all the time. We found everything funny, but when he came back from the jets he didn't laugh no more.

Fonz was fucking motherfuckas up in the projects with his gladiating skills. He was already cut up like Bruce Lee. He used to practice just as much as I did with the karate, boxing, basketball and baseball.

I was just a little better at everything, but he was great competition. Once they turned him into the Ultimate Folks he was never the same.

Before he left to the Jets Pauly just had the power over him. Pauly on the other hand was just a real wicked human being. He had to have a demon in him working overtime. Pauly had no sympathy for nothing.

Pauly's dog assaulted my dog Tiger. Pauly had this big ass German Shepherd named King. Everybody back then named there German Shepherd King seemed like.

I never walked my dog with a leash. I had the dog well trained. I could sick em on you if I wanted too. Anyway every time Pauly saw me walking my dog. He'd fuck with me.

First he would sic King on Tiger. My dog could go, but in the end. King would be choking the shit out of my dog, by biting his neck. My dog's legs would go stiff and looked damn near dead.

My dog was smart he would play dead for a second. I'd try and break it up and Pauly would interfere. By doing his karate moves on me. Pauly was the one who walked around wearing the karate gee, karate shoe and carried numb chucks.

Pauly and Lucas Folks on Prairie thought they were Bruce Lee for real. Every time I tried to break the dogs loose. Pauly would jump up in the air and try and kick me in the chest.

He would say, "get back Colo let them fight" while jumping in the air and kicking at me. His dog felt more sorry for Tiger than Pauly did and let my dog go. Once King let him go.

Pauly started yelling at his dog. "King why did you let him go?"

Tiger was playing dead good. As soon as King let Tiger's neck go he was up and out scratching down the alley to the crib. If it were up to Pauly he would have let his dog kill my dog.

Pauly was a straight bully. When he was trying to kick me he wasn't connecting. I could have probably flipped him, but I didn't even try. I'd just grab his foot before he got me with the full impact. He never took it that far for me to snap.

He really did, by sicing his dog on mines.

I always said, he was going to be one of the ones, I got back when I got older. Pauly was a real bully and thief. He helped turn Fonz into a goon, because he wasn't like that, when we were in the eighth grade.

Fonz was cool as you wanted to be. We were always sparred doing all the karate moves we saw at the show. We mimicked the moves just like they did it. We tried everything except the phony flying shit.

The tiger, the snake and the drunken monkey styles were practiced. We we'd jump on banisters on cars while posing in the different style. We used to have fun, fucking each other up.

I still got a scar on my stomach from when he clawed me across the stomach. Once he did that I gave him one of the Bruce Lee scars across the chest. Sliced him with the claws while make the waaaaHHh waaaahhhhhh sound.

Anyway we break in Half and Half's house, broad daylight. Fonz and Pauly got in some kind of way and opened the door. I don't know what else they got out the house. They were just stacking stuff at the door.

As soon as they brought the stereo to the door, I was out. I grabbed that bitch and I was out. I got what I came for so I am out.

Pauly was like, "hold up, damn Colo".

I paid him no attention and broke wide with the stereo.

I ran across Calumet to pitch fork alley, to the house. Pitchfork alley was the back route to my house. I get to the crib and I put the stereo component up under the steps in our house. I was going to figure out something to tell Mom on where I got the stereo later.

A couple of days went by and the police came by the house. My Mom answers the door. They tell her they had reason to believe that I broke in one of the neighbor's house.

She calls me to the door, but doesn't let them in the house. First I know she couldn't believe it or maybe she could.

She says, "Colo the police are here and they said you broke in somebody house. Do you have a stereo?"

I said, "oh no mother they got me mixed up".

She looked at me on the steps with that look. She then turns to the officers and told the officers that she'd look around.

She looked at me with the evil eye and said, "if you done broke in somebody house I am going to crucify you boy".

I got nervous when she went on the search. She checked all over the house then went to the basement and found it. When she found it I was out the back door. She was talking about taking it and me to the police station.

That was not going to happen. I skate over to Emus house to get my alibi. Emus always had my alibis. I get to his crib and tell him the deal. All you got to say is we were playing strike out with me.

My mother gave the stereo back to the police and was waiting on me to get home. When I came back my story was straight.

I told her, "yeah I had it, but I bought it for ten dollars, cause we didn't have one. I was buying this one for the house. I didn't know it was stolen I bought it at the end of the alley".

It was conceivable because a whole lot of shit gets sold in the alley. The alley is like the store for thieves to sell their stolen stuff. I kept a few dollars in my pocket working my paper route so I had money. Whoever, seen me, saw me walking down the alley with it. I had to tell them what they already knew. I was walking down the alley with a stereo. All while I was stealing the stereo and bringing it home.

I was saying to myself, "I look hot running down this alley sweating, with this stereo in my hand, while huffing and puffing".

The story was I was playing strike out with Emus at the skyway. Dude who sold it to me was in a car and showed us the stereo.

He said, "give me ten dollars for the stereo".

I gave him the ten dollars, cause we needed a stereo. I didn't know it was hot. What was a thirteen year older doing breaking in somebody house?

They had to see me coming out the crib for me to get in trouble and they didn't see that. I never went in the house I was just on lookout. She told the police what I said and I never heard anything else about it.

I was a juvenile and as long as you keep your mouth shut. You weren't going to jail. If you didn't get caught red handed, momma came and picked you up, just keep your mouth shut.

We were schooled to this fact. We could do all the dirt we wanted to do, before we turned seventeen. Don't believe that your record follows you throughout your whole life.

After turning seventeen you have to pay a bond to get out. If convicted it goes on your permanent record. Your juvenile record would be sealed. Oh yeah! One more thing! They can lock your ass up at seventeen. Most states eighteen was the age, for charging you as an adult. Chicago dropped it a year, because we were much more criminal minded.

Your Juvenile record couldn't be used against you back in those days. That's why the younger niggas went on the stains. We were schooled to how much time a particular crime carries, Tadpole.

What's the difference between a felony and a misdemeanor? When we did get caught one of the OG's would come get us out. Worse case scenario, you had to go to the auty home. I ended up with nothing on that stain. I also didn't tell and the hood knew that!

At this time in my life I was so out cold with the lies I told. I used to make up the lies for niggas in the hood in trouble. I'd tell them to tell me everything. Once they gave me the specifics. I could make a concrete lie up for them, to get them out of trouble.

Emmet and I were on the same page, mentally, he could lie too. My nephew in law Derek was spending the night at our house. My Mom would tell Derek to keep an eye on me.

I kept tearing Harvey Collins off for those cookies that came in the tube. I'd steal those cookies and cook them in the oven at the crib. One day Derek asked me because I kept having the cookies.

"Where did you get these cookies? You don't have any money".

I told him, "Emus sold me the cookies out his refrigerator for a dollar". I got to pay him back. He had caught me coming in with the cookies and no bag.

I was standing on our porch when he asked. Just so happened Emus bent the corner.

I'm like, "oh shit, I didn't get a chance to tell Emus so he could corroborate my story".

He said there's Emus right there and asked Emus, "you sold Colo these cookies?" Emus looked at me and said, "yeah".

Derek didn't believe and asked, "for how much?"

Emus answers, "I sold them too him for a dollar".

I then looked at Derek with the look and said, "why are you tripping Derek?" You don't want me to eat no cookies? He knew I was a thief and he was trying to catch me. He wasn't like the guys around the crib he was into church. The guys around the crib would tell me to go get them some.

I caught Emus later and asked, "how did you know how much?"

He said, "we shorties we ain't going to sell nothing to each other for more than a dollar. I said cool cause this nigga was on me. He used to smell my finger when I didn't even smoke weed. Out the blue he would tell me to come here and he'd smell my fingertips.

I'd look back at him and say, "you be tripping".

Freight Job

I thought I was through with stains, because the stereo was a close call. I had a little money coming in off my route. I didn't have to do stains. I was warding off niggas trying to steal and pull me in on the job. I never was the one looking to break in someone house. I wasn't the one to steal someone car.

This is how I got talked into doing the freight job. It was the music again. The neighborhood was hitting the freights like clockwork. I'd never go, but I'd be in the dungeon when they came back. Emus brother, Slick Coole, had this saying or something he said all the time.

When he tried to con you into going on a job he'd say. "You don't work, you don't eat, you don't work, you don't eat".

The first two times I didn't go and they came back with all type of shit. After narrowly escaping the last episode I wasn't trying to hit stains. The thing that got me was the tape recorders they got of the last stain. Those were hot back then and now look at technology.

They've got boxes and boxes of those tape recorders. Everybody in the hood had one of those tape recorders. We could record externally off the radio. From grandma all the way down to the baby had one! Everybody except me!

You know I was itching to go, but stayed strong. We still didn't have a stereo in the living room. Everybody had a tape, for you to throw in the boom box. You kept a tape in your pocket for music on the porch.

When you didn't have a box you had a master jam tape. I loved staying up catching the music and making tapes. I didn't tell them I was in yet, but I was thinking hard.

Again, I was going on an adventure with the boys in the hood. The lure was to get the music, anything else I probably wouldn't have gone. They tried to get me to go the first two times and I was straight. Maybe they got some stereos this time. I got these records, but no stereo to play them on.

Todd was like, "cuz I'm going, you going? The boxcars will be up there on Sunday just sitting".

That's all I needed for Todd to say was, he was going.

I thought and said, "yeah let's go". So far it's Pauly, Fonz, Big D and Slick Coole. We are all going to meet up about 8:00 o'clock, right before the sun comes down.

Todd told me to come by a little earlier and we'll smoke one before we go. Sunday come and it's on. I go by Todd's house and smoked one in the basement. We were amping each other up by saying, "we going to hit train hard!" After smoking the weed, it was about 8 o'clock so we headed out.

Now for some reason Todd and I switched one of our shoes. I had one of his and he had one of mine. I still till this day don't know why we switched shoes. We walked down the alley and meet up with everybody.

We catch Slick Coole coming out the crib in the back. We holler for a second then we go get Big D. Big D came out dressed in all black. Black boots, black hat, black shirt and black pants. We started giving it to him.

Slick Coole said, "Big D, who you think you are dressed like, it takes a thief?"

We laugh at him a little more, because he stops to think.

He paused for a second and then says, "fuck y'all I'm dressed for the occasion". Pauly and Fonz pop out into the alley from the back of their crib. Everybody is on time.

Fonz and Pauly knew how to get in the boxcars. All they had was some vice scripts and a screwdriver.

I'm like, "damn that's all you need to get in those motherfuckas".

Pauly and Fonz knew the deal on breaking in and getting into shit. All we had to do was walk down the alley. Go up behind the little industrial buildings. Go up the hill, get past the foliage and to get to the tracks. There would be miles of boxcars sitting on the tracks.

The plan was to hit them and bring the shit back to Fonz, Pauly and Big D's crib. Their crib was the closest to the tracks. Drop the first load off and then tell the rest of the hood it's on!

You need help bringing all that shit down. Once you into some shit! You ain't got to worry about getting any help, unloading. The hood will see you coming down with the shit you got. They'll immediately want to plug and get in on some of the action. They'll look out, until we ready to go back up.

The sun is going down so we head up. It's was about a five-block walk from Big D's crib. We get to the tracks and crawl up the hill to see what was happening. The hill was about an 1/8 of a mile to the top.

We had our zones for the lookouts. We had all immediate areas in each direction covered with surveillance. It was equivalent to a three or four block radius we could cover with four guys on lookout. The railroad police patrolled the area constantly. Especially, since the hood was hitting them hard.

After about five minutes of feeling everything out. Fonz jumps up, while we continue to survey the area. Fonz and Pauly have been hitting the freights, a long time. We were just along for the help. Fonz looked like a pro thief, how he hopped, jumped and then low crawled to the train.

He crawled to the side of the train and scaled up the ladder making no noise. He goes to work and the rest of us stay on security. I was watching in my zone like a hawk. My head was pivoting backwards and forwards on a swivel. All while I'm up there I'm thinking. "I can't get caught, cause my momma is going to kill me". This is what's literally going through my head at the time of the stain.

Once in the boxcars, we would take turns in twos, hitting the train. While the other stay on security until we all clear the train. Next, set up security coming back to the crib.

Fonz went to work with the scripts and tried to crack one and couldn't get in it. He goes to the next one. This box further from me, it is in Todd's zone. He couldn't get that one either.

Fonz then jumped off and came back. The same way he crawled up to the train. He came back the same way and tried to reevaluate. We had the job set up like seasoned pros. I wanted to be the first one in the boxcars. I wanted to get it and go.

Pauly was setting everything up. Next thing I know I see a motherfucka dressed like Big D, crouched down. He was trying to get closer, but trying not to be peeped. He was looking in the same direction we were looking, up at the boxcars.

I whispered and said, "shh shh y'all see that, it's a motherfucka over there peeping us in all black?"

Pauly answered whispering back, "yeah right Colo".

I'm, saying to myself, "like I don't see what I'm talking about. I am on security so I am on security. Just cause I'm a young nigga. I don't see a man in all black".

Everybody gets down and looked in the direction I was pointing. The officer couldn't see us looking up at him. He doesn't know it's a team of niggas watching him. He was trying to get Fonz, but couldn't locate him anymore. Dude moved again. This time everybody peeped him, because you heard the rocks move.

Todd broke first. He was at the spot just, before you get on the tracks. We could have just quietly back down the hill and get the fuck on! Once Todd broke you could hear him running.

I was a little further down, but closer to the rails. That's how I peeps him, first. I was the last one to jump in the wind. Todd cleared the hill before I even got going. We were running like a motherfucka back to the house. We hear screeching tires.

Slick Coole says, "Oh shit they're coming in our way," the way to get out. "It's a trap".

We tried to turn around hit the hill and come down somewhere else. By that time we thought about it, four or five cars were on us. The railroad police on the hill had trapped us in the middle. We were cold busted.

They jump out with the heat yelling at us, "get the fuck on the ground". Todd got away. Coole, Pauly, Fonz and I were caught. No one knew where Big D was hiding.

The script was if we got caught. We were just playing around up there, soldier games. This was conceivable the oldest was seventeen. That was Pauly and Fonz.

As kids we always played back there, but not on the tracks.

The police asked, "Why were y'all running?" We saw somebody up there dressed in all black so we broke.

Fonz threw the shit out of those vice script he used to try and get into the trailers. He slung them up on the hill. That was a smart move, I saw him do that. Once he saw the officer he threw the tools first and then ran.

This was before we ran down the hill. They need the intent not the actual break in the boxcar. Fonz knew that and got rid of the vice scripts and screwdriver quick. They had us on the ground looking for tools to break in the boxcars. They kept asking us where are the tools. If they found the tools that would be all they needed, to go ahead and prosecute.

Next thing you know! The twisters were bringing Todd back in a squad car. Todd is trying to tell them. He doesn't know us. They brought him back to the crime. Todd had them on the run when they were boxing us in behind the Industrial spot.

Todd told us later, "I almost got away. Police sees Todd coming from behind buildings turned his car and tried to hit him with the car. I jumped over his car and hit the hood moving. We were athletes so we were going to run and once in the hood. There is no way you going to get caught. You know to many gangways and people who will let you chill until they roll.

Todd says he gets somewhere and hid, because the dude chasing him, was fat.

Todd said, "he thought dude left, but he was just sitting somewhere lurking until he came out".

Todd thought he was in the clear and was trying to get to the house. That's when they came out from all areas circled and pounced.

Todd kept saying, "what y'all want, why y'all on me?"

The officer cuffed him and brought him back to where we were.

Todd kept saying he didn't know us. "They had brought him back to the crime".

I am thinking to my self, "what crime Todd?" I didn't say nothing cause that was dumb ass hell. We were just up their playing.

I had on one of his shoes on my feet though! They put us in the back together. Todd says give me my shoe. You can't say you don't know us when you look at our shoes. Now that was dumb.

Now Todd and I were trying to switch shoes while we in hand cuffs. Somehow we changed the shoes though! Todd should've gotten away, but where's Big D. They take us to the station on 171st & South Chicago.

They got us all in the room and we tell them the story. It was just Slick Coole, Todd and I. Fonz and Pauly were seventeen so they took them to lock up. The rest of us were juveniles. I was the youngest so they keyed on me. I'm looking green, but they just don't know, they can't break me.

Coole and Todd didn't know how I would respond under pressure. I just stuck to the story. They took me in a room by myself and tried to interrogate me. Police pulled a chair up while I was still standing and said to me.

"Yeah we know y'all were trying to break in those boxcars".

I looked astonished by bucking my eyes and said, "break in the boxcars, oh no officer. We were just playing around up there on the tracks. We always play up there".

The officer says, "I would believe you, but your boy Fonz and Pauly said something different. They said, you were the one trying to open up the trailer".

I looked bewilder and replied in low smooth tone. You can't let them see you sweat. "I didn't break in no trailer nor did I see anybody breaking in the boxcars. I stopped and look inquisitive then said, "why would they say that?" I was playing it to the fullest. "We were just up there, playing soldier games on the hill".

The officers said, "you might as well tell us, they told us it was you".

I looked the officer in the eyes with an easy voice, "I don't know nothing about breaking in any boxcars officer, but if they said I did it, then they must have done it. I didn't see them do anything though! We were all just up there playing around".

Police officer said, "Okay yeah right".

What they were trying to do was wait until we got into the boxcar. We needed to break the seal. The railroad officer had to see Fonz on the boxcar. I saw him looking up on the boxcar for Fonz.

The railroad officer couldn't see him low crawl back. He thought he was still on the boxcar when we broke. As long as we didn't break that seal and start unloading they didn't have a case. They couldn't find the vice scripts either.

We were straight and our security worked. Come to think about it I saved everybody by peeping the officer, first. I did it again by keeping my mouth closed and sticking to the story. They didn't find the screwdriver or vice script so they didn't have anything on us. The only way they could get us is, if we told on ourselves.

I come out the room Todd and Coole was like, "we heard you, you told Columbus.

I said, "I didn't say shit".

Todd and Coole was on me, "Yes you did we put this glass to the wall and we heard you tell it all".

I said it again, "I didn't say shit, but the script that was it". About a hour later Mrs. Stables, Todd's mother, comes through the door.

Police officer tells them we were up on the tracks. They're not supposed to be on the tracks.

Mrs. Stables said, "I told y'all to stay around the house why was y'all back there?

Todd says, "just playing momma".

Coole and I agree in unison, "yep just playing Mrs. Stables".

Everybody and their momma and grandmamma knew we were hitting the freights. Everybody momma knew except mines. You know why they knew, because they were the customers when we got back from the freights. That's one thing about the hood. We didn't call the police. Nobody never told, not even the parents. They knew we were devious. We were little mobsters, Andrea.

Mrs. Stables turns to the officer and says, "I know all these boys I can sign them all out".

Todd mother signs us out and takes me to our house and left and said. Okay Colo see you later. She didn't even say anything to my mother. I was like boy that was close. We didn't have no court or nothing. Pauly and Fonz I bond out. They weren't charged or they case was SOL. Looking back at it. This was the beginning we were little mobsters, a thief ring.

Todd kept joking though saying, "I told the whole thing to the police".

Which they know it wasn't true, because everybody came home. I was convincing to the police. This comes from years of training. My mother could break my lies down. Now she can't even tell, anymore.

She was way better at her interrogations, because of the physical factor. It was too easy just answering questions without the pressure of a beating. We had somebody for every thieving crime you could do, Tadpole.

Another thing about it, if the police caught you, we weren't even worried about you telling. You were just caught and took what you had coming. Next time be faster.

What about Big D what happen to him? Andrea asked.

Oh yeah! Remember we were laughing at Big D, because he was dressed in his all black hook up.

He was the only one that didn't run. He just sat down and chilled blended into the darkness. When it got dark enough he came down.

Big D said, "they were looking for a long time for him".

He could hear them over the walkie-talkies, looking for what Fonz threw.

He heard the officer saying, "it's got to be around here. He had it in his hand".

Dude did peep Fonz the first time he tried to get in the trailer. He didn't peep the lookouts. It was a trap and our security prevailed. That's the only way all those squad cars was on the site that quick. The freight job was old.

Big D said, "I just didn't move for hours".

He sat up there until it got pitch black a few hours and then came down. They used to laugh at Big D, but he was smarter than you think. They didn't have to worry about me up there anymore.

Once they got your name or know the game. It's over for you, because if you get caught up there again. Now they got history on you. I helped a couple more times, but that's after they got it down the hill. I shelved the freight job.

My Guys at the Robe

My first year of high school was a rough transition. I didn't go in with any of my guys. John went to Stemietz, Fester went to CVS and Stace went to Whitney Young, I believe. Most people from Rock Manor went to Communication Metro Semieon of CVS.

The older ones from my class weren't fucking with me anyway. I went to the Robe without a buddy. My first day of school I was already disappointed. I didn't make the team over the summer. My whole reason for going to the Darobe didn't make sense now. I walked up to Darobe by myself the first day of school. You know they throw pennies at the freshman. I'm like what's this shit about.

I am tackling this monster by myself. When you graduate out of grammar school you had a support group. You either clicked in with your eighth grade class in high school. Another click was the one from around the crib. My guys around the crib that went to Robe were much older than I. They weren't fucking with me like that I was still a kid!

I basically had to fend for myself in this vicious new cycle. Stanley Darobe was a new school it was built and opened in 1976. My sister went the first year it was built and operable. She had graduated from Darobe and was going to Illinois Circle by the time I came.

This was one of the roughest schools in the city. It based right in the middle of where B.D.N. and the BGN's originated in the Englewood district. This is where my world opened up. I had to make new friends. It was like, a new world, new adventures of trials and tribulations.

City Boy

I clicked with this dude named Eddie Harmon. We had most of our classes together. His street name was Cityboy, for short we called him City. He was my mellow in high school. City kind of look after me my first year, of high school. He was in the B.G.N organization.

The first day of classes we plugged, because we walked the same way to all our classes.

He was like, "you in here too".

We even had lunch together. Dude came from Texas and they put him a year back in the sixth grade. He got to high school a year late and I came a year earlier. That's the only reason it was possible for us to be cool.

What impressed me about Cityboy is that he was banging. While banging he was still pulling his grades. I was pulling mine too so that's really how we clicked. I knew I'd be able to pull mines. At that time I wasn't gang banging. I held out with hopes of joining a team, which was futile.

We hit it off well, because like I said, most of our classes were together. He had a little click that was off 172nd and Racine. City introduced me to all of his boys. Ruffhouse, Bob, Lucky D, Snake and a few more Folks who I was cool with once we clicked.

One of his boys came up to him with a problem and he handled it. Crazy John used to be on Darobe football our freshmen year. Dude was a big bully and always tried to punk someone smaller. John would be peeping you out, to see if you were soft.

Once he seen you were soft, you were a target. He had this crazy routine he would do to check you out. He'd make crazy faces and noises. He'd stand over you in an aggressive way.

Your body language always gives a mark away. That's when a bully pounces on you. The way you stand and the way you look back at the bully. He can see it in the eyes, if you were a mark.

The eyes meant a lot. The way I used my eyes is to peep out that a nigga who is looking at me. I would look away like a mark, once and even twice to lure you in to thinking I was a mark.

On that third look I look back straight into whoever eyes, that's trying to mark me out. On my face there's a little small frown. I had a deadly stare, with one eye squinted just a little bit. When it was a one on one, stare down. 95% of the time they'd back off.

I have to look like I know something you don't know. You could be on the bus or bus stop, on the train or walking down the street. You look back at em like, I am the wrong nigga to fuck with, but don't say nothing.

What you're doing is letting them know, you ready so you can't surprise me. The pussy ass niggas will back off. 80% of them are hoes by themselves.

Tadpole, you have to have an instant mask that appears when you sense danger. The only way it works is, if you peeps the danger before the engagement. Before you're about to be a victim of a stain.

Once you are about to be moved on, by opposition or just bullied in school. When they see no heart in the eyes, you were a mark. He'd then go forward with the bully or the smashing. You could basically pick out who were the marks by looks. Crazy John knew whom to try.

If he is a real bully, you just letting him know you're ready. A real bully don't give a fuck about no eyes, he is still coming. You really just pissed him off by looking back at him. He's coming at you regardless. That's when plan two comes in effect. Soon as he gets in range, bust him in his shit.

A real bully knows how to fight and usually bigger. He's used to beasting motherfuckas, that's how he eats. This is how you get your P's up or down, because it's going down, Andrea. What you are doing is letting everybody else know through this action that you are no hoe. Strike first!

Cityboy and I were walking out the building after 9th period.

Lucky D ran up and said, "Crazy John tried to fuck with one of the Folks".

City said, "who?"

Lucky D replied "Ruff House".

Just as he said it, John came walking out of nowhere.

City said, "let's smash his ass. I don't like his ass anyway. He's always trying to bully somebody".

City and Lucky D took off running up to John.

City said, "John what 's up, that's my Folk's, what's up now nigga? Fuck with somebody your size".

I can see it in his eyes that the crazy shit, was wearing off quickly.

John replied slowly while looking around at the situation. He says hesitantly, "What you want to be up?"

City just blazed him quickly. Lucky D gave him a couple of shots. John took off running. They couldn't catch him. I guessed that football training paid off that day. Dude jumped in the wind.

That day I was kind of glad it happened to him, because he would mess with people. He never messed with me, but he did check me out. I am a black ass nigga and black niggas seemed to be thought as a beast. He sensed I was ready.

John was getting some of his own medicine. The next day I thought it was going to be on. He was on the football team and usually the football teams run together. Nothing was said and City didn't give a fuck either.

After that situation Crazy John wasn't Crazy John anymore. He was just John. He wasn't that crazy when he felt those blows. He got out like Carl Lewis. A crazy motherfucka is about to fight to the death.

He was just acting crazy, because he wasn't crazy no more, after getting hit. He was sane cause he knew, how to run. His brain was processing the situation correctly. He was about to get smashed. So no, he wasn't crazy.

City wasn't buying it, dude ran away without throwing a punch. In those positions you fight for a while. Just to show them you are no hoe. You might smash them both then your legend grows. The only time you run is, if it's a mob, wasn't no mob. City wasn't worried he carried a heater back in our freshmen year anyway.

City said, "if they want some of me, come with it".

He then showed me the missile in his satchel. You'd look at City and you wouldn't think he wasn't cut like that. He looked like a normal guy. I had more of a thug look than he did. He had the hands. He was quick, but we never slap box each other our freshmen year!

Not only did City bang, but he was also a straight hustler. Cityboy made money and never was broke. He shot dice, played get like me, played cards and sold weed. I reiterate what impressed me the most. He still went to class and got good grades.

City was like my big brother in high school. Even though we were in the same grade. He was 15 and I was 13 my freshmen year. We were both black as hell, but I got him. I was just a little bit darker. I'm always winning, but this competition I wanted to lose.

He had a caring way about gangbanging. It must be, because he was from Texas. He wouldn't bother you for what you are so that's what I liked about him. He'd just snap, if a motherfucka tried to fuck with him.

Folk's back then used to be ruthless at the Robe. Folks would fuck with you for no reason. He wasn't like that! He took up for the peons or neutrons. You weren't a peon or a mark, if you was cool as hell. You did not have to bang to make it through school. I was cool as hell my freshman year and I was a nuetron.

Dave and Slept Rock

I had two other friends in high school. Cassius Mckinney we called him Slept Rock and Dave Sterling. Cassius and I got to know each other in Mrs. Smit swimming class. I loved to swim so if I had a free period. I would sneak in during any class and go swimming. I would cool out until everybody jumped in the pool.

After she calls attendance I would sneak out and jump in the water. At first I didn't know Cassius at all. He'd see me trying to sneak in and always rat me out. Once he saw me jump in the pool.

He'd yell out, "Mrs. Smit he's not supposed to be in here swimming this period". Mrs. Smit would take notice and kick me out. "Get out the pool Columbus".

Cassius was about 5'4" back when we first met. I thought he look very easy to smash. He had pissed me off. I couldn't get mad though, because he was right. I wasn't supposed to be in there swimming. I was just mad he was telling like a pussy. Don't nobody tell on you, you got to get caught is how I was cut.

This nigga was telling on me. He didn't want me swimming in the pool. I never saw anybody tell like that before.

Cassius was literally telling and calling her, "Mrs. Mrs. Smit Mrs. Smit that dude is not in this class".

Now who do that? This wasn't his first time doing it. Class was almost over when she put me out anyway on this occasion. I leave and go get dressed and now the class is over for him too.

Now dude coming in the locker room and I looked at him and said. "Man you a trick ass nigga".

He replied, "nigga this ain't your class, go to your own class.

I look at him and said to myself, "this must be some funny acting straight nigga, fuck him. I don't know any nigga who just go tell the teacher". I just put my clothes on and went to my next class.

At the beginning of the year we took one of those test. The test was to evaluate what level you are on in the freshmen class. Well after the results came back they said I needed to be in an honors division. Dave and I were cool already. We already had a couple of classes together and hung a bit. Dave liked cracking jokes. He was in my division too.

I was still trying to sneak in Mrs. Smit swim class on my free periods. Mrs. Smit was cool, but she wasn't having me once Slept Rock wired her up. Most of the time I could be in the pool and she not know it.

I used to tell Slept Rock, "you're a hoe ass nigga for telling, like a bitch". He'd be on the same shit, but I guess those words sunk into him.

The next day we got a little cool, cause he snuck me in the class himself. When I saw him I was, "here goes this bitch ass nigga".

He saw me and said, "hold on she's looking I'll let you know when she not. He goes in like he's the look out and waves me in so I could jump in the pool. Now he's cool and helping me.

I used to love swimming. I was coming off the high diving board doing all sorts of flips. I was backstroking, doing butterflies and everything.

Larry Driver had swim class with me and he was on the wrestling team. He was a freshman, but he had to be at least sixteen. Dude was strong than a motherfucka. This is one nigga I didn't want to see coming.

He had swimming with Slept Rock. I know I call him Slept Rock sometime and Cassius others, I always did that! The days I got away with swimming on my free period. I had to see Larry Driver.

Larry was terrorizing the class, girls and boys. Larry had a way of grabbing your neck and one of your legs. This is while clutching his hands together locking you in his grip. I found out later, it was a wrestling move called the cradle.

You have to swim away from him before he gets you in that position. You're just not going to let him do it. He did it cause you couldn't stop him. Larry would swim you down, grab you then manhandle you. That's when the fun begins for him. Once he got you like that, it was over for you.

You would have two arms trying to get loose. One leg will be left scraping the bottom of the pool. The other leg is locked with one of your arms and neck.

He'd drag you into the deeper part. Like a shark would do their prey. He could still stand up, but you couldn't. He was taller than us so he'd drag us to a part where you can't put your foot down.

As he pulling you in that the direction you start to panic. You really panic when your toes are barely scraping the bottom of the pool. He's dragging you, deeper and deeper in the water.

You try and stay calm and say, "all right Larry cool out," without losing your cool.

The terrifying part is the dragging of you to the deep. You were almost begging dude to stop by saying, "please Larry cool out".

He keeps dragging you to where he wants you. After getting you there he just begin dunking you over and over again. That's just to get you under control. Once he got you sedated he'd drag you deeper and begin again. Your arms and legs would be flailing up and down in the water. All you could do was hear him laugh as you go up and down.

You'd be under water damn near about to panic while taking in water. Naw fuck that, you are panicking. Larry then would bring you up for air then down again. It was like a shark having you in his jaws. You go down, bubble bubble gurgle gurgle.

Sometimes you didn't hold your breathe in time and you swear you were going to die. He'd bring you back up and the terror he saw on your face, amused him. He'd look in your face and laugh at the face you made.

This kept making him do it, more and more. Water is going down your throat and nose. You are coughing and snotting. This is completely terrifying, all in fun for Larry.

Now when he caught Slept Rock it was the funniest shit. When it was on somebody else it was the funniest thing to me. I'd be laughing so hard, because a person face would have (terror), stamped on it.

The desperation on your face when you were trying to get away was priceless. He did the girls, but he was light with the girls. He probably was just trying to be touchy feely with them. When he got to us it was for real.

You felt you were going to die at that moment. I love when he got Slept Rock, cause he talked so much shit. He was a trick at the time to me, still. That's how I know how to describe it so well. I watched Larry dog his ass out. Man while he was dunking Slept Rock he had this horror looking look on his face. He was scared than a motherfucka.

I 'd be laughing sitting safe on the side of the pool. Once Slept Rock saw me laughing so hard, his punk ass would say.

"Get Columbus, get Columbus Larry". Larry would stop look and start coming after me. He'd jump out the water and was literally chasing me around the pool. When he caught me believe me I was trying to get away.

I stopped running to keep from looking like a hoe. The girls were looking and I couldn't run one more step, but I wanted too. I tried to have my serious face on when I told him to cool out. He would then wrestle with me outside the pool until he could throw me in the water. Once he got you in the water it was his domain.

I'd try swimming away. The terror and anticipation of him catching wouldn't let me swim fast. Larry would grab me and here we go. He wouldn't stop until you got Mrs. Smit attention.

Every time he let you up for air you had to call out, "Mrs. Gurgle bubble Mrs. Smi then down. Bubble bubble gurgle gurgle, up again. Mrs. Smi Larry, down again, bubble bubble bubble, up Mrs Smit cough cough. You are trying to get the words out before he dunked you again.

I swear I think she sent him at us in the pool. It took her too long to see what he was doing. I am in the middle of the pool getting dunked and she doesn't see it. It seems as, if she kept her back turned to the pool.

We weren't whispering, we were yelling her name. "Mrs. Smit", shouting loud as hell.

She finally would holler at Larry, "Larry stop", then he would let you go.

You immediately start struggling against the water to get the fuck away from him. Once you get to the side while coughing. You want to fuck him up. Too big and too strong and he was just playing. Slept Rock was falling out laughing at me.

He asked, "how that shit feel Columbus? You was laughing your ass off at me".

I'd say, "fuck you, your hoe ass sent him at me", while still coughing.

That whole year Larry was the terror dome. Larry would see you in the hallway. He'd grab you while you are trying to go to class. He would then starts to practice his wrestling moves on you. First he'd knocked your books out your hand and it was on! I'd give him a run for his money, but dude would be too strong and too experience.

It was sickening when you seen Larry coming down the hallway.

I wouldn't say it out loud, but under my breath, "ol shit here come Larry". I don't remember him being Folks either. One thing Larry did was tighten my wrestling game up.

I started getting good with other folks I'd wrestle. I could never fuck with Larry that year. He had me at home lifting weights, doing pushups, sits ups and everything. When he grabbed you he did it in front of everybody. I was tired of the humiliation and I had to get stronger.

I started lifting more weights, because I had to get stronger. Wrestling is a match of strength and will. When you can't get out of a hole my hands means nothing. A nigga who can wrestle will fuck you up.

I can box, but if a motherfucka grabs me and wrestles me down. He's got the power of me. He can do what he wants to do to you. Boxing can't help you when someone is locking you down, in a wrestling hole.

Wrestling a motherfucka will sap your strength, quickly. Larry is imposing his will on you to where you can't move. You can't move and everybody's looking at you subdued in the middle of the hallway. I'd still struggle and try everything I can, but it's no good. I had to learn how to wrestle.

Sometimes he would let you go and wouldn't fuck with you.

He'd walk by and just say, "what's up?"

Most times he didn't fuck with you. Once every eight days or so, he'd grab you. He had me on pins and needles when I saw him. You had to be ready. I got to get stronger. He didn't grab Cassius in the hall, because he was a peep squeak. I did give him a little match.

This is one of the reasons why we started fucking with motherfuckas coming down the hallway. Larry taught us that. Slept Rock was mean and whoever was around nothing good would happen. Bad things happen when Slept Rock was around. His laugh meant the cloud was over your head.

It's about to rain on somebody parade. He was so much fun though! Slept Rock and I would tag team motherfuckas coming down the hall later on! Just like Larry did us. He didn't tag team us he didn't need a team. Cassius never helped when Larry had me. He just watched and laughed. We'd later be wicked to niggas like Larry was to us.

We'd chase them down and bang whomever we caught. We'd bang their body from the neck down. We'd be slamming you too the ground. Cassius was always fucking with Mark Pack.

Mark was a neutron and was cool, but when Cassius saw him. He'd practice his punching on him. He'd tell Mark to punch back, but Mark wouldn't. I didn't mess with Mark he was cool. He was too weak, physically. This was perfect for Cassius

Mark didn't have any strength. He walked a little like he was afflicted. Every time he saw Mark outside he would chase him home. When caught, Cassius banged him ugly to the body, nonstop with mean intentions. He went home with bruises all on his body, cause he was real light skin.

I used to tell Cassius to cool out stop messing with him. Mark is not punching back. Mark's scariness burned like fuel in Cassius. When Mark balled up to protect himself. Cassius eyes lit up and he would just start whaling on Mark. Mark would break out and run. He was a bully to Mark.

I used to hold Cassius back while Mark ran. One day Mark mother came up to the school looking for Cassius. Mark pointed him out and Cassius ran from the confrontation.

She yelled while running in his direction, "come here this is my child you beating on".

He yelled back, "show him how to fight, as he got more istant from her". His mother went and told Bonner. Mr. Bonner called Cassius down to the office the next day. When Bonner seen how little Cassius was he tripped.

He asked Mark, "you scared of this peep squeak".

His mother couldn't believe how small Cassius was and asked Mark. "Why are you running from this little guy?" Mark just looked as, if to say, you have no idea.

One day Mrs. Miskel our Home Economics teacher saw us in the hallway playing. We were slamming desk around, running and grabbing folks beating them and laughing.

Mrs. Miskel couldn't believe what she was seeing. She had come out her class and into the hallway, cause she hears the commotion. She's watching us while looking over her glasses, in disbelief. We didn't know she was watching us at first.

She would say after she got our attention. "You and Cassius are the stupidest, ignorant little boys I ever saw in my life".

Cassius and I would look at each other and bust out laughing. Her face looked like a picture of disbelief. This was after we got cool, because you know I couldn't stand his ass at first. How we really got cool cause even after he'd sneak me in, I didn't trust him.

When the test result came back I had to move. My regular division teacher Mrs. Barnes was astonished, because of my behavior in class. My behavior didn't coincide with the results that came back from that test.

Dave and I used to clown too, by cracking jokes with each other. I couldn't help it I used to clown at Rock Manor. The next day I was transferred to Mrs. Van Smith honors division and guess who was in there, Cassius.

To my surprise we hit it off. Cassius, Sterling and I had most of our classes together. We all like to laugh and crack jokes. We always used to wrestle and slap box in the hall.

We started chasing other people catching them and smashing them. Niggas didn't want to see us three coming. We were the three amigos in school. They didn't have to be our size.

They could be tall, fat, and skinny or whatever, we would fuck with you. Later on Ronnie transferred in the Robe. We had a lot of classes and he ran with us. When we got bored we would signify and spar each other.

Most of the time, Cassius and Sterling teamed up on me. Especially, when it was nothing to do they'd laugh and come my way. I used to play catch him, smash em already in the hood.

They fucked me up, but I was giving it back to them, when it was two on one. My gear was okay, just okay. Therefore, giving them more to talk about. It always seemed as, if they teamed up on me.

I was used to it though, being from Rock Manor. The whole classroom would team up on you at Rock Manor. This was a different stage though!

We had Mrs. Marchman for African American history class. Slept Rock and I would be in there making up songs from TV programs, but talking about each other.

Slept Rock was short, but had a big ass head in high school. I targeted his head all the time when going at him. The song went like this, King Kong you know the name of king Kong, ten times as big as man. Big head, you know the name of big head, he come to school with those cheap ass cloottthesssss and those plastic shoooesss.

Slept Rock wore baggy dress pants all the time with dress shoes. That was the style in those days. While staying with the tune I would say, "and those plastic shoes and hold the note, plastic shoeeeeeessss in a low tone like the cartoon".

Slept Rock had some shiney ones on that I never cracked on! I was waiting on a good time to bust him out. We were taking a test and it was quiet so I was saying it like in a whisper. This was the moment I needed.

Everyone looked down at his shoes and fell out while taking the test. He had them on and we were cracking so it was the perfect opportunity.

I had the whole classroom cracking up. Yeah, we would be singing the song during test time. It was quiet the teacher could hear too and she couldn't help from laughing.

I'm talking about on the floor laughing, the whole class. Slept Rock was a beast and mean spirited with that talk about shit. He had no mercy, but I got him this time.

Slept Rock was ignorant he just wouldn't stop. I cooled out and finished the test. He was still trying to get me back. I had him for the rest of the day. I finished taking the test.

It was a killer blow, cause he still had on the shoes. All somebody had to do was look at the shoes and replay the song in their head. They'd bust out laughing out of nowhere.

All I had to do was say, "and those plastic shoes" part of the song and the laughter would start.

He kept singing different songs trying to get me back. Mrs. Marchmen finally got fed up after asking him on several occasions to stop.

She said in a stern voice, "Cassius if I knew, if I knew, you were going to be my child".

Her face shows frustration so Slept Rock started laughing at her. I could tell she wanted to say something, but she was trying to word it.

After looking at him laugh she gasped, "Oooh you're just so stupid and ignorant. If I was going to have a baby and knew it was going to be you. I would have an abortion".

Everybody in the class was like, "damn damn" and busted out and started laughing at him. Now no teacher ever told me that. She cross the line, Slept Rock snaps back. Mrs. Marchmen had the short Afro look.

Slept Rock said, "If I knew I was going to have a ball head ass, ugly ass mother like you, I wouldn't come out". Slept Rock didn't care anymore she hurt his feelings. He took the gloves off. He was coming back hard, teacher or no teacher. She left it alone after that and told him to finish the test. He said a couple of more things. I don't even want to repeat them, but she shouldn't have opened that door.

Making a Name

It seemed in high school everybody trying to make a name at your expense. When you don't quite fit in, you get fucked with for sure. There was no way around it. That first year I didn't gang bang in high school. Therefore, it subjected me to be called a peon, mark or a neutron. I was a neutron meaning I just wasn't plugged. I was cool though! I held my own.

My new friends I met were banging, Dave Sterling was riding with B. G.N. Organization. Cassius wasn't banging yet, but all of his friends from the hood were GD.'s so he was straight.

I was less known and didn't have too many friends. I didn't go in with my crew from grammar school. The ones I graduated with were older than me and weren't fucking with me, because I was young. Rodell's brother Chris was going there too, but we rarely kicked it.

I had to prove myself with all of Cassius and Sterling friends. Cassius eventually would get me to slap box everybody from his hood. Sterling and I used to wrestle and body punch all the time. His skin was too light to slap box and wouldn't do it.

Dave was strong and had a wrestling background. When we wrestled he would always get me in holes I couldn't get out. Now I expect this out of Larry cause he was big and strong. Dave wasn't big like Larry. He shorter than me, but well cut up. Dave and his cousin Westly also boxed coming up at Morgan Park.

Dave was tight with both boxing and the wrestling sports. I used to always wonder? Dave was shorter than I. Why I couldn't get him in wrestling? In body punching he was a little more pronounced with his combinations. Every time he hit me with combination, chest, ribs, arm, arm, ribs and chest.

I had the strength of a thirteen-year-old guy. Dave had the strength of a person in training. He was also was turning fifteen. When we were at a stalemate he could out endure me and still get me. He kept putting me in that damn cradle. That's what it was the cradle.

I'd be struggling not for him to grasp both of his hands. He had my neck and my leg trying to lock me. The same thing Larry was doing to me in the water. Dave did it to me on the gym mats. Dave would be laughing while telling Slept Rock while we were in a clinch.

"Slept Rooock ahha hahh hhaah hha I abou ahhhh hh I'm about to put him in the ahhha hhha in the cradle".

I would be struggling for him not to put me in the cradle. Dave was just strong as fuck.

He'd get me in the cradle and say, Slept look ahhh hhha I got him in a cradle. I'm thinking to myself, "that's the same move Larry was putting me in the pool".

Dave was the first person who showed me about serving a pumpkin head to a Stone. I just watched I did not participate. Not just smashing a Stone, but smashing the opposition with several people. Pumpkin head style!

Dude came to school with a red hat on….. what he do that for? He must didn't know about the Robe. By ninth period everybody knew he was getting smashed in school.

Dave said they were going to move on dude who came with the red hat. Tadpole, Dave was calling it his freshman year for the Black Gangsters. Meaning they were moving on his command. Dave walked up and the mob encircled dude in a 360. Dave looked and stole on him without saying anything and kicked it off.

They smashed that boy for about a whole minute. Slept Rock and I were watching from a distant the whole thing. Dude was trying to escape running and jogging. He was running the way I walked home from school.

After Dave stole on him it was like flies on shit. It seemed as, if the beating was an hour long, but was probably only a minute. It was about twenty Folks out there at the time.

Each one of them put it on him. It was flying kicks, stomps and many many punches being administered. He also got hit with the cane he had brought to school.
They left him in the street and dude was shaking into a convulsion.

Right then I said, "I would never ever jump on nobody like that, that was totally wrong".

I was looking at Dave face after he kicked it off. It gave him pleasure to kick it off because he was smiling. After hitting him he just stepped back and the mob went to work.

That shit wasn't right. I felt sorry for dude all, because he had a red hat turned to the left. Yeah that shit wasn't right. I can see, if somebody went one on one. Two on one, but that pumpkin head was ridiculous!

Other than that Dave impressed me. He was short and could handle his own. He had heart like my cousin Todd. Dave was probably the toughest little shortie freshmen that came in that year on the radar scope. I flew underneath the radar-scope, because I know I had to be in the top five. It might have been me but I was a nuetron. One other thing about Dave he never got high or drank. Dave had two ways of kicking it. He acted a fool with us sometimes laughing and playing around.

He also was calling so he had a different way with the mob than when he was with us. He carried heat too and was focused with the gangbanging. He made sure everybody was up on the laws and literature and knowing every aspect of the BG nation. Even when he got older he didn't drink or get high. Everybody else was getting it in! I on the other hand, had unforeseen problems.

Dave, Slept Rock, Westly and I were cutting school. We went to Dave house to get bubbled. Only Dave wasn't drinking. He was just playing with his gun loading it up and spinning the barrel. This is what he did to have fun.

After drinking we drank the beer and was half way buzzed. Cassius and I were looking at each other, with the, what's up with this nigga look? I started getting an uneasy feeling in my stomach about Dave.

Dave started pointing the gun and clicking it at us. He was laughing and shit, we didn't. We didn't know, if he was putting the bullet in or not. We were shying away from the gun. We move like roaches when the lights come on! We are telling Dave to cool out. He just kept laughing and clicking. After a while we stopped flinching, because we knew he didn't have bullets in the gun.

His face had a mad look on it and he said, "Oh y'all don't believe I'll put a bullet in the gun".

He got mad and loaded one bullet in the gun and started clicking. We started running all over the house trying to get out the way. Dave is crazy he was putting the bullets in the gun. Next he was spinning the barrel and pulling the trigger.

We thought he was still bullshitting until we were trying to get in the closet and it went off. Booomm, as the smoke filled gunpowder hits the air. This is the first time I smelled gunpowder.

After the smoke cleared the look on our faces told the whole story. This nigga is crazy with a gun.

Here go Dave, "aw look at y'all, y'all scared" and started laughing.

Dave shot the gun in his house, in our direction. This nigga is crazy.

We like, "damn Dave you got the bullets in the gun. We thought you were bullshitting. It's time to go" and we all left".

Dave was the real deal. He definitely had the juice. A lot of the guys that were plugged were wearing mask of toughness. They look like you shouldn't fuck with them and carry all of these tough nicknames.

Baby Bill, Dollar Strong, Smokey Man and all sorts of names. They carry these reputations that make you avoid conflict with them. Dave didn't have a nickname and he was dead serious.

Same thing happened to Earth, when he got moved on, Dave was there. Earth is Slept Rock hommie off the block. He stayed a few houses down from Slept Rock. Slept Rock and I were coming out the school after ninth period. We walked up to 169th & Normal and we see they got his boy surrounded. Eddie McDuff and Elgin had him surrounded with the BD Folks.

Earth had a .357 magnum on his waist.

Slept like, "that's my man Earth and there's my cousin Hoolio across the street".

Earth didn't pull it out though he was just posted like, fuck with me. He was standing in the six-point stance because he was a GD. I don't know what it was about.

He let them get too close though and Eddie McDuff grabbed him from behind. They snatched the gun from his waist and they beat that boy close to death.

Hoolio was with him, but he got away. Hoolio was Slept Rock cousin and they lived on the same block too. They beat him so bad he didn't know his name. Dave ended up with the gun somehow. He came to school with it and showed it to us the next day.

Most of these guys were from Cassius way across Halsted. He would pit bully me with anybody ready to go.

He would say and ask boys around the crib, "my boy cold as hell you think you can fuck with him?"

I would say, "Cassius cool the fuck out, at first".

His boy from the hood would say, "come on". Cassius knew I was good, but he wanted to see how good his boys were. Everybody is bad when they're jumping on you. When it's one on one, it's a totally different story.

I 'd usually get the best of his guys when slap boxing or the other guy would quit. He had me slap box his cousin Kenny our sophomore year. After a couple of air swings, that missed.

He saw how I was cut and said, "he was straight".

I add those to my victory count. When you quit or don't take the match. When you are a goon you can't turn down a challenge. Win or lose, goons go to work, regardless. That's the job of a goon to move out.

Slept Rock and I are in the gym with some of his guys off the block. One of his guys off Halsted name Gearl wouldn't slap box me. He was a skinny light skinned dude. I took him lightly.

Everybody was shying away from me now. He said he'd wrestle me though.

I said, "fuck it let's wrestle". We get on the mats and start pawing at each other. We lock up and before I knew it. I was up in the air and getting slammed on my back on the mat. I hit the mat wondering what the fuck just happened? This skinny nigga was super strong.

I immediately get up and say, "let's slap box". He declined and was straight with the slamming. He didn't even want to wrestle anymore.

I looked at him and said to myself, "never take nobody for granted".

Other than Gearl, Slept and I soon realized. Most people talked and looked tough with our experiment. If you are scared to defend yourself, you'll get bullied. I went through that with the Hawk in the third grade.

It makes it much easier for the bully to take advantage of you. When you're an easy mark. Most bullies want things to be easy. They don't need confrontations so you got to make it hard for a bully.

That's why I used to say, "that nigga got his mask on!"

He looks like you should just give up and make it easy for him. When you talk to him though you realize this guy is no tougher than you. He's using his mean looks and dressing thuggish and cocking his hat to throw you off.

This was your first line of defense coming up. This was to let people know you are made. It's a mob behind me whether you see them or not. Next, was to talk a good game. The dog's bark is worse than his bite. My bark was the opposite. You barely heard it, but you felt the bite. Like one of those sneaky ass dogs that let you get close than snap at your ass.

Getting Robbed

I wasn't as popular as Cassius and Dave. I had to go through it the hard way. Find out who was who, because I wasn't plugged. I got robbed a couple of times by shorty Dave and Ebert they were GD Folks off of Halsted. Well not really robbed, but tested. Ebert used to fuck with me every time he saw me.

He was a little short nigga talking about running my pockets. Now this is another dilemma! You see they were Folks. I wasn't banging at the time. This was about the same time Todd and I started saying we were cousins before I plugged. That's when he took me under his wing.

I had back up though! Spider G, Sacks, Nino, Freddie and Dickie Lee were going to the Robe. Most of them were in higher grades. All of them were on some team, except Dicky Lee.

They rarely kicked it with me at the school. I never ever went and got help from the hood anyway. I figured I had to handle it myself. When they weren't around what was I going to do? Where I'm from, if you are challenged you must meet the challenge or you's a mark.

Ebert always was saying a little slick shit, because he was Folks. Here I am bigger than this guy, but he had the mob behind him. I wasn't up to getting smash like Dave did that Stone. I admit I kind of stayed away from them guys, if I could. When I saw Ebert I didn't want no smoke, I avoided them.

During our freshmen year Cassius and I went to the sock hop at the Robe. Shorty Ed was a little guy who stepped his ass off. He was the best stepper I knew. He did it all. Shorty would spin about twenty times in a row. After his spins he would do about twelve splits.

Pop up from the split and slide about fifteen feet in one move. His turns were so intricate. Shorty Ed used to tear the floor up. His shoes would be smoking when he came off the floor. He'd have the whole gym watching him step. He'd get a lot of ooohhh and awwhhhss from the crowd.

Ebert and shorty Dave caught me afterwards. This was another Dave and he was Folks. I was walking Cassius back his way to the crib after the sock hop. I still never let on to everybody I was just thirteen years old at the time. I was trying to figure my way around things. I should've been going the other way I'm the thirteen-year-old and Cassius was fifteen.

I walked his way so we stayed together until my bus came in the other direction. I began to walk him up to Halsted as far as I could, because he wasn't catching the bus.

Once my bus came I was going to jump on going in the opposite direction. We did that so we stayed together at least part of the way home. This is for protection for both of us. I don't know why? I could have been by myself.

Dave and Ebert popped out of nowhere.

Ebert said, "give me your money mark" and started reaching for my pockets".

He had his hand on my pockets and then ripped them down and my change flew out. I didn't have much money, but they couldn't have it. I started wrestling with Ebert and Dave picked up my change. After he got the little change Dave told Ebert lets go.

Ebert let me go and they walked away. They got like 80 cent so I said fuck it. I said to them while they were walking away, "awe, y'all can have that change, it wasn't shit".

Slept Rock just stood there and laughed all while it was happening. He never even thought about helping.

He laughed and said, "damn they took your change".

I looked at him crazy, because he literally watched me instead of getting those niggas off me. I said, "it ain't shit". Now I ain't got no bus fare. I had to hopped the bus home at Halsted.

That's one thing about Slept Rock he liked to see your downfall. He was no help to me. This was the difference from the crib and school. We would've scrapped if I had one of hommies from around the crib. Usually, Cassius was always starting shit for everybody else to get rallied up. That was Slept Rock a bunch of mouth back in the day.

He liked to see people fight and see people get fucked up. If I didn't know no better, I would have thought, he set it up. It just seemed he should have helped me due to the fact. He knew Dave and Ebert and he never said get off my hommie. It was two against one I would have helped him that's why I walking home his way.

I walked to Halsted and hopped the bus. While riding to the crib I felt like a mark. Worst the nigga with me thought it was funny.

I said to myself, "The next time Ebert fucks with me, fuck him and his mob". These niggas got me going the other way when I see them. This was going to stop somehow. I was a mark for real. I was trying to avoid confrontation. I learned from the Hawk in the 3rd this isn't going to stop.

A few days later Slept Rock and I were cutting class. We were in the washroom playing get like me for quarters. Who walks in the bathroom? It was Ebert and Dave my assailants from the other night.

Dave was cool he was really just was along for the ride. Ebert was the bully. Ebert came right at me. I was up against the wall standing. He walked up to me and looked me in the eyes with the grim face.

I am looking down on him while he's looking up and he says. "I should steal on your mark ass". He then starts putting on his gladiating gloves.

I looked at him and said, "yeah right". I just didn't believe he would do it. I turned my head a little and looked at Slept Rock. Before I looked back Ebert stole on me, bam bam. He didn't hit me twice, but my head hit the mirror behind me.

I wasn't stunned from him stealing on me. I was stunned, because I just didn't' believe he did it. This is how you do in high school no 3:15.

I looked at Slept Rock and of course he starts laughing again. Now this happened in a fraction of a second. Bam, look at Slept, he laughs, I snap and I got to work and move with the quickness, Bing@##*^@ bam**#@ boom boom choke.

This is the Hawk all over again. Every time I needed too. I would just put Hawk's face on you. I started smashing Ebert ass. I two pieced him and knocked him in between the bathroom stalls. I gave him the three pieced in the stall boom bam bam. I was on him. I get him in the stalls and start talking and fighting. "You are a pussy ass nigga and you fucking with the wrong one bam, bam".

It something that snapped in me and I turned into a warrior. Once that button is pushed I'm in the mode to hurt you.

I grabbed him by his neck and start slamming him in the stalls.

I asked him while smashing him, "You are going to steal on me, you pussy ass nigga?" I hit him one more time and Dave broke it up just in time. Now it's too late I am wide open, ready to fight. Big Ronald, popped in my head, I better finish him.

Shorty Dave saw I was fucking him up bad and broke it up.

Dave got in between us saying, "cool out Columbus, cool out Columbus, letting me know he was no threat first.

He saw what I did so quick or he knew he was wrong. Dave was supposed to help him, but he didn't, that was his Folks. I thought I was going to have to fight both of them by myself. Slept Rock was just standing there laughing until I went to work.

Slept Rock didn't know I was a beast. Nobody knew, because this was my first fight at the Robe. Shorty Dave got in between us and broke it up. Slept Rock never move to break it up. He just looked amazed while saying, "dammmmnnn". Ebert had to be held up by Dave. He grabs him up out the stalls and walks him out the bathroom.

Ebert staggered out the bathroom dizzy than a motherfucka. He took up the whole hallway trying to walk. He was holding his head where I connected and I drew blood.

Dave literally had to hold him up as he walked down the hallway. He had no idea how I was cut. He never bothered me again. As a matter of fact I never heard him bother anybody else again.

Slept Rock of course was just standing there watching. After seeing me go into action. He looked at me different. It was like he found out I was Bruce Lee. I was still mad not thinking about what he was thinking.

Dave and Ebert started walking the other way. I yelled to him, "I told you to leave me alone nigga".

Afterwards Slept Rock said, "damn you fucked Ebert up and quick too".

The only reason I didn't fight him was because he never hit me. The little eighty cents, two on one was petty. All that shit Ebert used to talk didn't bother me I avoided him.

When you hit me than that's when I really don't have any control over my actions. My mother always told me. Don't snap unless a nigga put his hands on you. You have no reason to put your hands on him. Ebert really thought I was scared of him. I was scared of mob action, on my ass and that's it.

Slept Rock never saw me real fight up until that point. Once he saw how quick I turned to mashing this nigga. It was unbelievable to him.

He just kept saying, "you fuck him up, you fucckkkeddd him uppp". He kept reenacting it, blow for blow. That's all he did was take pictures. Of course he went around the whole school and told them how I fuck Ebert up. I liked the cosign part. This was the beginning of my legend. I really am a nice guy. These skills I got, I could be fucking with a lot of people, but I don't.

One more thing I am younger than everybody. I didn't really want any smoke. This was the training I got at Rock Manor. You got to gel with volatile motherfuckas. From then on Slept Rock knew I was no punk and the secret was out. He knew I could slap box but that's different than fighting.

He saw how fast I was with those bare knuckles. He saw me talk to this nigga while whooping him. He saw my eyes change to destructive aggressive mode. In fighting, he knew now I was an assassin. Just think the nigga who was walking next to you the whole year. All this time was Muhammad Ali and I was undercover as Colo.

My motto was don't fuck with nobody, if fuck with, put it on them, ugly. I want have to do any talking, everybody else would. Slept Rock especially, he couldn't wait to tell everybody what I did to Ebert. He told City and Sterling. He told everybody from around his crib. It was so many GD's around his house.

Niggas started to know me and I didn't know them, because of my hands. Niggas didn't use to say nothing. Now they're walking by saying what's up to me? They still didn't know really. All they knew is what Slept Rock told them. This will soon change. He told all the Folks he knew what I did and how I did it. I felt good about that.

I went through some emotions when they strong-armed me for the eighty cents. I said while on the bus home, "they going to think I am a mark and they going to come again". I prepared myself mentally. The only thing I was worried about was Ebert getting the Folks on me, but that never happened. He probably was embarrassed. A neutron smashed him.

That's how my freshmen year went. Remember, I was younger than everybody else Cassius was fifteen. Whatever circle I was in I was always the youngest. I never let on how young I was for fear of getting picked on like at the Manor. They just never knew and that's how my freshmen year went. I was just trying to hold my ground and fit in the school.

I got my one-day of glory. We had inter-divisional games during division time. All freshmen divisions played each other in a basketball game. I started playing on the whole courts.

I went to the Iron Park to tighten up my whole court game. I also played on Darobe basketball court during gym periods. I had gotten comfortable playing whole court. We go down to the locker room to get dressed.

We come out the locker room and into the gymnasium. The stands were crowded with everybody in the whole school watching. Teachers, students, security, everybody was in the gym and it was loud. Cityboy and Diago were in the same division. They were talking shit to me before the game started.

I immediately got butterflies but I was charged. I see when I get the butterflies I respond well. It's like my system and nerves start to combust. It was like a 454 big block engine starting up. I was playing guard and I was aggressive. I was bringing the ball up and they sagged their defense into a zone. It was a spot in the dungeon where we shoot free throw from for twenty-one. It was about the same distance as the top of the key on the court. I walked the ball up and I wasn't gunning. I'm dribbling and crosses half court and I had no pressure.

I did what I would do in the dungeon. I pulled it and it went all draws. The crowd got charged. We get the rebound and I bring it up and the same exact thing happened. I bust them out the gate with two jumpers and now the crowd was on my side.

I then got down on defense. First I ripped City at the top of the key and I took it all the way down and laid it up.

We were up like 12-6. Diago brings the ball up the court and we went man to man. I checked him and knew his moves already. When he went to do his move I ripped him. I went down and dropped a behind the back dime, to my teammate and he hit.

On the next time up the court they went man-to-man. I busted the zone up. City comes out to stick me and I get a chance to display my handles. I begin crosses in between my legs. Gave him a hesitation and a shoulder shimmy and went down the lane and scored.

The gym exploded. I took four shots and I hit them all. That's all I did, because I got my teammates off. We won the game like 16- 10 and the bell rang for the next class.

After the game City and Diago come over and said I got lucky.

I said, "naw I got game". For at least a week the teachers and the students were coming up to me. Man you can play why don't you try out? The teachers made me feel good that day. Mrs. Smit even said it.

She was in charge of Darobe development team. I asked her could I try out, but they had their squad already. The varsity basketball coach was at the game. He told me I had a good game. I knew I had a shot to make the team. I just said next year I was going to try out for the squad, but now they know how I am cut.

Inspiration out the Hood

The best thing for me was to see what I saw my freshmen year. I saw Slick Freddie, Spider G and Dickie Lee graduate out of high school. Now these were the goons from the hood and they've graduated and walked across the stage. This impressed me a lot.

I said to myself, "if they could graduated, it's no way I'm not going to walk. I didn't have to get good grades just passing grades and I'll graduate.

This is the wrong attitude to take. I will find that out later. I'm transforming myself from off nerd status. I am starting to be cool and known throughout the school.
It was no reason I couldn't get all A's.

I settled for C's, my theory! You get the same amount of credit for passing. Why try harder? This is what you call outsmarting yourself. I didn't know anything about GPA or what it means to colleges. I wasn't on the team. I didn't think college was going to happen at the time.

I had failed my first class, wood shop. I just couldn't make it to that class. The class was boring and early. We worked with planes and straightening wood. I should have taken auto shop. I missed sixty days out of that class hanging out in the game room early.

My mother came up to check on me during teacher parent conference.

My wood shop teacher looked at me and asked her, "is this your son?"

She replies, "Yes this is my son".

He then said, "I know his name is on my roster, but I rarely see him".

He goes and gets the attendance book and shows her my absences. My mother looks at me and wants to knock my block off in the school. What could I say I wasn't there and I failed? I went to King Martin summer school and got my credit so I could play the next year. The only thing is while I am in summer school I can't try-out for the football team. I didn't think about that while I was cutting class. I chopped my foot off.

My old Man

It's been a couple of years since I found about my biological father. During this time we were trying to build a father and son relationship. My mother worked it out where he'd come get me and keep me for the weekends.

My mom always told me, "what ever I think about him, always respect him. Whatever you feel good or bad. You must honor and respect him. This man helped bring you into this world. You wouldn't be here, if it weren't for him".

I had been cool with him all the time. Ever since I known the man he used to give me scratch. My mother didn't know how much money he used to tear me off. I saw he was a beast when he thought I was being attacked.

I used to wonder why she always said that constantly, honor and respect him? I'm old enough to know how we get here, especially being in high school.

Anyway he'd come and pick me up for weekends. When he picked me up he would always go get my sister Trina. She stayed on 95Th & Throop. This was Stones neighborhood. We'd grab her up and we'd go out to dinner and see a movie.

The first movie he took me too was Eddie Murphy Raw live on stage. My mother would never take me to see something like that! It was rated R too oh no. She sheltered that stuff from my ears. Here I am with the old dude at the movies. He's not only let me see the movie. He is in the movie theater cracking up eating popcorn. I just look over at him like, wow.

Now this is a reverend at the church. He is enjoying this Eddie Murphy, Raw. When I went over to his house on weekends he'd just take me to see the rest of my brothers and sisters. One time he took us to Great America.

He took me after the time I was supposed to go with the church. He was supposed to meet me at the church and give me the money to go. The bus left without me on it and I was devastated. He came, but he was late and the bus was gone. He gave me a couple dollars and told me he'd take me later.

I'm glad it happened that way, because I went a couple weeks later with the family. This would be the best time with my two sisters. Regina and Trina and my brother Butch, we all went.

This was one of the best times of my young life with pops. My sister Trina was around my age. Trina was only six months older than me. Regina was the oldest by four years. We got on all the rides in the amusement park. We went to restaurants and hung out all day. I will always remember that day. That's the day I felt like a Cody, I felt home. I remember it like yesterday.

My father claimed me when he took me around he's friends he would say. "This is my son Columbus ".

My mother, she rather it stayed a secret. No my mother claimed me. She just didn't want anybody to know her secret. I was born out of wedlock. I don't know how I got here, but I damn sure knew he was claiming me. It felt good to me. If he's my father, I wanted to feel it.

He made sure I felt love from his side, once I found out. He brought me an acoustic guitar for Christmas. I wanted an electric guitar like they played in church, but it was straight. He told me I should learn off this guitar. I thought those guitars were for country singers.

It felt good having more family. Now I know a little more about my family history. We would go out west and see my sister Margo. She had three kids my nephew, Harvell, Lil Charles and his sister Muffin. Harvell was about seven years old. My sister Margo was about ten years older than I am.

I went in her room and she had this bowl of weed and about five joints rolled.

I say to myself, "wow this would never go on at my house. I know the old dude see the weed like I do".

I am already starting to see it's different on the old dude side. They were things being hid from me on my mother side. My father was letting it all hang out.

He owned the building he lived in and stayed in the basement apartment. He had the basement decked out though! My room was off to the side of his room, where he slept. My old dude had a bar with all these different kinds of liquors on the shelf. He's got a little small kitchen with a nice living room and small bathroom.

My Pops stayed by himself. The spot was real chill and comfortable. It's not uncommon for you to live in a basement apartment in Chicago. He rented out the first and second floor.

It was a nice building, 2233 W. Marquette & 167Th street. He had a remote control garage door. He had two cars one was 1980 Cutlass Oldsmobile and the Caddy. One thing I liked about my old Dude. He kept a pistol in his right suit coat pocket. He kept that thang. I would pick that up from him.

One weekend I was over there indulging in his bar. He doesn't know I drink. I was in his candy store of liquor as far as I was concerned. He'd leave and I'd get bubbled than a motherfucka while he was gone.

When he came back home and he'd bring me some food for me to eat. In the morning when he cooked he had a special way of making eggs. Still till this day I don't know how he did it. I should have paid attention. He'd get up and hook me some stuff up. When he didn't fix breakfast I bust some Frosted Flakes up.

I cooled out drinking his liquor. I noticed one time he came in from work and looked at the bottle I was drinking out. He looked at me and I was straight bubbled, but I played it. I was sitting there eating a snicker. He looked back at the bottle and kind of shook his head, but didn't say anything. I think he was shaking he head, because he knows I'm not drinking it. I am too young.

This is how he found out I was drinking. It was Sunday and he was taking me back home. I had to get ready for school. He had a case of Old Style beer sitting at the back door. He never really drank them they just sat by the door. Every weekend on the way home I walked by the beer and start to salivate but I never took any.

I said to myself, "this time I'm a grab a few when it's time to go home". I loaded up about six of them in my bag. I was going to drink them with Rodell when I got back home. He was my drinking buddy at the time. I got three beers for Rodell and three beers for me. I jumped in the car and we heads home. I get home and he drops me off. He gave me a couple of dollars and he drives off.

My sister opened the door for me so she was trailing me. I dropped my bag in the hall and it was opened just a little bit. When I sat it down it was cracked and you could see the beer in the bag.

She told me to hold up and looked through the crack and saw a can of beer. She told me to hold on!

She grabbed my bag and opened it took out one and asked me. "Rev Cody is giving you beer?"

What was I going to say, I said, "yeah be cool, he let's me get down".

She asked again, "Reverend Cody is giving you beer? I don't believe it!"

Did my sister pick up the phone and call him? I was hoping he didn't go straight home, but he did. Not only did she call him. He answered and she asked him did he give me the beer?

I am standing by the phone, looking at her like, "you bitccchhh".

The old dude answers her. "Of course not, that boy got beer?"

My sister lets him know what it is, "it six cans of Old Style in his bag".

She cracked my face open. It probably cracked, my old dude face open.

He said, "Old Style" He tell my sister to hold on and goes and checks his case. He comes back a few seconds later and he tells Barbara, "I'm on my way to get him".

She says okay and hangs up the phone. I was so mad at my sister I didn't say anything. He was at my house in approximately ten to fifteen minutes.

I'm like, "oh shit" he had never disciplined me before. I'm wondering what's going to happen? He tells me to get in the car. I get in and says nothing to me at first.

He then asked me did I steal the beer? I told him I took the beer.

He then asked me, "boy you are drinking? You ain't nothing but thirteen years old".

I just looked at him and said, "sometimes".

He shook his head and looked bewilder. He probably began thinking back. It was you in my liquor. He gets me back to the house and tears a hole in me. This was the first and only whipping I would get from him. I was already thirteen going on fourteen at the time. I had to accept that one I got cold busted.

I rather he whipped me, than my mother and that's for sure. I love my sister, but she crossed the line with that one. Now I know she was concerned. Her little brother is going the wrong way. I am out here drinking beers at thirteen years old. She could've just poured it out. She could've given it away anything, but call him and tell on me.

I never told on my sister about anything. When he dropped me back off I wouldn't say anything to my sister for about three weeks. She starts talking to me and I'd start to humming and playing like I don't see her.

Whatever she was talking about I would just drown her out, by humming. She gets mad one day and start to roughhouse me. I wouldn't fight her back so she beast me. I had a lot of respect for my sister and wouldn't hit her. She slung and threw me around like a rag doll.

She beast me enough to where I said, "it will never happen again".

I knew she would try again, because I was passive. She tried to show off in front of her boyfriend one time. She grabbed me one day. I looked at Dewayne and I didn't want him thinking I was a hoe anyway.

Wayne I say, was a pretty good guy. He was brown complexion and well fed but not fat. He was thick. Anyway she was showing off. She didn't know the love I gave her by not fighting back. She was almost on my momma status as far as respect.

Only thing she wasn't momma. I grabbed her ass back and start slamming her against the walls in the hallway upstairs by her room. Just like my momma did me, when Hawk chased me home. I didn't do her scandalous, but I showed her my strength while I was smiling.

While I'm slamming her against the wall I ask her, "what you going to do? You can't do nothing".

I was letting her know you can't get away with the strong arm shit anymore. Dewayne broke it up and told her, "you better leave that boy alone".

He took her in her room and started talking to her. She didn't put her hands on me anymore after that. After that I started talking back to her and everything. She caused me to get my ass kicked.

It was still an adjustment period, because it was two different types of living. Right away I knew this was my family though! My brothers and sisters on my father side was about it. They hustled some type of way, stole, boost and wasn't about to take no bullshit. My father's house was the street part of my family.

My brother Butch owned a bar. It felt like I was home. I always felt different at my mother's house. I was a big circle trying to fit in a small square, at mom's house. It's like I knew something was totally different about me. This was before I found out he was my dad. She knew too, that's why she constantly was on me.

As a kid I always wanted the bad guy to win at the end of the movie. I was always mischievous and did what I wanted, even knowing the consequences. The things we'd be laughing about at my father's house. I'd get a whipping for it at my mother's house.

My sister Trina used to always call pops an old baldhead. You make me sick with your old balded head. The old dude was 66 and balding. I would be laughing on the inside, but on the outside, I got a straight face. At first I didn't know how he was going to take it.

I thought Trina was crazy. Sometimes pops would laugh. Sometimes he would say watch your mouth girl. He then would rub his head searching for hair. We'd both crack up.

Trina would tell him, "I don't know what you searching for, ain't no hair up there".

Pops had a good sense of humor. He cracked jokes and everything. I said to myself, "this is it, this is where I belong. My old dude crack jokes. This is where I get it from, him".

My mother would've slapped me out the chair. Emus, if my mother heard me say that to my father. You old baldheaded, to any grown up and especially my father it would be hell to pay. There were two total different types of households.

My mother never drank and he's got a bar. I guess it was for company, because I rarely saw him drink anything off the bar. I was the black sheep on my Mom side of the family. Over here I fit in cool.

At my mother's house I just didn't fit in mentally. I get over here and I damn near feel normal. I never saw my father steal anything or do anything wrong. His offspring's gets out here and get it in, however you can. We are very smart. Genetics is a motherfucker and we all look alike.

You can tell soon as you see us together. That's my brother and that's my sister. I look different from my siblings on my mother side. We didn't come from the same seed. You know your brother and sister's on your father's side of the family. These are your 100 percent brothers and sisters.

These are your blood sister and brothers on your father side. Anybody can be the carrier and it still 100 percent of the same seeds. Your mother's blood is poisonous to the child. If the blood somehow, penetrate the bag it would kill the child in the womb. The mother is the carrier of the man seeds. I do look like my momma too though!

On my father's side we got these, noses that say, they're Cody's. Something in the spirit gets passed to the kids, because I see the difference. My kids never saw anything I've done, but they've got some of my characteristics in them. I just got to cut this corner, because I can attitude. Everybody else is sleep and I am the slickest person around.

My old dude also showed me how he didn't fuck around. My nephew in-law Derek was seven years older than me. We were body punching in the church bathroom. Now Derek big ass hell banging me because that's what he did. I looked up to Derek, because he had my back.

He played for Harper High School. He didn't go to college, but tried out for the Chicago Bears. He didn't make it, but he tried out. He was making sure I could take a punch and I was no hoe. Derek went to the same church as we did. He'd see me in the vestibule and say, "you ready for me?"

I would say, "are you ready for me?" We then would go in the bathroom and get it in, body punching. Derek and I was going backward and forwards throwing blows, bang bang boom, boom. I would get off and then he would get off.

My old dude came in the bathroom when he was letting loose on me. Door opens he sees him whaling on me. I'm bracing myself trying to find my opening. Derek doesn't see him but I do.

I kind of stop and it looked like he is beating me now. I stopped, because we're not supposed to be playing in the bathroom. Derek turns and looked over his shoulder. He sees me looking at my old dude, that when he stops. He didn't know he was my old dude neither.

My Mom said, "don't say anything to nobody, so I didn't".

My old dude eyes almost bucked out of his head.

He squinted his eyes in disbelief and said, "nigga what you hitting him for, like that? He said it loud as hell and jumped in his face.

Derek was like, "Rev Cody we just playing".

He said, "nigga that's my son and I ain't' never hit him like that. You don't play with him like that. Nigga don't touch him no more".

Derek says, "Rev Cody I was,"

Pops cuts him off. "nigga I said don't touch him no more. I don't care what you were doing".

He said this while looking him dead in the eyes, steely. Derek is big ass hell and my old dude is old, but he was not buying it.

Derek said, "okay Reverend Cody" and left the bathroom showing respect. Cat is out the bag too.

My old dude reached for his pocket. "I'll kill that nigga for messing with you". I notice he clutched his pocket. We both went to the urinal and took a pop and son piss. I didn't say anything, cause we shouldn't been in there playing.

I knew I was about to get tore off too. We washed our hands at the sink. After he finished he reached in his pocket and gave me a couple of dollars. That felt good knowing he'd kill something for me.

Reverend Bracken

I was still going to church with Moms. I really like church. We had a live church congregation. The church was live. Mr. Wooten was the conductor. I learned how to sing. The range I sung in was tenor.

I was in the streets, but I was getting my church lessons. I knew something was wrong with me. I couldn't stop stealing.

I'd tell myself, "Okay Colo don't steal". I would be cool, until it was a chance to steal. I didn't go out looking to steal, but if it was a chance it was no question. I'd have money in my pocket and didn't think about paying for the item. I thought about stealing shit all the time.

I used to ask myself, "why you can't stop stealing? It was like something inside of me says, "take it". I was sitting on the front seat with my church buddies Eric and Sticks.

Reverend Bracken was about to lay hands on us at authercall. He was in motion. Everybody he laid hands on was starting to feel the spirit. He laid hands on me and I felt nothing. I always wonder why I wasn't feeling like everybody else? I wasn't catching the spirit or the Holyghost or dancing in the spirit. I wasn't going to fake catching the spirit.

When my Mom is in the spirit people have to hold her down. My mother was strong in regular life. When she was in the spirit she had the strength of ten men. They had to encircle her and not let her damage herself. That's one thing about the spirit I never saw anybody get hurt while in the spirit. They could be falling down the choir steps in the spirit and after they come out of it. They would be good.

This was a very aggressive spiritual dance when she caught it. Some people might fake it, but you knew whom. When the music stops and you go sit down, that's fake. I thought those were the people who faked it. My mother never stopped, because the music stops. Believe me I was hoping she did go sit down.

While the preacher was preaching she'd still be in the spirit, dancing. After about ten minutes she would calm down. My mother never faked being in the spirit. My mother would've never let her hair down like that knowingly. I was trying to see how did they get like that and what did they feel?

It was my turn and while Rev. Bracken was laying hands on me, I peeked up. He was looking at me with an inquisitive look on his face. I closed my eyes again and he went to the next person. I wondered what Reverend Bracken saw? I figured he saw that I wasn't shit or maybe he sees a demon or something. He just had a look on his face. The face made me want to ask, what did you see? I was really was trying to investigate what was going on inside me.

Reverend Bracken has power and I saw it with my own eyes. I was sitting on the usher board and one of the deacons had died during the service. This is while the pastor was preaching. He had stopped breathing and then took his last gasp of air. The congregation finally got Rev. Brackens attention. Reverend Bracken stopped preaching, because now he saw what was going on!

He walked down from the pulpit and laid hands on the deacon. He put his hands on his forehead and prayed. After the prayer the deacon came back to life. It was no act and I couldn't believe it.

I did wonder why didn't the nurses give him some sort of resuscitation or assistant the deacon? You know like it's an emergency. Dude was sitting there for a few minutes not breathing before they got pastor's attention.

I watched him take his last breathe and his head roll to the side. I was watching to see was he still breathing. He came down and the nurse came with the oil and Rev. Bracken put some in his hand. After that Rev Bracken gripped the top of his forehead and head with his hand. He started praying and he came back to life before my eyes. I just knew he probably seen how corrupt I am. I wondered did he see any light at all?

My mother always told me I was going to do big things. She said the spirit told her this fact. I was like, "the spirit. Okay Mom". I'm trying to see, but I say, "I don't know about that," to myself! "Right now, right now, I am a young criminal and can't help it".

I was in church with the O G constantly. She was trying to work that devil out of me. I sat on the front seat trying to get filled with the Holy Ghost. Every Friday night or early Saturday morning I was in church. Reverend Bracken would have authercall, if that's the right word. These are the people who were saved and accepted Jesus as their savior trying to go to the next level.

Now when you're trying to go to the next level! You got to be filled with Holy Spirit. Some Fridays the spirit would tell Reverend Bracken to lay hands after his teaching. Eric played the organ and Junior played the drums and I played the bongos. We were the youngest one's sitting on the front seat.

Like I said when it came my turn for him to lay hands on me. He squinted his eyes and it was something different about his look. It was different from what everybody else, was getting. I always wondered what did he see? I think Eric got filled with the holy spirit that night. It might have been another grown up too. It was only two who got filled that night. I on the other hand drifted closer to the devil's plan shortly after that night.

My conscious

On Halloween I used to love it. I was so smart. My mother and sister made us up for Halloween. Even if we had masks or costumes I'd still make myself up underneath. Sometimes we didn't have money for costumes, but we had fun making each other up.

We would go house to house and I would get a double up. I'd have the mask on at first the first time through. The next time I 'd take the mask off and get another piece of candy.

Sometimes I knew they caught on, but they gave it to me anyway. Another way is to say you have two bags and then say your little brother couldn't come because he's sick. This bag is for him. Don't forget the money they were handing out. Some people would throw money in the bag. When we got home my mom would take the bags. Issue us out some and put the rest up. She had to or we'd of ate all that candy as quick as we could.

Well I was getting too old to be tricker treating anymore. I had to graduate to bag snatching. We were all aware of the bag snatchers and made sure we weren't sleeping. When the older teenagers would walk by I'd walk across the street.

You can see when people are up to something. I never got my bag snatched. You had to wait around until everybody filled there bag and then snatch it. This one year I said I was going to snatch a bag.

I had waited in a cubbyhole and watched while smoking a joint. Once it got dark enough and the bags were just about filled I made my move.

I popped out of nowhere and whisked by shortie and snatched his bag. He didn't even see my face. I looked back at him and he was running behind me.

He was shouting. "Give me my bag, give me my bag" and then he stopped fell on the ground and started crying.

I felt bad immediately, but it was too late I'm all in. I was gone I hit a couple of alleys and was in the wind. I got to the crib with bag so I got away. I couldn't get away from my conscious though! The look was engrained in my head, the look of his disappointment and hurt.

The first few pieces I ate. I thought about him running after me with the disappointed look on his face. I felt bad, but I ate his whole bag of candy. I didn't do it anymore though I shelved the bag snatching. It would be shit like this that I'd wonder about? I didn't feel good while eating the candy even though the candy was good.

After my freshmen year I get a summer job. I had a hookup from Lamont Old dude, Mr. Paxon. We had to go to work on 55ᵗʰ & Garfield. He had a hook up with the summer Cedar Program jobs for the youths. The job was to learn how to speed-read. This is the first time I started making some money in a long while.

I think it paid four dollars an hour. The only thing about it, it was located on 55th and Garfield. That was a Vice lord neighborhood. I was plugged by then and transition had been made. I am a full fledge Black Disciple. Trey for days and BD for always, was our saying. I have transformed myself totally. I am no longer a nerd I am a street nigga. You know what Andrea I am feeling good from the 1738 let's eat.

Summary

This is how a person could start gang banging. This is how you start stealing. This is why we fall into a pathway of destruction. Columbus history was stolen and it's nothing in the well to draw strength.

Columbus was seeking to examine his sins that he knowingly was committing. He was brainwashed slowly by community and family. His way out the ghetto playing sports is now a fore-gone conclusion.

He knows now this isn't how he's going to get his Mom out the hood. Columbus hopes of playing in the pros, was his main reason for breathing at first. Now he knows he only have one-way out. He has to graduate high school and do something else.

He is now a deeply entrenched street nigga whose dreams were shattered. The death of his two best friends deeply affected his psyche. He has packed it away into his subconscious.

His spiritual foundation obtained in church is what aids him in the streets while confronting evil! Check out how the demons in him that are fighting for control. Get the next book in this Quadology series called, "Young Mobsters!"

Go to You Tube and pull up OTKvideos for live interviews with eyewitness account. This manuscript has a lot of Ebonics that was left to give the reader, an inside view of street language. I left it real so don't be offended. Names and places have been changed, because of the embellishment on some factual parts.